The CANADIAN NIGHTINGALE

Bertha Crawford
and the Dream of the
Prima Donna

JANE COOPER

◆ FriesenPress

Suite 300 - 990 Fort St
Victoria, BC, V8V 3K2
Canada

www.friesenpress.com

Copyright © 2017 by Jane Cooper
First Edition — 2017

All rights reserved.

No part of this publication may be reproduced in any form, or by any means, electronic or mechanical, including photocopying, recording, or any information browsing, storage, or retrieval system, without permission in writing from FriesenPress.

ISBN
978-1-5255-1740-2 (Hardcover)
978-1-5255-1741-9 (Paperback)
978-1-5255-1742-6 (eBook)

1. BIOGRAPHY & AUTOBIOGRAPHY, WOMEN

Distributed to the trade by The Ingram Book Company

Dedicated to my mother, who listened to the whole book and remembered all the opera stories from her youth.

TABLE OF CONTENTS

Preface.. 1
    Overture – The Inspiration of Albani 3
Introduction – The Dream of the Prima Donna 6
    Entr'acte – A Child Takes the Stage......................... 14
Chapter One – An Inheritance of Ambition, 1858–1895.......... 17
    Entr'acte – Every Phoenix Needs a Fire 28
Chapter Two – Music in the Family, 1895–1903 32
    Entr'acte – Life Is a Gamble................................ 44
Chapter Three – The First Rungs on the Ladder, 1903–1907....... 47
    Entr'acte – Competing for the Metropolitan Prize 65
Chapter Four – The Pinnacle of Choirs, 1907–1909............... 68
    Entr'acte – A Satisfactory Picture........................... 79
Chapter Five – Riding the Rails, 1909–1911..................... 82
    Entr'acte – Sailing into Uncharted Waters................... 93
Chapter Six – Crossing the Atlantic, 1911–1912 97
    Entr'acte – The Singing Lesson............................109
Chapter Seven – An Italian Interlude, 1912–1913...............112
    Entr'acte – Backstage at the Opera 125
Chapter Eight – A Year in Warsaw, 1913–1914..................129
    Entr'acte – A Brush with Fame 143
Chapter Nine – A 'Canadian Nightingale' Takes Flight, 1915......146
    Entr'acte – A Narrow Escape..............................166

Chapter Ten – Adrift in a Storm of Change, 1915–1918 169
    Entr'acte – The Great Train Robbery 190
Chapter Eleven – A Return to Stability, 1919–1921 194
    Entr'acte – The Myth in the Making 211
Chapter Twelve – Transatlantic Times, 1921–1923. 214
    Entr'acte – Wrapping Up the Album. 239
Chapter Thirteen – Choosing Poland, 1924–1926. 242
    Entr'acte – A Stage in the Air. 252
Chapter Fourteen – Public Lives and Private Dramas, 1926–1934. 255
    Entr'acte – The Final Return 267
Chapter Fifteen – An Uneasy Return, 1934–1937. 270
    Requiem – Packing Up the Pieces 283
Epilogue 285
Acknowledgements. 287
Sources 291
    Archives and unpublished materials 291
    Bibliography 292
    Newspapers 303
    Notes 307
    Picture credits 331

Some Places Bertha Performed in Poland

POLAND 1921-1939
— Poland's national boundaries
--- provincial boundaries

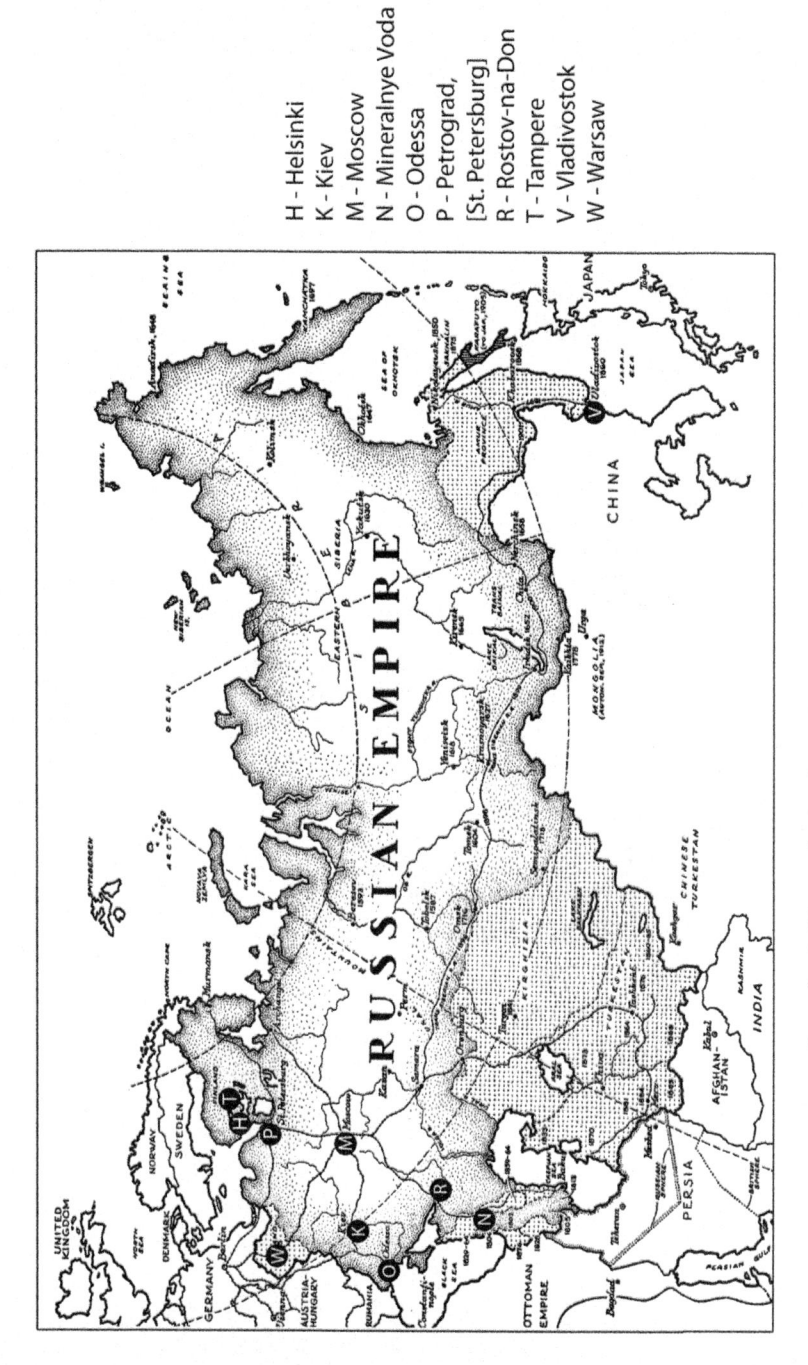

H - Helsinki
K - Kiev
M - Moscow
N - Mineralnye Voda
O - Odessa
P - Petrograd,
 [St. Petersburg]
R - Rostov-na-Don
T - Tampere
V - Vladivostok
W - Warsaw

Bertha's Travels in Russia, 1913-1918

After the Opera

Still the perfumed air is throbbing
    With the passion of the song!
How the spell of love and music—
    For a moment swayed the throng.

Thou, Isolde; thou, Aida;
    Melisande with loosened hair;
Thais temptress; mad Salome,
    Pagliacci's wailed despair,—

Can you hold them with your magic,
    Beauty, wealth and fashion there?
Is the ecstasy forgotten,
    As they clatter down the stair?

Have the splendour and the glory
    Left untouched this careless throng?
Is there one who yet remembers
    That the heart of love is song?

—*Theatre Magazine*
(Republished in *The Toronto Sunday World*, January 22, 1911)

PREFACE

*I*n the fall of 1924, my great-aunt Margret Tregear was in Poland, working for the Quakers on a refugee relief project. In December, she went to a performance of the Warsaw Philharmonic Orchestra, and subsequently she wrote home to her friends: "There was a ripping Orchestra, and an English singer, Berta Crawford, very Italian in style. She did wonderful things with her voice, and chose mainly operatic things or songs with heaps of trills and cascades of notes . . ."

Nearly 90 years later, I was editing Tregear's letters for publication and, out of curiosity, I Googled 'Berta Crawford.' The first hit that came up was an obituary from the *New York Times* which revealed that, in fact, Bertha was a Canadian who had worked for years in Russia and Poland. How unusual, I thought. A Canadian singer working in Poland in the 1920s? Farther down the page was a link to an entry in *The Canadian Encyclopaedia of Music*, but it was only four sentences long. My curiosity was piqued. There had to be more to her story than that.

With a little time on my hands, I thought I would conduct a minor experiment. Just how much can one find out about a forgotten singer using new online resources like digitized heritage newspapers? I found quite a few references, but every new fact only inspired new questions. Consequently, before I realized what was happening, I was caught up in the challenge of completely reconstructing a lost life. Inevitably, it became clear that the Internet alone would not be enough. Visits to libraries and archives in Toronto and New York only whetted my appetite for archival research, and before long I had booked my tickets to Warsaw, with plans for St. Petersburg percolating in the background.

The beauty of a historical biography is that it provides a focal point—one woman's life—from which you can justify reaching out in any number of directions to learn new things. You can dig through genealogical resources to find her relatives, many long dead, but happily, some still alive. You can read contemporary biographies and novels to understand how her chosen career was represented during her life. You can travel to many of the places she visited and lived, finding some drastically transformed while others are surprisingly unchanged. You can read the newspapers she read—online, on microfilm, or in dusty paper volumes—and, by doing so, find yourself immersed in both the social conventions that delimited her world and the politics that several times altered the direction of her life. You can get a taste of many of the people she met through other authors' biographies, both online and in print. And you can listen to almost all the music that she sang, at home via YouTube and on great opera stages around the world.

Chasing Bertha Crawford's life has led me down so many unexpected roads. I invite you to follow the same journey and see what surprises you find.

Jane Cooper

Overture – The Inspiration of Albani

Evening, May 1, 1901. Grand Trunk Railway, Simcoe County, Ontario, Canada. Bertha slips in and out of slumber as her head bumps gently against the carriage window of the train, which is trundling home across the sleeping Ontario countryside. She is exhausted, slumped sleepily in the corner of the compartment. But her fourteen-year-old head is still spinning. What an evening! When has she ever seen sights and sounds like this? And when can she see them again?

Bertha has seen professional singers in concert before, but nobody who appears in her village of Elmvale compares with tonight's performance at the Grand Opera House in Barrie. The international opera star Emma Albani is on a cross-Canada tour with her four-person company from London, England. Albani looked so serious and dignified when she stepped onto the stage. Bertha expected her to be wearing something colourful, or maybe pure white like in the photos she has seen. But she found that Albani looked even more impressive dressed as she was in court mourning for the recently deceased Queen of England and Canada. Albani's heavy black satin dress was lush with embroidered side panels, a deep hem covered in jet and silver sequins, and just a hint of white chiffon and lace around her neck. She expertly swung the long train around to fall in a rich black pool beside her as she took her position beside the piano. Her diamond necklace and tiara seemed all afire from the footlights. She looked as regal as the monarch she was mourning.

"Oh Daddy, doesn't she look splendid?" Bertha whispered to her father, who was sitting between Bertha and her older sister in the red velvet seats at the centre of the Opera House floor.

"Well, she's holding up pretty well for a woman of her age," he murmured to himself.

Bertha wasn't really listening. "She looks like a queen herself," she sighed.

Queen Victoria died only three months before, but Bertha knows from the papers that Albani was one of the monarch's preferred singers and was especially invited to sing at the late Queen's memorial service. Bertha thought about how romantic that must be, to be the favourite of a grandmotherly queen—and to be loved by everyone else. The audience around Bertha wouldn't stop clapping, and Albani hadn't even started to sing. Wouldn't that be something, Bertha fantasized, to be applauded like that?

It was the first time Bertha had heard many of the songs Albani sang. Some were in German, others in French or Italian, hinting at exotic affairs in faraway lands. But there were a few in English that she could understand, too. Bertha was entranced when the violinist or the flautist played a complementary part and the instruments made a duet with Albani's soaring voice. And then Albani sang a vocal duet with the lesser known English contralto Muriel Foster, which reminded Bertha of all the duets she sings with her sister. If only the Crawford sisters could sound like that, Bertha thought.

As the concert went on, Bertha almost succumbed to a building pressure in her chest. She found herself breathing in time with Albani and wanting to open her throat and sing along. Coming out of the theatre, she desperately wanted to try to make a sound like that right away. She was on the edge of singing as they crossed the lobby.

"Daddy, did you hear how she sang that phrase?" Bertha asked, and she had already inhaled and opened her mouth when her sister Lucia jumped in.

"Bertha May, don't you go making a spectacle of yourself, singing in the theatre foyer!" Lucia blurted out. "Tell her to wait until we get home, Daddy."

"Well, now, lassie," John Crawford said to Bertha, amused. "I think you are going to embarrass Lucia if you start doing your impression of Albani right here, you know."

"Oh, but didn't you think she sounded grand? I want to sound like that some day!" said Bertha, taking her father's arm.

"Wouldn't that be a fine thing?" her father mused. "Maybe someday you will."

INTRODUCTION –

The Dream of the Prima Donna

When Bertha May Crawford (1886–1937) was born in the small town of Elmvale, Ontario in 1886, the highest aspiration for a girl with musical talent was to become a prima donna, the leading lady of the opera stage. The woman who could win a place as a prima donna with a major opera company could take centre stage and top billing, travel the world, and earn a substantial living. When Bertha was still a child at the turn of the century, opera stars were the biggest international celebrities. Indeed, the top opera sopranos—women whose carefully trained bird-like voices could sing melodies that soared to the highest notes, like the Australian Nellie Melba (1861–1931) and the Spanish-born Italian soprano Adelina Patti (1843–1919)—were the highest paid entertainers in the world.

Bertha may have been born in a rural community, but she could have fed her musical dreams by taking a short train journey to the city to attend performances by some of the biggest international opera stars of the day. During Bertha's youth, stars such as Adelina Patti, French Canadian soprano Emma Albani (1847–1930), American soprano Lillian Nordica (1857–1914), Scottish-American soprano Mary Garden (1874–1967), French soprano Emma Calvé (1858–1942), and Italian tenor Enrico Caruso (1873–1921) came to Toronto, and sometimes even to nearby Barrie, on concert tours. Travelling American opera companies, like the National Grand Opera Company, the San Carlo Opera Company, and Henry Savage's Grand English Opera Company, put on full performances of popular European operas in Toronto every year. As she was growing up, Bertha probably grabbed the opportunity to see performances of French and Italian operas like *La Boheme, La Traviata, Rigoletto, Pagliacci, Aida,* and *Carmen.*

Canada's first international opera star, Emma Albani, inspired young singers like Bertha Crawford to think that they too could have a professional career.

Of all these visiting stars, the prima donna whom Canadians of Bertha's generation were most familiar with (and took the most pride in) was the soprano Emma Lajeunesse, better known by her stage name Emma Albani. Born in Chambly, Québec in 1847 and educated in Montréal, Albani was proud of her Canadian identity all her life, although she moved to Albany, New York when she was still quite young, and she lived most of her adult life in England. From an early start singing in the church in Québec, Albani went on to study opera in Paris, France and then in Milan, Italy under the noted Italian singing teacher Francesco Lamperti. Based most of her life in London, she appeared often in opera at Covent Garden and in oratorio recitals around England. She toured extensively around the world and returned to Canada to perform in 1883, 1890, 1901, 1903, and 1906. A booklet advertising the musical talent of Toronto in 1897 chose Albani's photo to be featured on its frontispiece and, even though she lived in England, labelled her the "Canadian Queen of Song." Albani was the first Canadian to be an international opera star, and aspiring singers across Canada looked up to her as a model of success.

Young singers like Bertha were encouraged by the press to view prima donnas like Albani as almost mythical heroines. The public imagination was fed with tales of their characters and careers through extensive newspaper coverage of their travels and travails, and more directly by the women themselves. There was something of a craze for operatic memoirs and autobiographies, and many of the great North American opera stars and musicians of the era published personal stories of their rises to fame. During her lifetime, Bertha would have been influenced by the accounts given in autobiographies like Amy Fay's *Music Study in Germany* (1880), Emma Albani's *Forty Years of Song* (1911), Clara Louise's *Memoirs of an American Prima Donna* (1914), Lilli Lehmann's *My Path Through Life* (1914), Geraldine Farrar's *The Story of an American Singer* (1916), and Kathleen Baird Howard's *Confessions of an Opera Singer* (1918).

From books like these, Bertha would have absorbed a consistent narrative that came to define her life—what might be called the dream of the prima donna. The legend goes something like this. The talented young North American singer studies hard. Her gifts are recognized early as she develops her musical grounding in sacred music in the church choir. Inevitably, she is encouraged to leave her home and go to Europe. Only in Europe can she get the kind of training and exposure she needs to become the star she is destined to be. She perseveres to find the right teacher and follow the correct lessons. She struggles with new languages and customs. Her money is stretched thin. Her modesty comes under threat, but somehow she preserves her reputation. When at last she is discovered, she attains almost immediate success on the stage without compromising her art or her virtue. Her achievement is measured by the number of major opera houses she sings in as she tours across Europe and around the world. As an ultimate mark of real celebrity, she becomes intimate with other famous musicians, titled nobility, and, most importantly, royalty. And when she finally comes home to North America, she receives a rapturous welcome. Bouquets cover the stage and newspapers heap praise. It was a dream to enchant any young musician.

This epic tale of the rise of the opera star is always told as the story of a modest girl lifted by her uncompromising commitment to music—and her personal hard work—far above her previous station in life to the peak of society. Canadian-born mezzo-soprano Kathleen Howard (1884–1956) could not sum up her life in opera without including details of her interactions with the Kaiser's court during her time in Berlin. Emma Albani's proudest reminiscences in her autobiography are not of her greatest moments on stage, but of her personal correspondence with Queen Victoria. In a society still defined by class, royalty sat firmly at the top, and there could be no higher mark of success for a singer than recognition by someone wearing a crown (or, at the very least, a tiara).

As a child, Bertha may have been caught up in the fairy tale aspects of the dream of the prima donna. Sometimes the girl finds a Fairy Godmother, in the form of a patron or a teacher, who lifts her out of domestic drudgery and sends her up to the palace—first the theatrical palace of the opera house, and then to real palaces with real royalty. A wealthy patron might help by giving useful introductions or paying for the costs of lessons or costumes. A well-informed *protettore* might even give vital advice about the operatic marketplace. Mary Garden owed her success to a rich patron, Florence Meyer, the wife of a Chicago department store magnate who funded her studies in Europe. Sometimes, the prima donna meets a Prince Charming, perhaps a manager or a fellow singer, who sweeps her off her feet and sets her down on the stage. Emma Albani married her manager, Ernest Gye, who, for better or worse, kept her feet on the boards for many years. And everywhere the prima donna appears, she finds an adoring public that is as devoted to her as her ubiquitous lapdog. Emma Albani's Maltese terrier, Beauty, even followed her onto the stage at Covent Garden once.

Eventually, the singer becomes so famous that she is universally recognized by just one name. Just as the name Cinderella stands alone, so was Emma Albani known simply as 'Albani,' and opera audiences everywhere knew that 'Patti' meant Adelina Patti and that 'Melba' referred to Nellie Melba. A prima donna might even become immortalized through eponymous cuisine. People around the world still eat the Melba toast and Peach Melba that were named for Nellie Melba and the Chicken Tetrazzini favoured by the Italian coloratura soprano Luisa Tetrazzini (1871–1940).

The road to stardom for a Canadian singer like Bertha was clearly mapped out. Stars, like the American dramatic soprano Lillian Nordica with her *Hints to Singers*, and Lilli Lehman with her *How To Sing*, gave very specific advice. The experts suggested that before a singer went to Europe, she needed to get a sound foundation of musical training and experience singing in churches and in concerts at home in North America. When she got to Europe, she needed to find an experienced specialist in voice production, who would build her vocal and physical endurance so she could last through demanding operatic roles. The North American singer would do well to begin by perfecting her English diction, which was best done in England, singing in oratorio and concerts, and where she could also acquire a cultured stage deportment. She also needed to master modern languages, ideally French, Italian, and German, so that she could pronounce correctly and understand what she was singing. If opera was her goal, then she was encouraged to spend three to six months in Italy, where she could work with a specialist in the operatic repertoire to learn a minimum of three or four classic Italian operas, memorizing the full singing parts and taking coaching in the standard dramatic action. Italy had the added advantage that it would then be possible to stage a 'soft debut'—an engagement smoothed by some payment to the theatre management—in one of the more than eighty small opera houses, where a failure would be less embarrassing, and a success could lead to bona fide offers of further work.

But as she grew older, Bertha would come to understand that, however carefully these detailed instructions were followed, there were no guarantees. The dream of the prima donna is a simplistic account that glosses over the ambiguities of real life. Like all fairy tales, the story is a poor guide for what the heroine should do when real life deviates from the standard plot. It doesn't explore the compromises a singer might have to make—as might happen during a World War, a revolution, or an economic collapse like the Great Depression—or the price that might be exacted for those trade-offs. Bertha might have found a more nuanced exploration of the risks inherent in a prima donna's career in some of the popular contemporary novels that featured prima donna heroines, like DuMaurier's 1894 bestseller *Trilby*, or the trilogy that F. Marion Crawford began in 1905 about a soprano who takes to the opera stage.

In the end, though, these prima donna narratives are equally vague about how the heroine will survive after she leaves the stage. Prima donnas' memoirs always leave the singer with her success secured and only a hazy image of what it really means to 'live happily ever after.' There is scant advice about how to safely invest your savings to last into old age. Emma Albani, for example, had to be rescued from penury in the 1920s after her wealth disappeared in poor investments. In fact, the prima donna often has to resort to teaching—a profession that can never generate an income equal to what she earned during her best years on the stage, or support the lifestyle she has become used to. Still, these harsher realities are glossed over in the public story, and even as the fans themselves age, their prima donna is remembered as fixed in her prime.

Perhaps Bertha found personal reasons to discount the risks of chasing the prima donna dream. The myth of the prima donna had additional resonance in the early years of the twentieth century because the myth, and sometimes the reality, dovetailed in some important ways with the ideals of the 'New Woman.' In the 1890s, when Bertha was an impressionable young girl, the first wave of feminism was rolling into the consciousness of Canadian communities large and small. The novel idea that a woman could have a career, earn her own living, and control her own destiny was being articulated as Bertha grew up. The New Woman could remain single, be well educated, stand up in public with confidence, and travel unescorted—things usually outside the experience of the women who had come of age only a generation before. Putting her considerable creative energy to work in the arts, both in literature and on the stage, the New Woman might even find independence from, and equality with, men. For some Canadians, this new vision was full of excitement and promise.

To Bertha, the prima donna would have looked like a prototype for the independent career woman. Indeed, the opera singer had to be well educated within her field, and she walked with confidence on the public stage. And that confidence could lead to influence beyond the theatre. For instance, Lillian Nordica used her theatrical experience to great effect as an activist for votes for women. A prima donna travelled widely and met a fascinating range of people. With fame, she gained the ability to dictate the terms of her contracts and the right to demand working conditions equal to or better than those of her male counterparts. For the talented few, financial security was a possibility. Those few who managed their earnings wisely, and who were careful to preserve their voices for an extended career on the stage, made a very good living, led independent lives, and even supported large families. Adelina Patti's earnings bought her a Welsh estate with a castle with thirty-four bedrooms to retire to.

But by the time Bertha was a young woman with her sights set on a career in opera, she would have known that making the leap from successful local singer to the international stage was a huge gamble. The popular newspapers Bertha grew up reading loved to highlight the successful careers of the small number of women who became true opera stars (and the large fees the best of them could demand). In 1903, the ageing but still famous soprano, Adelina Patti, was reported to have earned $10,000 for a 'farewell' concert in Toronto. This was probably an exaggeration, and, needless to say, the number of opera singers at the top of the profession were few—perhaps thirty or forty in the whole United States. More sober musical journals cautioned that the second tier of opera singers earned considerably less—perhaps $250 to $400 a month. While this might have sounded like a reasonable income for a girl from small-town Ontario living with her parents, it was barely adequate to cover the cost of living in a different city and the typical expenses of a performer, like having costumes made and keeping a personal maid.

However, professional singing certainly was a viable career for those few women who were really talented, and for Bertha it would have offered the best route to an independent career. In 1911, *The Toronto World* published an analysis of the earnings of singers and concluded that a soprano who worked as a church soloist and a school teacher—jobs that were easily combined—would be able to make a very comfortable income. In fact, according to *The World*, a talented singer who chose this less risky path would be much better off than a singer who left home to work in opera. But the gamble of chasing the dream of the prima donna would have tantalized Bertha with more than just financial independence. It held the possibility of adventure, glamour, and fame—perhaps an irresistible lure for a small-town girl with a big imagination.

Bertha Crawford pursued her dream of becoming a prima donna from the church choir in Elmvale, Ontario, across Canadian stages big and small, and onto the great opera houses of Russia and Poland, but her story is no fairy tale. The roller-coaster ride of her life follows the path of an actual artist, with highs and lows and the heartbreaks that real people encounter when faced with real dilemmas. By the time she died, aged only fifty, Bertha had sustained a career on the stage for thirty years and had seen more of the world than most Canadian performers of her time. Her voice and performances had been compared favourably with those of great coloratura soprano stars like the Hungarian Ilma de Murska (1834–1889); the Italians Adelina Patti, Luisa Tetrazzini, Olympia Boronat (1859–1934), Elvira de Hidalgo (1891–1980), and Amelita Galli-Curci (1882–1963); the American Marie Litta (1856–1883); and the Polish Ada Sari (1886–1968). But what had it cost her to keep that career going? And, as it came to an end, had she accumulated the reputation and money to make the struggle worthwhile?

Entr'acte –
A Child Takes the Stage

Evening, February 14, 1895. Presbyterian Church, Elmvale, Ontario, Canada. John Crawford is leading eight-year-old Bertha by the hand as they make their way through the church's double doors. Eleven-year-old Lucia skips ahead into the sanctuary with its rounded arched ceiling and new wood smell. The church is abuzz with noise. There will be no sombre church service this Monday evening. Tonight's entertainment is a children's concert and celebration following the recent dedication of the substantial new brick church, now the finest of any congregation in Elmvale.

The Crawfords, father and daughters, slide along the freshly varnished seats of a curved pew in the centre of the church, settling in beside their relatives. Bertha and Lucia chatter with the Walton girls, while John nods to his brother-in-law, David Robertson, and their Walton cousins, James, Chester, and Charles. Even with John's wife Maud at home with little Howard, the family fills up the whole pew.

David speaks over the children's heads to John. "Your girls all ready for their big debut?" he asks.

"Oh, I think so. They've been singing around the house all week," John replies. "Maud says it'll send her right 'round the bend if she has to hear those songs again."

But John is only joking. Both parents could listen all evening to their daughters harmonizing their pretty voices.

There is a rustle at the front of the church, and a hush descends as the choir gets up to lead the congregation in an opening anthem. Then everyone sits down as the village doctor and church elder, Dr. McClinton, steps up to the pulpit to begin his address. The twists and turns of how this new church came to be built are common knowledge across the village, but everyone takes pleasure this evening in reviewing them now that the job is done.

Listening to Dr. McClinton's retrospective on the church, John is drawn to take stock of his own personal life. He doesn't look back often. John Crawford is known as a man whose eye is firmly on the future. But for once he is remembering that day, nearly twenty-five years ago, when he came down the gangway from that nauseating rocking ship. He remembers how good it felt as he, his parents, and his brothers and sisters set their feet on the firm Canadian ground. Now, at thirty-seven, he has his own lovely wife and three children. Over the past ten years in this Ontario village, he has built a thriving tailoring business and owns some profitable properties on the side. Looking down the pew, he gives thanks for the camaraderie of his cousins and friends in the church, in the Elmvale Silver Band, and at the Curling Club. But tonight he is most proud to think that his daughters are growing up to be talented little singers.

The program is a long one, and the girls are not on until more than halfway through the evening. Lucia, determined to show off her relative maturity and decorum, is sitting quietly while she waits. Bertha, on the other hand, is fidgeting and occasionally kicking her high buttoned boots against the back of the next pew, as her feet swing clear of the floor. John reaches down to catch her knee, smiling at her impatience. He knows that she is itching to get up and show her stuff.

When their turn comes, Bertha marches up the aisle ahead of Lucia and stands as straight as a ramrod through the duet. Although she is singing the second part, Bertha's voice rings loud and clear, nearly overpowering Lucia's. Lucia leads sweetly with the melody, but in the end it is Bertha's strong harmonies that make the piece singular. John doesn't let out his breath until they are finished the song. Both girls, seeming a little overwhelmed by the applause when they finish, bob a quick curtsey before they rush back to their seats.

"Did we get it right, Daddy?" Bertha whispers to John as they sit down. "I took a really deep breath in the middle like you said."

"Shush, lassie," John quiets his excited daughter, but he has a pleased smile on his face. "You're not finished yet."

Bertha sits on her hands and sets her feet swinging again. It is a long time for a young child to wait. But then the girls are up to the front again, and John can see the familiar concentration on Bertha's face as they sing their way through the more complicated duet. Again Bertha's notes, pure and true, can be heard above Lucia's, showing breath control unusual for such a little girl and catching the attention of the people in even the farthest pews.

The friendly audience claps even louder for this second song, and Lucia blushes as she bobs again. But Bertha takes her skirt in both hands and, holding it out wide at both sides, makes a curtsey so deep and dramatic that her knee almost touches the floor. This gets a laugh and a second wave of applause.

James Walton leans across the pew to John. "It looks like you've got a natural performer there," he chuckles. John can only grin with agreement as his girls come back to his side.

CHAPTER ONE -
An Inheritance of Ambition,
1858–1895

Scottish immigrant, John Crawford, and his Canadian wife, Maud, had optimistic dreams about their daughters' futures. It would be their younger daughter, Bertha, rather than the elder, Lucia, who would take their ambitions to the greatest heights.

*B*ertha Crawford must always have had a natural ambition to sing, but she also owed much of the purpose and drive that carried her forward through her life to her family, and more particularly to her father. John Crawford's passion for music was as important to Bertha as his entrepreneurship, which provided the family's daily bread. If Bertha spent her life chasing the dream of the prima donna, it is perhaps fair to say that her father was living proof of the potential of the dream of the immigrant settler, who arrives with empty pockets on the docks at Montréal, and who, through hard work and immersion in his new community, fights his way up to middle-class respectability.

Bertha's father John Crawford (1858–1942) was born in Kilbirnie, a small industrial town near Glasgow, Scotland, into a solidly working-class family. His father was originally a flax dresser, and his mother worked as a factory hand and cotton weaver. Perhaps they met at the big mill in Kilbirnie, W&J Knox Threadmills, a series of hulking four- and five-storey stone structures that dominate central Kilbirnie to this day.

In fact, John Crawford's hometown was dominated by stone walls and slate roofs. Workers lived out their lives in stone cottages, working in stone mills and worshipping in stone churches, surrounded by low stone walls that separated the open fields from the compact village. Cobblestone streets curved and turned to accommodate an ancient landscape. The stone-built surroundings sent out a message to both the past and the future—that one's place and one's fortunes were also set in stone. Immigrants streamed out of these dark industrial towns in the Scottish lowlands to test the bright Canadian offer of a less class-bound society, where a person might rise on their own merit and hard work.

Bertha's father arrived in Canada as a thirteen-year-old child immigrant with his parents and four siblings in 1871; he was one of 3,400 Scottish immigrants who came through the port of Québec that year. At that time, half a million Canadians of Scottish descent could be counted among the 3.5 million people living in Canada. Two of those Scotsmen already settled in Canada were John Crawford's uncle, Andrew Crawford Senior (1831–1902), and his wife Sarah (1828–1892). Uncle Andrew was a tailor who had settled in the small community of Schomberg, Ontario, north of Toronto, more than a decade earlier in 1857, and who had probably paved the way for his brother's family, including young John, to make their way to Canada.

Apparently Canada did not catch Bertha's grandparents' fancy, for within a few years they took four of their five children back to Scotland, where they remained for the next ten years. Only John stayed on in Canada. This was not a particularly unusual outcome; up to a third of all Scottish immigrants to Canada returned home. Many others became serial immigrants, moving on to other destinations like Western Canada or the United States.

Bertha's father, however, saw a land of potential in Ontario, where he settled in, living and apprenticing with his uncle and learning the tailoring trade. In the early 1880s, John's younger brother Andrew Crawford Junior (1861–1943), also a tailor, came back to Canada to join John. The two grew up to chase their dreams in the rapidly growing towns and villages of southwestern Ontario. The rest of the family re-immigrated around the same time to Massachusetts and lived out their lives in the mill towns near Boston. Eventually, John would move on to Toronto, while Andrew moved several times, from Schomberg to Hillsdale to Penetanguishene, and then out west to Red Deer and finally to Calgary, where he finished his days. The Crawfords, it seems, were a restless brood, following opportunity wherever it led, however far that might be.

Maturing in the small Ontario village of Schomberg, John developed the skills that he would put to use as an adult, many of which he would pass on to Bertha and her siblings. John's educational base was probably laid down at a Scottish school in Kilbirnie, and he probably went on to complete some schooling in Canada. Clearly, as an adult, he could write a literate and well-argued letter, and he was more than competent at maintaining his business accounts and calculating accurately the potential return on a variety of investments. He raised his children in a literate household, and he passed on his respect for education and learning to his children, who turned up regularly on the honour roll during their school days. Tailoring remained the profession by which Bertha's father defined himself for the rest of his life, both in census reports and in town and city directories, but it is clear that the majority of the income that would eventually fund Bertha's musical studies was actually earned from investments in land and other enterprises.

Bertha's mother, Lavinia Maud Robertson (1863–1942), more commonly known as Maud, was not only a neighbour of the Crawfords, but also a family friend. Maud's father, Thomas Robertson (1831–1883), had immigrated from Kilbirnie to Schomberg in the 1850s, and he probably knew John Crawford's father back in the old country. In Scotland, Thomas had been a wage labourer like the Crawfords, working as a thread lapper in Kilbirnie's textile industry at the same time as both of John's parents worked in the factories. In Canada, Thomas became a self-employed wagon maker and wheelwright. He settled near Bertha's great-uncle, Andrew Crawford Senior, whom he undoubtedly knew well.

Bertha's maternal grandmother, Ann Isabella Walton (1834–1913), had deeper roots in North America. The Waltons were a Quaker family that had immigrated to Canada from Pennsylvania with the United Empire Loyalists. The Quakers, pacifists on principle, had refused to take sides in both the American Revolution and the War of 1812. Escaping from American displeasure, they were welcomed to Canada, but they had to work for their land like other homesteaders—by clearing fields, building roadways, and paying taxes. Bertha's mother Maud was raised in the Presbyterian faith of Thomas Robertson, but Bertha's grandmother Ann remembered her Quaker roots and must have taught some of those principles to her daughter, as well as to her grandchildren during her regular visits to the Crawford home during Bertha's childhood.

Bertha's parents were still young when they embarked on their long marriage one Tuesday in September of 1882. John was twenty-four and Maud was just nineteen, and their marriage was to last until John's death sixty years later. Witnessing their marriage was John's friend and soon-to-be business partner, Chester Walton (1858–1946), who was also Maud's first cousin. The marriage of John and Maud cemented in place an extended Scottish-Canadian family that would offer a solid network of support for Bertha as she grew up.

Not long before Bertha was born, her parents moved from Schomberg to Elmvale, Ontario. They were following in the footsteps of Maud's first cousins, James (1856–1914) and Chester Walton, who set up businesses in Elmvale in the early 1880s as cabinetmaker and baker, respectively. Later they would be joined by the Waltons' younger brother, Charles Walton (1864–1917), and by Maud's younger brother, David Robertson (1865–1938), both also cabinetmakers. John's brother Andrew Crawford Junior soon followed, setting up a tailoring shop only a few miles west of Elmvale, in Hillsdale, in the early 1890s. By the beginning of the 1890s, the six cousins were successful tradesmen and self-made men, building their businesses in the bustling economy of Flos Township and raising their children within the embrace of a large warm family.

The village of Elmvale sits about halfway between Lake Simcoe and Georgian Bay. In the final decade of the nineteenth century, when John Crawford was settling his family into their new community, Elmvale was a place in flux, and visually as impermanent as the fortunes of its people. The first European inhabitants had arrived a mere thirty years before, in the late 1850s, and they had laid down their streets in a precisely determined chequerboard. Their houses and stores were built of wood, many of which were thrown up quickly. Completed to varying degrees, some were not yet painted or were waiting for the finish of a front porch. Only the better few were faced with a layer of brick. Fences were inadequate and property lines loosely marked. Horse-drawn vehicles rocked and rattled along the unpaved streets. There were wooden sidewalks to keep pedestrians clean, particularly women in their long skirts, but the streets were muddy in spring and dusty in summer. There were winners and losers in a new settlement like Elmvale, but as John Crawford made the most of the turbulent Elmvale economy, he learned that opportunities had to be grabbed as they emerged, and that the people who take the initiative get ahead. These were lessons he would later pass on to his daughter Bertha.

When Bertha May was born on June 20, 1886, she already had an older sister Lucia Maud (1883–1961), who had been born two and a half years before. Still, there is no reason to believe that the arrival of a second daughter was in any way a disappointment to the Crawford family. On the contrary, both daughters were clearly objects of considerable pride for their parents. When Bertha was just a toddler, John and Maud took their daughters on their first international trip to Lawrence, Massachusetts, to introduce the little girls to their Crawford grandmother and aunts. However, many fathers yearn for sons, and John was no doubt pleased when Bertha's three brothers—Howard (1892–1940), Lorne (1898–1978), and Clarence (1901–1977)—arrived over the next few years. But John always seemed to hold a special place in his heart for his two eldest daughters.

Early on, John encouraged his girls to join him in his musical pursuits—something the brothers apparently did not take up. He persuaded his girls to sing in public at a young age, and sometimes even took the stage alongside them. When the girls were older, the local newspaper's social column regularly mentioned how John took his daughters along with him on visits to family, trips to local fairs, and farther afield to horse races. (One can only wonder whether Maud was annoyed or relieved to be left at home with the small boys.) In truth, it seems likely that right from the day of her birth, John Crawford thought that the arrival of baby Bertha was a harbinger of good things for his family.

Bertha's first friend in life must have been her older sister Lucia. Less than three years apart in age, Bertha and Lucia shared many important moments growing up. They were frequently mentioned together in local newspaper reports, which detailed them making social calls, becoming members of the Young People's Society for Christian Endeavour (Y.P.S.C.E.), and travelling together to visit out-of-town relatives. Often referring to them as 'the Misses Crawford,' the newspaper portrays them as a regular duo during their adolescence. But, most importantly, it was Lucia who initially paved the way for Bertha to take to the stage, as Lucia was the lead soprano in their childhood duets.

In the absence of any written evidence, we can only speculate about Bertha's and Lucia's individual characters and their relationship when they were young. However, it seems safe to read something of their youthful personalities from their later careers. In many ways they seem to have been opposites, and perhaps their different characters provided a balance that facilitated a close relationship. Bertha must have been the extrovert, as she clearly wanted a career on the stage, although she didn't perform on her own until she was a teenager. Bertha's later success suggests that she had inherited her father's drive and ambition, and that she could focus her energies when she had a goal she wanted to reach. On the other hand, Lucia was probably more like her mother Maud with her serious, staid Quaker roots. In fact, Maud rarely got a mention in the local newspaper, apparently devoting herself instead to private family life out of Elmvale's public eye. Lucia also seems to have been a more retiring character, and was remembered by her son and grandchildren as a quiet and unassuming woman in later life. In contrast, as an extrovert, Bertha was probably a social girl, happy to join in the whirl of an extended family's life.

The family photo at the beginning of this chapter shows Bertha and Lucia dressed in the fashions typical of the era. Like all young girls, they would have worn their hair at least shoulder length or longer. Fortunately for Bertha, her naturally thick wavy hair—probably chestnut in colour—would have suited the young girls' fashion of curling bangs and ringlets, although she probably kept it tied back at school. She probably often wore a white frilled pinafore over her day-to-day calf-length dress of dark wool, and a hat when she was outside. On her feet would have been leather boots with a row of buttons up the side, reaching above the ankle to meet her dark stockings. As her father was a leading figure in their village, she probably always went out neatly dressed, and it is unlikely that she would ever have been allowed out in the street in bare feet.

For several years, cousin Chester Walton lived next door with his wife and their eight children, including three daughters close in age to Lucia and Bertha: Eva, Edna, and Gladys. We can picture a gaggle of girls playing in the back yard of the Crawford's Queen Street brick block building, where they all lived in the upstairs apartments. After their homework and chores were done—perhaps with some of the brothers in tow—they might saunter down the block and around the corner to James Walton's home on Patterson Street to look for their other cousin of the same age, Ella. In the summers when the children were young, Bertha's father John and her uncle Andrew took their families on holidays together to camp on the shores of nearby Lake Orr. They would close down their tailoring shops and take a week or two away from the cares of business, spending the nights under canvas and the days boating and fishing on the lake. The mothers must have had some time to relax while the fathers were on the lake, before they had to deal with the challenge of turning the day's catch into a family dinner over the fire. Bertha and Lucia probably enjoyed the chance to swim in the lake, while the baby boys from each family crawled around and got dirty.

Bertha would have learned her more formal lessons at the Elmvale public school. Bertha started school in this fine two-storey brick building, where three classrooms were crammed with about 240 students total, including up to fourteen of Bertha's siblings and cousins. The Crawford children often appeared on the honour roll, although in the early years, Lucia turns up more often than Bertha and looks to have been the more serious student. For Bertha, who was probably quite a lively and outgoing child, staying focused on the dry work of reading and arithmetic in those big classes—and refraining from humming her favourite songs—may have been more difficult than it was for the quieter, more studious Lucia.

The Elmvale Presbyterian Church looks much the same today as it did in 1902, when Bertha sang at a celebration for the installation of a new bell.

While Bertha's weekdays were busy in school, her Sundays were almost always devoted to church. Raised in the Church of Scotland, John brought his family into the congregation of the Elmvale Presbyterian Church as soon as he arrived in the village. Bertha spent her early years attending church every Sunday in a small, crowded wooden building, looking up to the minister at his high pulpit as he delivered his sermon to the congregation below, and listening to the choir sing. In 1894, a fine new brick church was built which, during the Crawfords' time in Elmvale, was the biggest church in the community. The new church had seating for more than 600 people and a balcony for the choir and organ. Bertha's family spent many hours in this building, and much of that time was spent singing.

Bertha and Lucia's first singing appearance to be reported in *The Elmvale Chronicle* was in a children's concert to celebrate the opening of the new

Elmvale Presbyterian Church in February 1895. It must have been an exciting evening for Bertha. The program opened with an anthem sung by the choir. Then a group of ten Sunday School children sang their first song. Following that, there were several recitations, addresses, and more Sunday School songs before Bertha and Lucia got up to sing their first duet. The newspaper didn't record which song they sang, but perhaps it was "Raindrops on the Roof" or "Light After Darkness," two duets that the girls sang on other occasions. After two more recitations and another address, they sang a second duet.

Was Bertha nervous at this first public concert? Probably not. At least not about the audience, which was a friendly crowd made up of school friends, neighbours, and family. And her older sister would have been singing the soprano lead, while in these early duets Bertha sang the subsidiary mezzo line. While there is no way of really knowing, it is easy to imagine that in this early concert, Bertha's biggest motivation was to please her father.

It is very unlikely that Bertha and her father were already pondering a career in opera for her when she was just a child singing in the church choir. But the legendary life stories of many of the great opera stars of the day, including Emma Albani, always start with the star's early appearances as an infant prodigy, with their remarkable singing voice heralded from a very young age. John Crawford certainly felt that both of his daughters had beautiful voices when they were still children, and he had his daughters showing off their vocal talents by singing duets in public from the time Bertha was only eight and Lucia eleven.

But only a few months after that church concert, musical pastimes would have to be set aside as the Crawford family dealt with the biggest crisis of Bertha's youth. The great Elmvale Fire of July 7, 1895 started in a harness shop at 1:30 a.m. on a hot dry Sunday morning. By daybreak, it had consumed more than twenty-five buildings in the central part of the village, including many of the main street businesses and the homes of the businessmen's families who lived above the stores. Also gone were the skating rink, the public library, and every hotel and liquor store in the community. *The Elmvale Chronicle* estimated the total loss at more than $52,000, of which only $17,000 was insured.

One of the biggest losers was Bertha's father, who lost his brick block building, which contained his tailoring shop with Bertha's family home above it and two stores they rented out. He also lost an implement building and another rented house. Describing Bertha's family's losses, the local paper noted that "The only things saved were a piano, a dressing case, and three chairs. The piano was turned end over end into an adjoining yard." Clearly, even in the heat of a crisis, the family thought that music was a priority. Although watching her family home burn must have been a traumatic experience for nine-year-old Bertha, saving the piano—and the family musical evenings it enabled—was an important compensation.

While a fire on this scale may sound like a major catastrophe to a reader today, in fact the Elmvale Fire of 1895 was neither particularly large nor surprising for the time. For instance, five years later, in April 1900, a fire that started in Hull and spread to Ottawa burned more than 3,200 buildings, left more than 14,000 people homeless, and cost more than $6.2 million in damages. The great Toronto Fire of 1904 burned through twenty acres of the downtown core, destroying 104 buildings, many of them multi-storey factories and warehouses, for a loss of more than $10 million. In towns where the majority of the buildings were wood frame with cedar shingle roofs, and where water supply was primitive or non-existent and there was no firefighting equipment, it took little more than a small fire and a stiff breeze to turn an accident into a calamity. At the turn of the century, an Ontario community that had not experienced a multi-building fire was the exception, not the rule. Families braced themselves for disaster and learned to keep life's ups and downs in perspective.

Bertha would have been too young to understand much about the fallout of the fire, but it seems clear that John Crawford already knew that the successful businessman in the era of fire had to be stoic and resilient. In fact, the Crawfords had been burned out in Elmvale before, in October 1891, so John knew what it took to rebound from a setback. Only a month after Elmvale's 1895 fire, he was building temporary quarters from which to run his business. By October, he had rebuilt his block of shops, was running his tailoring business, and soon was renting out space to his brother-in-law David Robertson's furniture shop and Sneath's general store.

John was an optimist at heart, unbowed by the challenges of life and always ready to grasp a new opportunity. *The Elmvale Chronicle* described him as a "pusher" and lauded his "enterprise and characteristic pluck." As he rebuilt his businesses after the 1895 fire, the paper observed that "[i]t will take several fires to dishearten John in his fight with the world." He was energetic and "always 'on deck' practice or no practice." He built helpful connections with the powerful men of the town, curling on a team with the reeve and the bank manager, and serving together with other influential men on the board of the Agricultural Society and as a village trustee from 1895.

By this time, John Crawford was well on the way to being one of the most prosperous businessmen in Elmvale—and one who would be able to invest in his daughter's musical career. From a modest start with his tailoring business, over his years in Elmvale he built up a profitable network of investments in land, buildings, and enterprises. As a merchant tailor selling fabric and making clothes, he advertised "Custom Made Clothing at Ready-Made Prices," turning out wool suits for between $6.50 and $15.00, and pants for $2.50, for cash or on credit, with a "complete stock of goods always on hand." At one point, he also invested in a livery stable, and at another point in a bakery, both with Chester Walton. After the 1895 fire, he rebuilt his brick block building with space beyond his own business needs so he could rent stores to fellow entrepreneurs. In 1896, he built a bakery beside his brick block, where his wife's cousin Chester Walton would set up his business. The store John rented to Sneath's Dry Goods in 1897 was reckoned to be one of the finest in town, sixty feet long by twenty-five feet wide, with white walls, a varnished wood ceiling, and plate glass windows fronting onto Queen Street. By the end of 1897, John had completed a second brick block and was landlord to at least six businesses including his own, and he was paying taxes on at least five properties in town.

Indeed, it seems that Bertha's father did not allow the setback of the great fire to interfere with his long-term drive to accumulate the capital he needed to support the ambitions of his children. In the 1890s, he couldn't have known exactly what those ambitions would be, but he was a practical man, and he knew they would require money. By the age of forty, Bertha's father was a prosperous middle-class businessman who aimed to pass on to his children a life far removed from the expectations he had been born to in Scotland. And it was his daughter Bertha who would take those ambitions to the greatest heights.

Entr'acte –
Every Phoenix Needs a Fire

Midnight, July 7, 1895. Yonge Street, Elmvale, Ontario, Canada. Nine-year-old Bertha is sleeping fretfully beside her older sister, Lucia, tangled in her long cotton nightdress, with unnecessary blankets kicked to one side. She is drawn out of her drowsing by the unusual sound of her parents' raised voices in the hall.

"Maud, get the bairns out! And don't forget the deeds. I'm going out to help." And then her father John's usually measured steps are discarded as he crashes down the staircase and out the front door.

Both girls come abruptly awake. The bedroom is bright—not with candlelight, but with a deceptively pleasant glow coming in through the open window. The room, still holding the heat of a stifling Saturday in July, is rapidly filling with smoke. Strange noises and voices float up from the street below.

Their mother crosses directly to the window and slams the casement down. Her tone is unusually sharp. "Lucia, you remember what to do? And Bertha—take Howard down into the yard, away from the house. And don't leave him!" With that, she is out the door.

Lucia jumps up and starts pulling their dresses off the hooks on the bedroom wall. The smart matching frocks they'd worn to sing their duets at the church concert only a few months ago. Last year's worn school dresses. Yesterday's pinafores. Random linen from the top dresser drawer. No time to sort. She struggles to tie up the corners of the bedspread.

Bertha drags her two-and-a-half-year-old brother Howard and his quilt out of his crib and stumbles down the stairs and outside. She dumps him down on the ground at the back of the yard, but he doesn't wake. She turns towards the back of the brick block building that houses their home, her father's tailor shop, Mr. White's drugstore, and Mr. Broderick's liquor store.

She stands transfixed by an enchanting sight. The flames from Hunt's Hotel across the street reach so high she can see them over her family's building. The sky is filled with small fairy lights, floating far and wide from who knows where. One settles down near her on the packed earth by the stables. A burning shingle. She ought to stamp it out, but her feet are bare. It smoulders on without catching. But when she looks up she can see that several flaming shingles have landed on the roof. In no time they are burning brightly, luring more fuel into their little fires from amongst the cedar shingles, which are bone dry from the summer's drought.

Lucia comes spilling out the back door, clutching the bundle of clothes and bedding, and nearly careens into her dazed little sister. Following Bertha's line of sight, she turns and hollers for their mother. "Ma, the roof's caught already!"

Maud comes out clutching the dressing case full of family papers. "Good God, not again," is all she says. Bertha is aware that her mother has seen this all before, only four years ago. "Lucia, go and find your father. He's out in the street somewhere with the men."

Then Lucia is gone, sprinting around the corner.

Bertha watches the strange sight of her mother hopping from foot to foot, then dashing back into the kitchen and dragging out two chairs. She dives back in again to fetch a third. Then, just as suddenly, Maud loses her nerve and sits down to watch. What else can she do? Bertha knows they have only two buckets—no pump, no hose—and an eroding sense of faith.

Then suddenly John is back, out of breath. For all of his strong bandsman's lungs, his thirty-seven years are starting to show. Uncle David is hot on his heels. They pause to take stock. The roof is fully flaming now. It will be minutes, not hours.

Bertha can see that her father is weighing the odds. "What do you think, Davie?" he ponders. "We rescued it the last time. We cannae let it go this time, can we?"

Bertha has heard her mother often enough, chiding her father for his Scotsman's stubbornness, but she knows that it is something her mother loves in him. "Are you going to get the piano, Daddy?"

"Och, I do believe we are, lovey." Then the two men dive through the back door.

An agonizing minute passes. Out in the yard, above the crackling and the hissing, the men's thumping and scraping can just be heard. Bertha creeps onto the back porch and stands in the open door. They are stuck on the threshold between the back parlour and the summer kitchen.

Her father turns and sees her. "Christ Almighty, girl!" He never swears. "What do you want?"

"My dolly. It's upstairs."

He swings around and grabs her by the shoulders. "Bertha May. *You* are *my* doll. And I intend to play with you tomorrow. So get out of the house. Now!"

He shoves her, more roughly than she has ever known him to handle her. She's shocked. But then she catches the look on Uncle David's face, and it is one of pure fear. He's trapped behind the piano, still inside the house. She is out of the way in a flash.

"And a one and a two and a three!" With that, they lift together and, letting out a demonic howl, drag the great weight across the summer kitchen, onto the porch, and over to the edge of the back steps. Carried on by sheer momentum, the piano hangs briefly over the edge and then tips and slides with surprising decorum down the steps. When it reaches the bottom, it rocks forward and comes to a decidedly undignified rest on the ground, end up. It plays a ghastly off-key chord that vibrates on the night air.

At just this point, all three of the Walton cousins—James, Chester, and Charles—round the corner of the building at a trot.

James has an undertaker's dour sense of humour. "Well, I can't say we're surprised to find you playing the piano at a time like this. They'll be calling you the Nero of Elmvale by tomorrow."

There is a crack above as an upstairs window blows out. Glass sprinkles down. Without a word, the five bandsmen surround the piano and automatically glance towards the leader of their Elmvale Silver Band. James raises his head for his customary nod, and on the downbeat they heave together. The piano rolls forward onto its top, and then onto its other end, until finally it lands upright again. In a second movement, they lift and march it across the yard. And with that done, they are off to the front of the building to continue the fruitless fight.

Before he follows them, John stops and looks down at his girls.

Maud looks worn. "I just don't think I can do this all again," she says.

"Oh, it'll be alright, lassies," he says with a smile, and then he's gone.

"Good God," Maud says to her daughters. "Your father's actually enjoying this. He's already making another one of his plans. The building's not even burned down yet, and already he's planning a new one."

CHAPTER TWO –

Music in the Family,

1895–1903

*A*s Bertha was growing up in Elmvale, her father ensured that she got the kind of initial grounding in music that would open up the possibility of a future musical career. However, there is nothing to suggest that she was one of those children who endured long formal lessons and tedious practice at a preternaturally young age. More likely, to begin with, Bertha just soaked up the music that was all around her.

The most influential lesson Bertha absorbed in her early childhood was a love of singing, and the first place she experienced the passion for vocal music was in church every Sunday. John Crawford had a strong voice—he was admired as a tenor—and he was not shy about using his talents in public. When he moved to Elmvale and joined the local Presbyterian church, the elders quickly recognized his musical skills and appointed him to lead the new choir, which he did until 1892. Later, Bertha and Lucia were both members of the church choir with their father, and they would have developed a strong foundation in choral singing through their regular choir practices. That musical foundation was probably supported by frequent coaching in the front parlour.

Indeed, Bertha's musical training would have begun at the parlour piano, which John Crawford saved from the great fire in 1895. In the final decade of the twentieth century, a daughter who could provide musical entertainment was the pride of her family, and piano lessons were the common foundation of a young girl's musical education. And for an aspiring young vocalist like Bertha, the ability to play the songs she was learning and accompany herself during practice was a particularly valuable skill.

The piano on which Bertha learned to play—and beside which she learned to sing—would almost certainly have been made in Ontario. There was a boom in the Ontario piano industry from the 1890s through the first quarter of the new century, driven by the limited competition from foreign pianos, the ease of rail transport inside Canada, and the increasing prosperity of Ontario families. During this period, more than a hundred manufacturers produced pianos and piano parts in the province. In 1900, about 12,000 pianos were made and sold in Canada, many by companies with German roots like two of the most prominent, Heintzman and Nordheimer.

In an era when music in the home had to be homemade, the Crawford's parlour piano was the ultimate marker of middle-class civility. For an immigrant family, the purchase of a piano signified an important step upwards in Canadian society. Both a status symbol and a practical instrument, the piano was often the most expensive household item that an upwardly mobile family owned. But for the Crawfords, saving the piano from the fire was not just about preserving an investment; it was about saving a piece of their identity.

Many of the members of the Elmvale Silver Band were Bertha's relatives. John Crawford is holding the clarinet.

Beyond the piano in the parlour, John Crawford also gave Bertha an early and frequent exposure to ensemble instrumental music through his membership in the Elmvale Silver Band, the village's brass band. The tradition of the brass band was brought to Canada by nineteenth-century immigrants from Britain, where factory and community bands were a great source of working-class pride in industrial towns. Before radios, movies, or the gramophone, the brass band was the only source of public music in rural Ontario communities outside of the church. The brass bands of the era traditionally were comprised of tenor, alto, and baritone horns, as well as cornets, flugelhorns, trombones, euphoniums, tubas, and, of course, a drum.

Bertha had a strong personal connection with the Elmvale Silver Band, as the entire band was something of a family project. Not only was her father a keen member, playing both the clarinet and the alto horn, but her mother's first cousin James Walton was the band leader. In fact, along with James's two brothers, James's son, and John's brother-in-law, more than a third of the Elmvale Silver Band's fifteen members were related to the Crawford family. Practices and performances must have had the flavour of a regular family reunion.

When Bertha and her siblings were young, listening to brass band concerts must have been a big part of their lives. The Band's members played on the community's set of silver-plated instruments, and with their smart hats and sharp playing, the community was proud to support the Band's activities. During its heyday in the 1890s, the Elmvale Silver Band played annually on May twenty-fourth, on Dominion Day, and at the Elmvale Fair. In the summer of 1896, their "sweet strains" accompanied a party from the village on a civic holiday excursion on a rented steamer on Georgian Bay, travelling to Collingwood and back. All that summer, they played on the main street every Thursday evening, and in the winter they played at the ice rink for the skaters. But the biggest event on the calendar for all the bands in the area was the annual meeting of the Protestant fraternal organization, the Orange Lodge, held each twelfth of July. Every village aspired to send out a well-tuned band to lead their delegation in the big joint march.

It is obvious that the Crawford children grew up surrounded by music and musicians, from the piano to the choir to the Band. However, whether Bertha and Lucia actually had formal music lessons during their childhood—or indeed whether they needed them—is unclear. Their whole extended family was musical, and they may all have been mostly self-taught (or, rather, may have informally taught each other). As a church choirmaster, John must have been confident enough to coach his girls for their frequent singing appearances, and so he should be properly credited as Bertha's first singing teacher. There were also at least two women who gave music lessons in Elmvale, one of whom prepared girls to take the vocal exams offered by the Toronto College of Music, but there is no evidence that the Crawford sisters attended. Bertha is listed as the accompanist for her classmate Lulu Sneath when Lulu sang a vocal solo at an Epworth League meeting in 1901, so by the time she was fourteen, Bertha had somehow learned to play the piano well enough for a modest public performance. But long before that, she was prepared to sing in local concerts.

The Elmvale newspaper records at least fifteen performances in community concerts by Bertha and Lucia during their childhood and adolescence. When local organizations needed entertainment for a fundraiser or a social event, Bertha and Lucia Crawford were often called upon to sing their popular duets, and the girls also sometimes appeared in trios with their father. The majority of their performances seem to have been at their own Presbyterian church, but they also lent their talents to other worthy organizations like the Epworth League (a Methodist youth organization), the Women's Christian Temperance Union (WCTU), and the Women's Foreign Missions Society. In 1897, the young girls sang their duets as part of the program at a July strawberry festival organized by the Elmvale Silver Band. They mostly sang hymns like "Light After Darkness," as well as some of the popular songs that Victorian families sang around the parlour piano, like "Raindrops on the Roof."

While Bertha's enthusiasm for singing probably only grew with every performance, her quieter older sister Lucia may well have been beginning to think about other things. In 1899, as fifteen-year-old Lucia came to the close of her school years, and as thirteen-year-old Bertha had the end in sight, the future was probably in the forefront of their thoughts. This was also the year when Elmvale entered the age of electricity, and new light came into the Crawford household. The Village Council, including Bertha's father John, commissioned an electrical plant to light up the village. The new brick power house was temporarily manned by a young man from Acton, Ernest Pearson. Ernest was a gangly eighteen-year-old, but with his highly specialized cutting-edge knowledge of the world of electricity, he must have created a bit of a stir among the young people. Did Lucia form a 'friendship' with Ernest? Surely she met him. Perhaps they walked about, with Bertha in tow as a chaperone? But after six months, he had to return to his hometown of Acton. He made enough of an impression on the town that his leaving was marked in the local paper. And it appears he also left a lasting impression with Lucia, as he and Lucia would meet again more than a decade later and would eventually marry. But in 1899, Lucia and Bertha were still at school, and boys could not yet be a serious consideration. Even so, the sisters' paths in life were already beginning to diverge.

By 1902, nineteen-year-old Lucia Crawford had given up singing duets in public and ceded the stage to her younger sister Bertha's solo career.

Indeed, as they moved into their teen years, the musical relationship between Bertha and Lucia changed. Years later, in a 1915 interview with a reporter from the *Christian Science Monitor*, Bertha looked back on how her own and Lucia's singing had evolved: "I began to sing at my home . . . when a young girl. My parents were both singers and my sister and I used to sing trios and quartets with them. At first I always sang mezzo to my sister's soprano, but one day a passage proved too high for her. I was told to try it, when it was discovered that I could sing it easily. From that time soprano my voice has remained." We don't know if Lucia resented being demoted to the second parts in the duets, or if she was relieved to be unbound from public performance as she became a mature young woman. Perhaps she had never really enjoyed it like her sister and her father had. Whatever the reason, by the turn of the century, Bertha began to find herself more often performing solos rather than duets as Lucia increasingly retired to the musical sidelines. At the same time, with her high vocal range more prominently on display, Bertha began to attract the kind of attention that would encourage her to think more seriously about her singing.

As a young teenager in Elmvale, Bertha seems to have become more dedicated to her education in her final year at school, but she was also probably coming to the recognition that an ordinary village school was not going to contribute much to the subject she really wanted to study, which was music. While Bertha's appearance on the honour roll is spotty in her early years at school, she appears almost every month in 1900, which suggests she had buckled down in anticipation of the provincial public school leaving exams. But unlike Lucia, Bertha was not mentioned in the local paper as having passed those exams, so it is possible that she did not succeed. We do know that she did not enter what was called, in those days, a 'continuation class' (equivalent to modern-day secondary school) in Elmvale. Apart from her later musical studies, it seems unlikely that Bertha had more than six to eight years of formal schooling, which she completed by the age of fourteen.

In her final year at school, there were still about forty children in her class, and undoubtedly this was a tough challenge for the young teacher in charge. So perhaps the most lasting lesson Bertha learned from her school days was that teaching is a difficult job—and not one she ever wanted to take on. However, it is likely that she did develop some practical skills at school that served her well throughout her career. For instance, in late nineteenth-century Ontario schools, there was a strong emphasis on rote learning and memorization. A good ability to learn quickly by rote would have served Bertha well later in life, when she came to learn long opera roles in foreign languages.

While Bertha's formal schooling was limited, and although she lived in a small rural community, it would be a mistake to assume that she was condemned to a particularly narrow view of the world in her teens. All the big events and issues of the day during Bertha's childhood were aired in the pages of the local and regional newspapers. Certainly, she could have read news from far-flung countries and learned about the lives of the great entertainers of the day while still in her own community. *The Elmvale Chronicle* published its first issue in the middle of August, 1893, when Bertha was just seven years old. The eight-page paper focussed on local social news and regional politics, but it also republished long articles about international news and affairs not found in local newspapers today. It also carried serialized fiction and included plenty of health and household advice heavily influenced by advertisers of patent medicines and miraculous cures. The Crawfords would have had a subscription from the first months, as the family members—including Bertha and 'the Misses Crawford'—were mentioned regularly in the social column. John Crawford also occasionally ran an advertisement for his merchant tailoring business. Bertha and Lucia probably honed their early reading skills by pouring over the social column to see which Walton or Crawford was in *The Chronicle* that week, and their mother likely followed the serial when she had the time. Elmvale also had a public library and reading room, open six days a week, which, by 1899, carried three daily newspapers (presumably from Toronto), four weekly papers, and eight periodicals, along with nearly eight hundred books. If Bertha was interested in the world outside Elmvale, and surely she was, then she had many ways of learning about it.

The Crawford girls were encouraged to be independent and travel beyond the confines of Elmvale from a young age. Their uncle Andrew Crawford had moved his business from Hillsdale to Penetanguishene around 1897, and from the time Bertha was eleven, she and Lucia went on regular visits to 'Penetang.' Their parents would put the girls on the train in Elmvale, and their uncle and aunt would meet them in Penetang a short half hour later. Penetanguishene was a much bigger town than Elmvale, with a population of about 2,500 in the late 1890s, and must have seemed an exciting place for the village girls to visit. Their father also took them along on his trips to visit family, to the Schomberg Fair, and to New Market, near Toronto. They probably also went farther afield with him to see some horse races.

No one knows at what point Bertha determined that she could turn the family passion for music into her own career. But her first exposure to the early feminist debates about the potential for women to earn their own living and take control of their own lives would probably have been in her early teens, when the Women's Christian Temperance Union (WCTU) arrived in Elmvale. In 1898, when Bertha was twelve years old, a group of Elmvale women led by the local newspaper editor's young wife, Mae Gadd, set up a branch of the WCTU and introduced avant-garde ideas about women to the community. In a rural community like Elmvale, the WCTU presented the most practical example of the ideals of the New Woman, as the members strategized about taking local action to promote their political agenda of temperance. Bertha and Lucia were invited to sing at WCTU events, where they would have listened to Mrs. Gadd and, most likely, admired much of what she represented.

The WCTU, and the enthusiastic and confident young Mrs. Gadd, offered two contrasting influences on Bertha as she grew up. On the one hand, the WCTU presented a positive model for the progressive, active New Woman. It encouraged women to stand up for their rights and for the rights of others, and to work against violence against women and children; it also promoted votes for women and better education for all. The WCTU had been founded in 1874, with the goal of protecting the home from the 'ravages of alcohol,' and it took on the strategy to 'agitate, educate, and legislate.' By the end of the century, it had become one of the premier women's organizations in North America. It was known as a place where women were trained to think on their feet, speak in public, and run an organization, and it was also where they learned, in practical ways, about strength in numbers. As they came to understand the interconnection between social and political problems, the WCTU leaders saw the necessity for women to promote their causes through legislation. In 1894, the WCTU endorsed votes for women. Prominent Canadian women leaders like Nellie McClung and Louise McKinney got their start in political organizing through the WCTU.

On the other hand, for an aspiring performer like Bertha, the WCTU represented a movement which, in a much more subtle way, was opposed to the public display of passion and human drama that is at the heart of grand opera. The debate around temperance and the prohibition of alcohol was a microcosm of the larger Victorian narrative about the need to promote civilization through the management and control of nature. The Victorians aspired to control everything from the broad natural environment to individual human nature. The immigrants who came to Canada from the United Kingdom believed they had a mission to conquer nature by clearing the forests, ploughing the land, and laying out rational roads and streets in neat grids that defied the natural curves of the countryside. They extended that civilizing mission to their fellow human beings. The ideal Victorian woman encased her natural curves in steel-reinforced corsets and hid her limbs with cumbersome skirts and long sleeves—something Bertha would experience directly as she grew into womanhood.

As uncomfortable as they were with the natural body, the Victorians were perhaps even more uneasy with uncontrolled emotions. The British middle classes felt that their self-control and discipline—that infamous stiff upper lip—were what made them superior to the more spontaneous and relaxed Latin cultures, like the French and the Italians, not to mention their own intemperate working classes. They drew a clear separation between the righteous road of sober Protestant rationalism and the seemingly less controlled passions of the Roman Catholics. In rural Ontario, this discomfort was most evident when confronted with drunken, out-of-control men rolling down the streets from the hotels and bars. In Ontario cities, the distaste for, if not fear of, open displays of emotion—let alone sexuality—also expressed itself in the censorship of theatre and opera performances.

However, it is unlikely that the teenaged Bertha really grasped this contradiction when Canada's most celebrated prima donna, Emma Albani, came to nearby Barrie the year that Bertha finished school. At this stage in her career, Albani was a highly successful working woman, but despite making her start in the emotional whirl of Italian opera, she was really best loved in Victorian England as a soloist in the irreproachable world of religious oratorio. On May 1, 1901, the fifty-four-year-old Albani gave a concert in the Barrie Grand Opera House as part of a Canadian tour that took her from Halifax to Victoria. She brought with her from England a concert party of two supporting singers, a violinist, a flautist, and a piano accompanist. They performed a selection of opera arias and ballads, with Albani appearing three to four times during the evening to sing solos and join in duets. Predictably, Canadian audiences across the country gave the returning star an enthusiastic welcome and demanded repeated encores at all of her performances, confirming her status as an established national heroine who could still hold her own on the stage.

Albani's Barrie concert was advertised in *The Elmvale Chronicle*, and it is hard to imagine that John Crawford did not take his singing daughters on the short train ride down to Barrie to hear the famous soprano sing. The Barrie Grand Opera House, which opened in 1886, was one of the most impressive theatres in Ontario and was a popular venue for major touring artists, although it very rarely entertained full opera companies. 'Grand' was a somewhat inflated adjective for the square brick building, but it did somewhat resemble a medieval castle. Two square towers were attached to the front façade, and a balcony between them protruded over the circular arch that framed the front door. Did Bertha get her first taste of the magic sound of a professional opera singer in the Barrie Grand Opera House? Did the sight and sound of the Canadian Albani singing Italian arias inspire the fourteen-year-old to begin to dream that she might also learn to sing like that one day? It is entirely possible. The timing was certainly right. Bertha was just finishing school, and with her life opening up before her, she would have been at a particularly impressionable turning point.

Whether she actually saw Albani in person, or only heard about the concert second hand, Bertha's horizons continued to expand during 1901. She had her first experience with the excitement of international travel in September of that same year, when she and Lucia joined a party of young women and men, under the supervision of some stalwart members of the Elmvale community, to visit the Pan-American Exposition of 1901 in Buffalo, New York. The 'Pan,' as it was referred to in the local newspaper, was open from May to November 1901. An average of 50,000 people a day toured the exhibition. By the end of the fall, eight million North Americans had made the journey to sample the excitement of a massive public event unlike anything they could see at home.

The trip to the Pan would have exposed Bertha to more than just American progress. The exhibition covered 350 acres with pavilions demonstrating the latest technologies and wonders from around the world. Only a day's travel by train from Elmvale, the Crawford girls probably spent a couple of nights in Buffalo before returning home. They might have stayed in one of the big hotels in the city—up to six in a room—or in somebody's spare bedroom rented out especially for exhibition visitors. Given the dramatic events that Bertha experienced during her travels later in life, it seems ironic that her teenaged trip to the Pan occurred the same week that President McKinley was shot there—maybe even the very day. The President didn't die until some days after the girls returned home, but the shooting immediately ignited a national uproar. However, as the initial reports predicted his recovery, the Pan went on as usual the next day, and the girls would not have missed any of their fun due to the assassination attempt.

As Bertha grew more confident navigating the world beyond Elmvale, she also began to embrace the opportunity to appear alone on stage. In May 1902, with some fanfare, a bell was installed in the Elmvale Presbyterian Church tower, and Bertha was one of the "Elmvale talent" who sang a solo at the celebration. On one of her trips to Penetanguishene in November 1902, she made what may have been her first solo appearance away from home, at the Presbyterian church there. *The Penetang Herald* reported that "Miss Bertha Crawford of Elmvale sang 'Jesus Thou Joy of Loving Hearts,' with pleasing effect. She has a strong, clear, flexible voice and takes the highest notes with apparent ease. The congregation will be much pleased to hear her again." At an April 1903 Elmvale fundraiser in aid of the public library, she sang alone and then performed duets with her father, which brought enthusiastic applause and calls for encores. By 1903, when she was sixteen, Bertha had established a local reputation as a promising young soloist.

Bertha continued to inspire her father's pride—and his plans—as her singing developed. In 1902, John penned a letter to the editor of *The Elmvale Lance* that shows how his musical interests, and those of his daughter, were inextricably intertwined with other parts of his life. He opens the letter by highlighting an opportunity not to be missed: the County has offered a grant to build a hall. He moves on to lay out his personal assessment—that the community lacks a hall for large meetings and, more importantly, one "suitable for either a musical or dramatic entertainment. Neither instrumental nor vocal music can be properly heard, and therefore not properly appreciated." He brings his business acumen to bear, stating that debentures could be raised and calculating that they could be paid off in ten years. He proposes concrete action—that the Township Council and the Police Trustees must meet. And he insists that the common good must prevail—that the hall must be a community venture, not a private enterprise. This is Bertha's father in the essence: a man who can recognize a good opportunity, clearly articulate a need, make a sound business plan, and put forward a political action plan—and in all of this keep the public interest in mind. Although surely his unspoken agenda was to see Bertha singing in this unrealized hall, for who else in Elmvale would win more from such a venue?

Indeed, John Crawford was a master of the calculated gamble, as his success in horse racing showed. Most rural households in the 1890s would have had a horse or two, but John was noted for having "a fine drive in the shape of horse flesh." He enjoyed the "breeding, training and care" of good-quality horses, and he liked testing their mettle on the racecourse. In 1897, he and his wife's cousin James Walton formed the organizing committee for the New Year's Day village horse races in Elmvale, and eighteen months later, John bought himself a "dandy bicycle trotting sulky." Starting in the fall of 1898, he had several successful years in harness racing, running at least three different horses: Prince Wilkes, Princevale, and Bertvale. Building on previous successes at the local fair and the May 24 celebrations in Elmvale, John's horses took first prize two years running in the Barrie Ice Races on Lake Simcoe held each February. John took his horses on to regional race meets in Orillia, Creemore, and Penetang, and further afield to Toronto, Guelph, London, Hamilton, and Orangeville. Finally, after two dramatic wins at a meet in Bradford in 1900, he sold his best trotter, Princevale, for $825—and this at a time when an ordinary well-trained horse might bring $50 to $100, and when a village house on a lot could be bought for $500. Two weeks later, he turned down an offer of $200 for the yearling Bertvale, which he kept to race successfully two years later. John seems to have had a fine nose for speculating on a good investment, building up that investment, and knowing the right moment to cash out.

In retrospect, encouraging Bertha to follow her developing dreams of becoming a serious singer was probably the biggest gamble of John's life. And that gamble really began when he upped stakes in Elmvale and took the family to Toronto in May 1903.

Entr'acte –
Life Is a Gamble

February, 1900. Lake Simcoe, Barrie, Ontario, Canada. Bertha stamps her feet on the packed snow. Her felt overshoes are supposed to be waterproof, but they are damp from the slush that was outside the train station this morning, and now the cold is seeping in. But soon enough her feet will be numb, and she won't be thinking about them until after the final race anyway.

Bertha is standing in a clutch with Lucia and the Walton girls. Eva, Edna, and Ella have joined the Crawfords to see the excitement of the ice races in Barrie today. The collars of the girls' thick knitted sweaters stick up from under their coats, while their long underwear is well hidden under their wool skirts. They ball up their hands inside their mittens. The girls have strategically taken up a position far enough from their mothers that they can gossip without being overheard, but close enough that they won't get scolded for wandering around unchaperoned.

The crowd is predominantly men, and not all sober men at that. The tension has grown as the afternoon races have progressed. There are seven horses entered in what has been billed as the 'Championship of Ontario.' After four heats, the score is tied, with two heats to John Crawford's Princevale—a relative unknown—and two heats to the favourite, Dalton McCarthy. Of course Dalton McCarthy is tipped to win; the horse is named after the late local Member of Parliament who won more elections than most people can remember.

Steam rises from the groups of men, who are loudly debating obscure political allegories and discreetly passing around bottles. Intermittent whiffs of alcohol float by on the light breeze.

The girls squint in the bright sunshine that reflects off the broad, snow-covered surface of Lake Simcoe. Standing at a distance, the girls' mothers have their heads together, talking intently.

"Your mother looks perturbed, Edna. Do you think something is wrong?" asks Bertha. At thirteen, Bertha is full of questions, but not yet adept at figuring out the answers.

Edna glances across at her mother, who has a look of distinct disapproval on her face. "Oh, Bertha, you know Quakers don't approve of gambling."

"But you Waltons are Methodists, Edna."

"Well, we only go to the Methodist Church because there isn't any Quaker meeting in Elmvale. But you know our grandparents were Quakers. Anyway, Methodists don't like gambling much, either."

Bertha studies her mother and her Aunt Mary some more. "But why would they be talking about gambling today?"

At this, the older girls all roll their eyes and take the superior stance that having attained the grand age of fifteen or sixteen entitles them to. "Bertha May," Eva starts in a patronizing tone. "You see all those men over there, crowded around the man in the top hat? He's a bookie. They are all making bets on whether Princevale or Dalton McCarthy is going to win this final heat."

"Oh, I knew that," says Bertha quickly. But she hadn't. She's quiet for a while. "Well, I guess Presbyterians aren't so fussy."

Edna just laughs. "I don't suppose your father would be running his horse in all these races if he thought gambling was a big problem."

Bertha catches Lucia's look of embarrassment, and the realization dawns that the dazzling glare of the sun might be obscuring the darker side of the afternoon's seemingly innocent entertainment. The two girls wander away to where their father is checking his horse.

John Crawford is running his hand down Princevale's foreleg and examining a harness strap. The horse is still sweating from running four heats along the snow-covered racetrack, which has been laid out across the smooth, unobstructed surface of the frozen lake. Princevale is tired, but he can't be any more tired than Dalton McCarthy is. Bertha thinks her father looks confident today. She has heard him boast often enough that this horse is the best he has bred and trained so far.

'Uncle' James Walton and 'Uncle' Chester Walton come up behind John. "John, you've got half the ready money in Elmvale riding on your horse today," says James. "I wouldn't want to be in *your* shoes tomorrow if he doesn't bring it all home."

Bertha suddenly wonders if all of her 'uncles' are betting on this race.

John turns to young Billy Arnold, who is driving the sulky again today. "Where's your father got his money, Bill?"

Billy's father, Thomas Arnold, is an Elmvale horse trainer. Thomas has been helping John with his hobby for years and is a fine judge of horse flesh.

"Geez, I certainly hope it's on us!" snaps back Billy.

"Well, get out there and show them what we are worth!" John says as he slaps his horse's rump.

The girls back away as Billy steers the horse and sulky around and trots smartly to the starting line.

The seven horses line up, and almost instantly they are off. Princevale and Dalton McCarthy are leading again as the field comes into the home stretch; all of the horses are straining to complete this one last heat. The ice creaks as the horses pound by. The winter cleats on their horseshoes spit chips of ice left and right, and flecks of sweat fly off the horses' backs.

The noise of the crowd works its way up to a steady roar, and Bertha forgets her unease about the gambling as she loses herself in the cheering of the crowd. Even the oldest girls are jumping up and down like they are small children again.

The two leading horses are straining side by side, but then they start to separate. By the time they reach the finish line, Princevale is ahead by a clear length. The horse will be lauded as a provincial champion in the papers this week.

John beams at his girls all the way home, his prize money safe in his pocket. "What do you think about the chances for an unknown from little Elmvale now, eh?" he asks them.

CHAPTER THREE –
The First Rungs on the Ladder,
1903–1907

Is this the suit Bertha wore when she set out on her first international tour in January 1907? She certainly seems to think she is going places.

JANE COOPER

*I*n May 1903, the Crawford family left the village of Elmvale and moved to the rapidly growing city of Toronto. As she made her new home in the provincial capital, sixteen-year-old Bertha's opportunities to make something out of her singing voice expanded hugely. Indeed, while we can only guess at the reasons behind John Crawford's decision to move his family to Toronto, he would have been well aware that of all of his children, Bertha probably had the most to gain from living in a big city.

The family's move seems to have been carefully thought through. John Crawford sold his Elmvale tailoring business in May 1902 and moved the family out of their apartment in the brick block building and into a farmhouse he owned on the edge of the village. Only a year later did they complete the move to Toronto. On leaving Elmvale, John was lauded as "one of the pioneers of Elmvale . . . [who] has built or was instrumental in having built a large portion of the town" and who would also be "much missed in musical circles." Like a rite of passage for the successful immigrant family embarking on another stage of their voyage, the Crawfords auctioned off many of the possessions that had defined their rural life: old household furniture, vehicles, and harnesses—all things that the family would not need for their new urban venture.

Although the family got rid of unnecessary property, they didn't cut their personal ties abruptly. The social columns of *The Elmvale Lance* noted regular visits to Elmvale and the area by different members of the family over the next few years. The family came up for events like the Elmvale Fair and the Easter holiday, and John returned to the village regularly (probably to collect rent). When Bertha came back from Toronto to sing at the tenth anniversary of the Elmvale Presbyterian Church, Reverend McKay expressed the community's continued fondness for Bertha when he said that "We are proud to think of her as an Elmvale lassie."

However, as they moved into the new century, the extended family that had bound Bertha to Elmvale was rapidly dispersing. Cousin Charles Walton took his wife and son south in February 1902 to the Hamilton area. Chester Walton took his brood north in July 1902 to New Liskeard and Charlton, Ontario, to try his fortunes as a baker and postmaster in the northern Ontario clay belt. In August of that same year, James Walton moved east to Fenelon

Falls to take up a job as a furniture factory foreman. By the fall of 1903, the only family member of the Elmvale Silver Band still in the village was David Robertson, and he eventually brought his family to Toronto in 1906, settling down a ten-block walk north of John Crawford's new home. John's brother Andrew Crawford left Penetanguishene around the same time for Alberta. By the middle of the decade, the close-knit Crawford–Walton clan of the 1890s was scattered across the province and country.

The Crawfords' new home in Toronto was a three-storey semi-detached brick house on Palmerston Avenue with an elegant arched entranceway and ornate pillars holding up the deep front porch roof. It was probably more comfortable than living over the store in Elmvale (it had indoor plumbing, for instance), but it was not a particularly large building, and there certainly wasn't space for a stable on the small urban lot. However, John hung on to his racehorses for another season, presumably boarding them in Elmvale. He did not sell the colt and broodmare until the fall of 1903. He ran Bertvale in a race at the Toronto picnic for the Retail Merchants Association of Canada that summer, melding his leisure hobby from Elmvale into his new business persona in Toronto.

How John made his money in Toronto is a tantalizing question. Over the next decade, he apparently accumulated enough money that he could consider sending Bertha abroad to study music—an expensive proposition then as now. For the first five or six years in Toronto, Bertha's father ran a tailoring business out of the family home. It is not clear how many other properties John owned in 1903, but it appears he kept some Elmvale income-generating properties for several years after the move to Toronto. In October 1904, he sold a farm in Elmvale as well as one of his brick block buildings that was rented out as retail space. The brick block brought him $2,800.

Did John reinvest his money in the Toronto property market? Toronto's economy in the first decade of the twentieth century was experiencing a boom that was a welcome contrast with the final years of the previous century, which had been marked by depression. The cost of living rose as the economy improved, which made life very difficult for the poor, but provided opportunities for those with money to invest. The cost of first-class men's suits increased by fifty percent in the run-up to the First World War, which must have worked well for a tailor like John. However, the overall cost of living also went up by fifty percent, so his tailoring income probably just kept pace. In contrast, rental property was at a premium, and rents in some parts of Toronto doubled in the early part of the decade. If John built on his Elmvale experience to become a landlord in Toronto, he probably did well out of it.

If Toronto was a good place to make money from John's perspective, then from Bertha's point of view it was a place full of opportunities to sing. Toronto at the turn of the century was a city dominated by its churches; every church had a choir, and the larger ones employed four soloists to lead their choirs. In 1904, *Robertson's Landmarks of Toronto* described in detail almost 200 churches, many of them substantial buildings, serving a rapidly growing population which increased from 200,000 in 1901 to more than 375,000 by 1911. The book organizes the churches by denomination, a distinction Torontonians would have been acutely aware of even as the proposed union of the major non-conformist churches offered to shift the balance between the churches. While the Anglican Church of England was the largest individual denomination in Toronto in 1911 with 102,000 members, the combined membership of the non-conformist churches (i.e., Methodists, Presbyterians, and Baptists) exceeded that number with 146,000 members. Catholics were a much smaller group with 46,000 adherents, while the Jewish population in 1911 was only 18,000.

The churches that Bertha would come to sing in harboured the predominant Victorian Protestant morality that made Toronto a conservative place in many ways. Both work and play were discouraged on the Christian Sabbath. For many years there were no streetcars on Sundays, and boys might be arrested for playing in the streets on the Lord's Day. More generally, there were rules forbidding 'lewd books' and 'immoral plays,' and theatrical and musical performances—particularly those aimed at the more plebeian audiences—were subject to censorship by the police. Productions that included risqué material might be permitted if they appeared under the guise of 'high art' for the wealthy, but anything that smacked of the erotic or blasphemous was not allowed in the burlesque theatres frequented by the working classes. Many Protestants in Toronto considered all professional theatre—including opera—immoral, regardless of the quality of the music or dance. These attitudes were endorsed by popular community organizations like the WCTU, which Bertha knew well from Elmvale, and the Canadian Temperance League, which Bertha often entertained in Toronto.

Inevitably, the musical world that Bertha dived into in Toronto—the world of respectable music, that is—was defined by the close relationship between music and religion. The key figures in music in Toronto all built their reputations by producing church music, and choral singing and oratorio were the most popular musical forms. Occasional visiting opera companies drew good audiences, but when Toronto musicians put together local productions, they preferred to mount cantatas and oratorios based on religious themes. While Toronto did not have a permanent orchestra until the 1920s, or an opera company until 1950, it already had a reputation as the choral capital of North America in the early 1900s due to the quality of its church choirs, concert choirs, and choral societies. Almost all the important voice teachers also worked as choirmasters in the big churches. There were three prominent music schools—the Toronto Conservatory of Music, the Toronto College of Music, and the Metropolitan School of Music—and various smaller ladies' colleges and private seminaries that prepared students for music careers. Almost all of their staff members were also in some way connected with church music. This is not to suggest that there was not also vaudeville and burlesque theatre in Toronto, but for a respectable girl like Bertha, the obvious way to build a musical career was through singing in the church.

Soon after Bertha arrived in Toronto, she put herself on this conventional path by signing up for professional singing lessons with a voice teacher who had a reputation for preparing vocalists for soloist work with church choirs. Edward Washington Schuch (1848–1940) was born in England of German descent, and, like John Crawford, he immigrated to Canada as a child. Schuch studied at the bastion of the Anglican establishment, Upper Canada College, and, although he maintained an interest in German music throughout his life, his loyalties lay with the Church of England. He spent his early career scrambling through a variety of jobs—as an insurance agent, a canvassing agent for *The Globe*, a proprietor for an advertising agency, and a clerk in the Bureau of Industries. He does not appear to have successfully established music as his profession until he was in his mid-thirties. Schuch built his reputation in the field by singing as a baritone in church and in public concerts, and also by working as a music journalist. For ten years, starting in 1882, Schuch was the music and drama critic for *The Globe*. He then moved on to write for *Saturday Night* and to edit *The Musical Journal*.

Clearly, John had chosen a musician with broad experience to serve as his daughter's first formal voice teacher. Indeed, by the time the fifty-six-year-old Schuch took on sixteen-year-old Bertha Crawford as a student in 1903, he was one of Toronto's best known singing teachers, advertising lessons in "voice, culture and expression." He seems to have been an indefatigable man, expecting his students to be energetic and inspiring them to work hard towards their goals. In the photo of him that accompanied his entry in *A Souvenir of Musical Toronto* five years before he became Bertha's voice teacher, he had already lost most of his hair and had a smooth, domed forehead and an aquiline nose that contrasted with his drooping walrus moustache, so popular at the turn of the century. Schuch was considered genial and tactful, and he enjoyed a broad reputation both for successfully directing large choirs of amateurs as well as for training the individuals who made up the quartet of professional soloists that every large church in Toronto aspired to have accompany its services. Quartet choirs, fronted by four soloists—two women singing the soprano and contralto parts, and two men singing the tenor and baritone or bass parts—were enormously popular, and there was a great deal of music produced for this market. Many of the students Schuch trained went on to work as soloists with large church choirs in Toronto, and some even in Montréal and New York. But no student of his had yet moved on from singing as a church soloist to singing in grand opera or on the international stage for a lengthy career.

It would not have taken many lessons for Schuch to realize that Bertha, with her already agile voice and her remarkable range that reached from F below the staff up to F above high C, had the rare potential to train to become a true coloratura soprano. Coloratura singing, also known as florid or ornamental singing, is characterized by the exhibition of vocal virtuosity including runs, trills, leaps, and embellishments. The lyrics are often irrelevant, and coloratura phrases, which may have a simple melody sung on only one vowel, are designed to display the pure beauty of the voice. A well-trained coloratura voice sounds almost birdlike, which is why coloratura sopranos were often fondly referred to as nightingales. Shaping her natural voice with years of subsequent study, Bertha came to excel at this singing style and was known as a coloratura soprano throughout her career.

In other ways, Bertha was typical of the kind of young student who took singing lessons with Schuch. Most were in their teens and early twenties, and many came from the newly ascendant middle classes. Their fathers, like John Crawford, worked as tradesmen and merchants in fields like printing, stationery, and the wine and liquor trade. Their daughters had absorbed an ethic that respected hard work and the ability to earn their own way. With the growth of the feminist ideal of the New Woman, many of these young women were interested in having a profession of their own and earning their own money. Professional singing in a church choir was a highly respectable career choice for a young woman with aspirations and the requisite talent. For the family who could afford to pay for singing lessons for a talented daughter, the possibility of a good return on this educational investment was a compelling incentive. Schuch tapped into those desires, advertising his lessons in *The Globe* and *The Toronto Daily Star* by listing his many students who currently held positions as paid soloists with prominent church choirs.

While Bertha continued to expand her musical aspirations in Toronto, her sister took quite a different path. Lucia left her childhood musical adventures behind and learned to be a stenographer, taking dictation in shorthand and transcribing and typing letters and reports. She probably worked as a stenographer for several years, as this was listed as her occupation in the annual *Toronto City Directory* until she married ten years later. She may have worked in an office, but most likely she also used her training to help her father's business ventures. But like many women of the age, her stenographic career came to a close after she married and had children. Indeed, Bertha and Lucia came of age in an era when it was quite unusual for a woman to continue within a professional career after marriage, and in fields such as teaching, it was actually prohibited.

Predictably, shortly after Bertha arrived in Toronto, she put her singing lessons to work with her local church choir. By the end of December 1903, Bertha was mentioned in *The Globe* as singing with the choir in a concert at College Street Presbyterian Church. The church was only a few blocks from her new home and was probably the family's new congregation in Toronto. Whether this was a paid position is not clear. However, she was soon also appearing in the wide variety of other musical events that the large city offered. From the middle of 1904, Bertha's name begins to appear in the newspapers as a soloist in charity concerts in Toronto. For example, in August 1904, she sang in a concert in Guild Hall in aid of the Frances Willard Home for Girls. The Willard Home was a hostel run by the Toronto District WCTU to help destitute and homeless young women in Toronto find jobs as domestic servants and save them from becoming 'fallen women.' In November 1904, Bertha was one of the singers in a concert in Broadway Hall under the auspices of the Church of St. Mary Magdalen's Tennis Club.

While Bertha was obviously happy to sing at a variety of events and venues, it is unlikely that any of these smaller events made quite the same impression on her as the first time she sang on the stage of Toronto's premier concert venue, Massey Hall. In January 1905, Schuch arranged a large choral recital at Massey Hall to raise funds for the new Toronto Grace Hospital, a maternity hospital that the Salvation Army was creating by converting their women's refuge home. Bertha was one of four women soloists that Schuch chose to feature with the accompaniment of a Ladies Chorus of fifty women.

For an up-and-coming singer like Bertha, the stage of Massey Hall was an unparalleled place to perform. The Massey family, which earned its substantial wealth producing agricultural machinery, had built the hall out of a commitment to public service, and, for many years, charities and non-profit organizations could rent the hall at much lower rates than professional artists. From the time the 3,500 seat hall opened in 1894, it was renowned for its superb acoustics and immediately became the preeminent concert hall not only in Toronto, but in all of Canada. The interior was decorated with an exotic Moorish theme and was richly painted in reds, blues, greens, and golds. Banks of stained glass windows filled the hall with coloured light in the daylight hours, while both gas and electric lights were used at night. The hall was noted for the unusually good view that patrons had of the stage from almost every seat in the house. Artists came to appreciate the intimacy they could share with the audience members, every one of whom they could see from the stage, in contrast with the older theatres where many patrons were obscured in tiers of private boxes. During the eight years that Bertha lived as a young woman in Toronto, she sang in many charity and community events at Massey Hall, so it may have been on this stage that she first honed her talent for connecting with an audience—an asset that came to define her performances during her career.

Bertha sang many times in Massey Hall. At the turn of the century, this premier Toronto concert hall was frequently rented by charitable organizations at a discounted price.

Bertha would have cut a fine figure at the centre of any stage. At eighteen years old, she was a pleasant-looking young woman who measured up well to the standard of North American good looks for the period, the Gibson Girl. While not as tall as the illustrator's ideal model—she was somewhere between five feet, three inches and five feet, six inches tall—she was fortunate to have thick, wavy brown hair that could easily be shaped into the fashionable bouffant styles, where the hair was piled high and wide on top of the head. Her teeth, while somewhat prominent, were strong and white. She was slender, and her photographs suggest that she wore a structured Edwardian corset to achieve the desirable S-curve profile of a slim waist with an ample bosom and hips.

From these early days in her career, Bertha understood the benefit of making unpaid charity appearances. One has to assume that she was sympathetic to the fundraisers' causes, but Bertha probably also appreciated the personal benefits of appearing in a charity concert. It seems likely that, from her earliest performing days, she cherished the interaction with an audience—especially the sound of their applause, which she would never hear during a church service no matter how well she sang. And while these performances did not earn her any money, they presented important opportunities to gain exposure to music critics and to build her reputation.

Certainly, as a young singer, Bertha would have been aware of the effect of newspaper reviews on her reputation as a developing musician. Even an amateur musician benefits from the support and endorsement of music critics, and for a budding professional like Bertha, the word of important critics can make or break a nascent career. Therefore, she must have been pleased when, in 1905, *The Toronto Sunday World* reported on her performance at Massey Hall, saying, "[i]n a waltz chorus the solo was sung by Miss Bertha Crawford, who has an exceedingly bright, clear soprano voice and whose singing is full of promise." She probably clipped that review from the newspaper and stuck it in a growing collection in her album. Indeed, in these early days of recording, short of an audition, reviews or 'press notices' were the only way of representing an artist's experience and abilities to an agent. Singers like Bertha always had a sheaf or album of press clippings available to attest to their experience and successes—the equivalent of the modern resume or portfolio.

By the time Bertha took to the stage in the early years of the 1900s, most of the Toronto papers employed writers who specialized in covering music and theatre. By the middle of the decade, she was receiving regular press notices from local music reporters, including the 'grandfather of Toronto critics,' Edwin Rodie Parkhurst (1848–1924). An immigrant from England and an amateur musician himself, E.R. Parkhurst had a well-deserved reputation as an optimistic booster of the local music scene. He tended to write short and overwhelmingly positive reviews, preferring to encourage new artists rather than criticize them, leaving the reader to interpret any shortcomings by reading between the lines. In unsigned "Music and Drama" columns in *The Globe* in 1906, which are presumably Parkhurst's work, Bertha was noted for singing with "ease and grace of style" and for having a "clear soprano voice" that was "deserving of mention." At nineteen, Bertha had already caught the attention of a critic who would continue to track her progress in his columns in *The Globe* and in his own monthly journal *Musical Canada* over the next twenty years.

By this time, Bertha was earning more than just applause and exposure for her singing. Early in 1905, she got what was probably her first paid position as the soprano soloist at the Erskine Presbyterian Church on Caer-Howell Street in Toronto. Schuch must have introduced her to the choirmaster, Alfred Sturrock (1873–?), who had himself been a student of Schuch and who acted as both the baritone soloist and the choirmaster for the church. Sturrock was a fairly typical local singer who was working his way up the rungs of the Presbyterian church music ladder into the world of professional music like Bertha was. While working as a telephone operator, he also sang professionally, touring Western Canada in 1896 and even giving American vaudeville a try around 1900. But he kept coming back to the more respectable world of church music, and sometime in 1904, when he was still a young thirty-two, he took on the choir at the Erskine Presbyterian Church and hired eighteen-year-old Bertha Crawford to be his soprano soloist soon after. Another of Schuch's students, Ida Maw, held the position of contralto soloist.

For the ambitious young Bertha, it must have been hugely encouraging to get a paid soloist position after little more than a year of professional training—a firm affirmation that she had stepped onto the first rung of the professional singer's ladder. With its gallery full, the Erskine Presbyterian Church could hold up to 1,100 people—almost twice the capacity of the Elmvale church that Bertha was most familiar with. The Erskine Presbyterian Church was a white brick Gothic-style building, and its sanctuary had excellent acoustics. The congregation looked down from pews that curved around the main floor, slanting down to the pulpit in front of the organ. An upper gallery surrounded the main hall, supported by eight iron columns that led up to the gracefully arched ceiling. Large windows at the back and sides of the hall would have made the church bright on a Sunday morning, and a gasalier hanging from the middle of the ceiling would have given a soft overall light in the evenings. While Bertha had sung plenty of church solos as a member of her own church and as a guest soloist before, she must have felt an unusual swelling of pride the first time she stood up from her pew beside the organ and faced the congregation as an official paid soprano.

Winning the soloist's position was probably as important for Bertha's ego as it was for her purse, but getting a well-paid job in music when she was still eighteen would have reinforced her dreams that music held promise as a viable career. Indeed, pay for a church soloist was above the average earnings available to most women. The lower paid soloists at the biggest churches like the Metropolitan Methodist Church made about $300 a year in the middle of the decade and were only required to sing at Sunday services and practice once a week on Friday evenings. In contrast, women school teachers in Ontario earned on average between $246 a year in 1901 and $485 a year (for men and women) in 1911 for a five-day work week—and the women teachers of this period were better paid than most working women in Ontario.

But working as a church soloist offered more opportunities than just earning money—*if* you were in the right church. Bertha would have expected to be constantly improving her singing through her church work. Working under Sturrock, who had learned from the same teacher as she had, would have had its limitations. Did she begin to feel that she had learned all she could under Sturrock's guidance? Or was she looking for a more prestigious position with a bigger, better resourced church? Whatever the reasons, after little more than a year at the Erskine Presbyterian Church, something drove Bertha to look for a change. In April 1906, *The Globe* noted that she had taken the position as the soprano soloist at the Sherbourne Street Methodist Church, where the choir director, Arthur Blakeley (1865–?), was a locally renowned organist and music teacher in his own right. Located at the corner of Sherbourne and Carleton streets, the large square stone building had a distinct tower that dominated the street corner with its round base and square top. An ornate wind vane rotated high up on its peaked roof, pointing the way to Bertha's new assignment.

Blakeley had been born in England and had started his training as an organist there. The colonial mentality was still strong in turn-of-the-century Toronto, and a musician with English training was usually assumed to be better qualified than someone who had studied only on the Canadian side of the Atlantic. Blakeley immigrated when he was nineteen and almost immediately found work as a respected church organist in Toronto. By 1906, he had been the organist at the Sherbourne Street Methodist Church for twenty years, and for several of those years he had taught organ out of the Toronto Conservatory of Music. He also regularly gave well-reviewed organ concerts. Working with Blakeley would have given Bertha the chance to learn more demanding music, but it was still not enough to satisfy her itch for new challenges.

On a cold Friday in the first week of 1907, twenty-year-old Bertha took a step that suggests she was beginning to dream of taking her career well beyond the church sanctuary. On January 4, she climbed onto a train in Toronto, bags in hand, to embark on an international music career. She had taken a leave from her soloist position at the Sherbourne Street Methodist Church to join a concert party tour. A 'concert party' typically included three to five performers: a reader of entertaining writings, one or two singers, an accompanist, and perhaps another musician. Starting in the late 1860s with the Redpath Lyceum Bureau, American agencies known as lyceum bureaus established circuits that grouped together a number of small communities where there was a demand for a series of lectures and musical performances. The bureaus negotiated contracts between local organizing committees and performing acts of a guaranteed standard, and the acts would travel the circuit, performing at each community in turn. The bureaus distributed promotional brochures with flattering pictures of the performers, glowing descriptions of their talents, and quotations from the best newspaper notices about recent appearances. Many of the established musicians in Toronto regularly joined concert party tours in the U.S. on the lyceum circuits (later also known as Chautauqua circuits). In January 1907, Bertha joined their ranks and began her international career touring on a lyceum circuit across the southern United States.

'Elocutionist' Marietta Ladell introduced Bertha to the life of the touring musician when she took her along as a supporting act on a two-month tour of the southern United States in 1907.

This concert party tour, which lasted three months, took Bertha on a long series of engagements in smaller towns, starting in Williamsburg, Virginia and taking her through North and South Carolina, Tennessee, Kentucky, Georgia, Florida, Alabama, and possibly even Texas. Modest concert parties like these filled a niche market, performing in venues too small to attract larger touring companies, but still able to accommodate an audience of a couple hundred people. The economics of tours such as this demanded a careful balance between the expenses of the artists' fees, as well as transportation and accommodation, with the revenue earned from performing in community halls in small towns or in large churches in cities. A profitable tour required shows to be booked every night or second night in towns less than a day's train journey apart.

A concert party tour was an important test for an ambitious professional musician like Bertha. Aspiring young singers were warned by the established stars that they would never have a serious career unless they had the strength and stamina for extended travel. After all, the only way to reach a large audience and build a large reputation was through touring. Bertha got her apprenticeship in the life of a touring artist under the tutelage of the lead artist on the 1907 tour, Marietta Ladell (1874–?). The thirty-three-year-old Ladell was an elocutionist, or, in common parlance, a reader. Turn-of-the-century concert audiences were accustomed to being entertained by professional readings of dramatic or humorous stories, and they admired good elocution. Ladell was based in Toronto, but she was an experienced touring artist, spending several months every year reading to audiences in small- and medium-sized communities across Canada and the United States. In October 1902, the Crawford family probably saw her when she gave a reading at Vollmer's Hall in Elmvale, and they would have been familiar with her work in Toronto. In the middle of the decade, Ladell made several tours together with the violinist George Fox (1870–1913) and a complementary soprano singer. And in January 1907, that singer was Bertha. Ladell would have mentored Bertha in how to keep up with a fast-paced tour, changing hotels every day or two and making the best of constant train travel and mediocre restaurant food—and all while keeping fresh enough to please a new audience several evenings every week.

The violinist George Fox may have exposed Bertha to quite a different aspect of the artistic world. Fox began his career in Walkerton, Ontario as a six-year-old child prodigy on the piano, but as an adult he favoured the violin. His father was a German watchmaker who invited a music teacher to live with the family and train his young son. Perhaps it is inappropriate to speculate about Fox's sexuality based on minimal circumstantial evidence, but by the time he was twenty-one, George had left home to live in lodgings with his childhood violin teacher. He toured for several years with Ladell, but they do not seem to have been a couple. Fox never married, and by 1911, he had returned to live with his parents. In 1913, at age forty-two, he died of 'dissipation,' a polite term for alcoholism. Did his drinking mask a frustration with the difficulty of living as a gay man in his time? It is impossible to know, but it is interesting to speculate whether Bertha, in this first tour away from home—and away from the restrictive conventions of the Toronto church world—came to understand that human relations were more diverse than contemporary Protestant morality admitted to.

Bertha kept up with the pace of her first tour and collected good reviews on the road. *The New Enterprise* in Madison, Florida reported in February that "[t]he singing of Miss Bertha Crawford, the talented young soprano, was splendid and the rich voice of this young lady, the ease with which she rendered her numbers and the modesty and grace captivated all," and *The Atlanta Journal* thought that she "sang beautifully, marvellously . . ." Did these rave reviews from American reporters (albeit small-town reporters) give Bertha, on her first adventure south of the border, a taste for that special attention that expatriate artists get? Did these clippings find a place of honour in her scrapbook to tease her with thoughts of more exciting times during her duller days in Toronto? She was probably relieved to finally come home to Toronto in time to sing at the Easter services at the Sherbourne Street Methodist Church at the end of March, but there can be little doubt, in retrospect, that her first international touring experience was positive. However, she had also returned just in time to prepare for a significant appearance in musical theatre at Massey Hall—an appearance that had just as important an impact on the direction of her future career.

Bertha had first learned the leading role of Mabel in the Gilbert and Sullivan operetta *The Pirates of Penzance* for a production put on by Edward Schuch the previous year, in March 1906. The 1906 production was first aired over two evenings at Toronto's Princess Theatre, a modern theatre where touring opera companies often appeared. The event was a fundraiser to help the Toronto Argonauts rowing team get to England for the Henley Regatta, and it featured Schuch's students. Building on the success of the 1906 performances, the same cast reunited in the middle of April 1907 for a larger, improved production in Massey Hall. The 1907 version ran for four performances over three days, with tickets selling from $0.25 to $1.50.

The Pirates of Penzance is a light-hearted comedy about an encounter between a band of hapless—and single—pirates and a pompous Major-General hamstrung by a houseful of unmarried daughters, including Mabel. At the end of two acts of humorous antics and playful arias, the pirates reform, are forgiven their misdeeds, and—in a satisfying Victorian conclusion—are ultimately redeemed through marriage to the Major-General's daughters. This English operetta contains many musical elements that parody Italian and French operas, particularly Verdi's and Gounod's works. The parody is not a mockery, but requires good-humoured respect for the music, not to mention superior technical singing skills. Indeed, for the determined singer, Gilbert and Sullivan's operettas can be a stepping stone to more serious opera.

Putting together a production with ten soloists, a chorus of sixty, and an orchestra of twenty musicians was no mean feat for amateurs. Schuch may have chosen this particular operetta because he knew that, in Bertha, he had an unusually skilled young soprano whom he could count on to carry off the difficult coloratura work in the leading soprano role of Mabel, including the famous solo waltz "Poor Wand'ring One." And indeed, of all the cast, it was Bertha's photo that was featured with the advance notices for the production in *The Globe* and *The Toronto Daily Star*.

Bertha was fortunate that Edward Schuch was an Anglican and had no qualms about the moral implications of musical theatre. On the contrary, Schuch thought Gilbert and Sullivan's operettas were very suitable vehicles to showcase the talents of his students. On the other hand, members of the Massey family, who built Massey Hall, were strict Methodists who did not approve of any professional theatre performances, let alone operettas. Although by 1907 the hall was being used from time to time to present theatre and even opera, Massey Hall had been originally designed specifically to exclude the presentation of musical theatre. The showpiece auditorium had very limited space for dressing rooms and storerooms, and there was no real backstage space to facilitate dramatic productions. In the absence of an orchestra pit, the front rows of seats had to be removed to allow for the musicians to line up to the right and left of the conductor. Furthermore, for *The Pirates of Penzance*, the stage had to be extended, a proscenium arch had to be fashioned out of drapery, and special electrical effects had to be created—a process that took up several days before the show. Massey Hall was always an elegant space for concerts and meetings, but it was an awkward space to put on either an English operetta or an Italian opera. However, Bertha and her friends were undaunted.

For Bertha, who had previously sung mainly hymns and oratorio in church and sentimental Victorian songs in concerts, *The Pirates of Penzance* was an exciting opportunity to put her skills to work in a full-length production that required sustained attention to both singing and acting, as well as cooperation with a cast of other actors. Obviously, she found that she enjoyed being part of a team effort, and she enjoyed the challenges presented by the music. Mr. Schuch's Opera Singers earned very friendly notices in the Toronto papers, with Bertha leading the honours. *The Globe* felt she had "made a great hit in the waltz song ['Poor Wand'ring One'] in the first act" and was impressed with her "light voice of clear timbre and exceptional range." *The Toronto Daily Star* reported that "Her charm and naïveté of manner won the unbounded applause of the audience and her voice was heard to advantage in several melodious solos and duets." Bertha's good reviews were supplemented by calls for encores and bouquets of flowers, and no doubt she had great fun. Any nerves that she and her friends had on the first night were gone by the second, and if she had not previously realized that she had a knack for connecting with an audience through musical theatre, then she certainly knew it by the time she took her final bows in the role of Mabel.

For a coloratura soprano like Bertha, to finally have the chance to put both her singing and acting skills to the test in a role like Mabel may have been something of a life-changing experience. The operetta role gave her a legitimate vehicle (at least in the eyes of some) to fully act out her youthful *joie de vivre* on stage. With the costumes, the lights, the orchestra, and the harmonies of her fellow singers all coming together, she must have experienced firsthand the dramatic magic of the opera that has inspired many a singer. Moreover, she had her first taste of the kind of attention that a successful opera singer could attract. After all, in the international world of entertainment in this first decade of the twentieth century, there was no character more renowned, more glamourous, or more handsomely paid than the top opera soprano—the prima donna of the opera stage.

But if Bertha hoped to experience more of this exhilaration, it was not going to be in Toronto. There was no permanent opera company in the city, or anywhere else in Canada. And the international touring opera companies that came through Toronto all featured established singers with European training. For instance, the San Carlo Opera Company, which had arrived in Toronto just days after Schuch's *The Pirates of Penzance* 1907 production, was headlined by the American-born—but European trained—soprano Lillian Nordica. So, despite earning a good salary for her singing as a church soloist, having toured across the southern United States, and having starred in a large-scale amateur operetta production, twenty-year-old Bertha may not have thought that she had it all. Regular mention in the Toronto papers confirmed that, after four years in the city, she was established as a successful local musician. But did that just leave her yearning for something more?

Entr'acte –
Competing for the Metropolitan Prize

November, 1907. *Metropolitan Methodist Church, Toronto, Ontario, Canada.* Bertha Crawford leans over the rail of the gallery from her seat above the sanctuary. The patent leather tip of her boot is tapping against the cast iron end of the pew as she waits for her turn to audition. She looks down to the organ below and watches Herbert Wheeldon lift his fingers off the keyboard and tuck his feet up under the seat. He runs a finger around the inside of his celluloid collar, easing the sharp white line around his throat. Bertha can tell that he is hot. Perhaps he is not yet comfortable with the central heating in this church. Bertha has heard about those damp English churches and draughty cathedrals where he used to play. She thinks he will appreciate being warm better when he steps out onto Queen Street to walk home. But that won't be for another couple of hours.

Below her, the church doors swing open and shut. She feels as much as she hears the rhythm of women's boots crisply trotting up the stairs to join her in the gallery. Mr. Lamb, the choir librarian, is directing all of the competitors upstairs. Bertha expects that Wheeldon will ask them to sing from the front of the gallery, where this church's choir stands during the service. He'll want to hear if their voices can really fill the full vault of this large building. The

Metropolitan Methodist Church is the biggest and most important Methodist church in Canada, and the congregation expects choral singing of a quality befitting their stature and their building.

The door swings open again and boots clomp up the west aisle. Bertha is surprised to see Tom Weatherly joining Wheeldon below. Bertha was a guest soloist only a couple of weeks ago at a Thanksgiving concert at the church where Weatherly is the organist. She wonders what these choirmasters are talking about now. She sits back suddenly as the two Englishmen look up at her before they go back to studying their papers and talking quietly.

Bertha is uneasy, but not about the singing. She has been singing in church all her life. And she has been taking professional voice lessons for four years now. This church is bigger than most, but it isn't as big as Massey Hall. She knows for a fact that she can throw her voice to the back of the top gallery in that hall, so she doesn't think filling this space will be a challenge.

The first woman is invited forward to sing.

Bertha is confident about the quality of her own singing. Last week, she asked her teacher, Mr. Schuch, for his advice about the audition. Her balding, jovial mentor had just laughed.

"Bertha May, you have to give this one a try. An open competition for the top soprano soloist in Toronto doesn't happen very often. And what do you have to lose if you don't get it? You can always go on tour instead."

She could almost see him thinking, "But what a feather in my cap, if another one of my students gets that job!" At that, she had smiled inwardly, secretly proud of the idea that she might repay his years of encouragement by getting the most important—and the best paid—singing job in Toronto.

Another woman makes her way down the pew past Bertha. She stumbles across Bertha's foot, but Bertha doesn't notice; she is worrying about something else.

A month ago she signed a contract. She is supposed to go on another tour with Marietta Ladell in the United States. And now, if she wins this audition, she will have to break that contract, and that thought leaves her worried.

If John Crawford was concerned about the propriety of his twenty-one-year-old daughter trailing around America, chaperoned only by an unmarried woman of the stage and the dissipated overgrown boy who is her sidekick, he won't feel much better about Bertha breaking a contract signed in good faith.

John is a businessman, and he built the Crawford reputation on his commitment to fulfill a contract, regardless of whether it is typed up in duplicate or made on a handshake.

Bertha hasn't told her father about this audition. If she gets this job, will his pride outweigh his disappointment about her going back on her word? Or will he actually enjoy her comeuppance? She can just imagine he'll have to say, "Aye, lassie, I think I might have suggested that you were making a hasty decision about that tour..."

She thinks it through as she waits for her turn. Which would really be more satisfying? The brilliant but ephemeral thrill of the stage? Or the regular and profitable routine of a prestigious church position?

Below, Wheeldon and Weatherly put their heads together again. Wheeldon makes a note and checks the list. "Bertha Crawford?"

Bertha stands up. She looks around, taking in the elaborately painted ceiling arches, the towering gilt organ pipes, the soft evening light filtering through the stained glass. She looks down at the choirmaster, imported with such fanfare all the way from England. And she decides. "I want this job, and I am going to get it. I will worry about the rest later."

CHAPTER FOUR –
The Pinnacle of Choirs,
1907–1909

Bertha was very pleased with herself when she won the top soloist position with the Metropolitan Methodist Church on Queen Street in Toronto in 1907.

𝓑ertha seems never to have been afraid of change. In retrospect, it looks like she often sought it out. Perhaps she was driven by a kind of internal restlessness, a persistent nagging doubt that there might be something better waiting just around the corner or over the horizon. Or had she inherited a taste for adventure from her immigrant father? Regardless, she was probably often supported in her desire to reach for bigger and better things by others—family, friends, and colleagues—who persuaded her that her talents were not yet being fulfilled. It is not clear exactly when she decided that she could not be really satisfied until she had tried her luck on the opera stage. But in the first decade of the century in Toronto, there was a variety of musical opportunities to tantalize a singer, each with a promise of its own rewards.

In the fall of 1907, a particularly tempting opportunity for Bertha arose out of the forced 'retirement' of Dr. Torrington from the Metropolitan Methodist Church. The Metropolitan Methodist Church was a splendid venue for performing sacred music and, in many ways, had the best musical reputation of all the big Toronto churches. The cornerstone of the Metropolitan Methodist Church had been laid in 1870 and, soon after the church opened in 1872, up to 3,000 worshipers were attending on Sundays. A good part of the congregation was accommodated in a second-storey gallery that surrounded the main floor and was held up by iron columns beneath an ornately decorated ceiling. The choir's voices rang out from this gallery in an earthly imitation of a 'choir celestial.' The congregation's commitment to setting the standard for inspiring church music in Toronto was established early on, with the hiring of Dr. F.H. Torrington (1837–1917) as the organist and choirmaster in 1873. It was further enhanced in 1876 with the installation, at Torrington's behest, of the largest and most complete organ in the country, with its 3,315 pipes and notes. The church went on to build a reputation for excellence in organ and choral music that Bertha would have found very attractive.

However, in early 1907, after thirty-four years with the same choirmaster, the Metropolitan Methodist Church's Music Committee decided that it was time to replace Torrington. Controversy swirled about the aged organists' ouster. The scandal was a hot topic in the musical community—and in the newspapers—for the first half of 1907, while Bertha was still singing at Sherbourne Street Methodist Church and performing with her friends in concerts around Toronto. Bertha, like professional singers all over the city, took note as the choir, including the soloists, all resigned. A petition in support of Torrington was circulated. A book of letters of commendation was privately published. A farewell concert drew a standing-room-only crowd. But the members of the Metropolitan Methodist's Music Committee stood firm. Dr. Torrington was seventy years old, and in their considered opinion, it was time for a younger man to take the job. And as the preeminent Protestant church in the country, with one of the best organs in the country, it behooved their status that they should have an organist who was a Fellow of the Royal College of Organists (FRCO) in England. In July 1907, Herbert Arthur Wheeldon (1864–1943?), previously of St. Saviour's Church, Chelsea, from London, stepped into the maelstrom and accepted the appointment as the new organist and choirmaster. *Musical Canada* rapidly endorsed the new engagement with a biography and portrait that showed a neat man wearing a silk tie around a tall celluloid collar, with hair precisely parted, sensitive bright eyes, and a soft lower lip showing beneath a wide, slightly pointed moustache.

When English organist Herbert Wheeldon chose Bertha as the lead soprano for his new choir at the Metropolitan Methodist Church in 1907, her feet were set on a path that would lead to London.

Born in the English Midlands town of Derby forty-three years before, Wheeldon had first learned to play the organ from his father before articling as a pupil to the organist at Rippon Cathedral. He worked his way through a challenging progression of exams to become an Associate of the Royal College of Organists (ARCO), and earned a Bachelor of Music from Cambridge, before finally achieving the coveted FRCO. Along the way, he discovered that he also had a talent as a composer, and his works for organ began to be heard in recitals on both sides of the Atlantic. By the time he was enticed to Canada, Wheeldon was a musician of considerable reputation.

The new choirmaster would need to rebuild the choir following the resignation of Torrington's team. But first Wheeldon had to establish his credibility. Within days of his arrival, he began putting on organ concerts that brought regular audiences into the church. Did Bertha take an anonymous place in one of the back pews to listen and take measure of this new Englishman who was predicted to leap to prominence in the world of music in Toronto? Did she hear more about Wheeldon from his good friend and fellow immigrant organist, T. Herbert Weatherly, when she sang under Weatherly's direction in the Central Methodist Church's annual Thanksgiving concert at the end of October? Did Weatherly describe Bertha's singing in complimentary terms to his friend Wheeldon? Bertha certainly paid attention when, a few months after Wheeldon's arrival, he held auditions in November 1907 for four new soloists to front the re-established choir. Would this be the change she was looking for?

Beginning at the age of twenty-one, from December 1907 through to October 1910, Bertha was the lead soprano at Toronto's Metropolitan Methodist Church. The prestige of singing with the Metropolitan Methodist Church's choir, particularly for a singer as young as Bertha, cannot be underestimated. As her later publicity materials told it, "in competition with dozens of Canada's foremost sopranos," Bertha won "the premier church choir position in Canada." From 1908, Edward Schuch's newspaper advertisements confirmed her elevated standing, putting Bertha at the top of the long list of church soloists he had trained.

Bertha was crucial to Wheeldon's efforts to build a choir that equaled or exceeded the reputation of Dr. Torrington's choir, and she stayed in her job longer than any other soloist he hired at the time. The other three soloist positions each turned over more than once, but Bertha continued for three years. A contemporary essay in *Musical Canada* described the combination of talent and malleability that a choirmaster should look for in a soloist, particularly in the soprano, who inevitably was considered the star performer. She should be healthy and young, not yet set in bad habits. But she should also have the maturity to perceive the poetry that the composer had intended for his work. Apparently, even at this young age, Bertha had achieved that balance.

Moreover, she had enough restraint to know when to give precedence to the music and to her fellow choristers. Wheeldon would not have wanted a singer who thought that the choir was only there to back them up; he needed a singer who could weave in and out of the foreground as the music required. Bertha's extended time with the Metropolitan Methodist Church choir suggests that, by the time she reached her early twenties, she had mastered the characteristics of the ideal church soloist.

Less than four years after arriving in Toronto, Bertha's hard work and talent had propelled her to the pinnacle of the world of church music in Toronto. She was working under one of the best-trained choirmasters in the city, and, what's more, the financial benefits were excellent, particularly for a young woman. By the time she won her position with the choir in 1907, the church's Music Committee was spending a budget of almost $3,000 a year, with the top salary of $1,000 a year going to Wheeldon. Bertha signed annual contracts for each of her three years that gave her the second best salary of $500 a year—well ahead of the other soloists, who were paid around $300 a year or less. And this for a job that only required her to be present for Friday evening practices and Sunday services.

The Metropolitan Methodist Church on Queen Street had one of the wealthiest congregations in Toronto and could afford to pay top dollar for soloists like Bertha.

Bertha's correspondence with the Music Committee shows that, from an early age, she was hard-nosed about her earnings. Over the summer and fall of her first year at the Metropolitan Methodist Church, a controversy arose about the occasional absences of choir soloists and whether their salaries should be deducted if they were away. Bertha—who had missed some practices but had paid a friend to substitute—wrote a firm letter to the Music Committee, stating, "I should not care to, in future, pay a substitute and also have it deducted from my salary. Of course anytime I have been absent was either sickness or a concert engagement. Kindly advise me if it is not satisfactory . . ." She may have been young, but when it came to money, she was ready to stand her ground.

Bertha had plenty of opportunities to work as a paid soloist in concerts in addition to her church work. She frequently sang for public organizations like the Orange Lodge, the Canadian Temperance League, the Masons, the Western Hospital Board, the Toronto Railway Employees Union, the Baptist Young Men's Union, and the British Welcome League. But holding the soloist's position at the Metropolitan Methodist Church did not come without trade-offs. The paradox was that the more prominent her position became as a well-known church singer, the more her hands were tied in terms of what and when she could sing.

Outside of church, Bertha built up her reputation from the stage of Massey Hall, with its superb acoustics and intimate atmosphere. Stained glass windows, which are closed off today, let daylight into the hall during Bertha's time.

Initially, it seems likely that Bertha had to cancel plans for another American tour in the fall of 1907. It looks like she had agreed to travel with the Ladell–Fox Concert Party again in late 1907 and early 1908 before she knew about the auditions for the Metropolitan Methodist Church. Brochures must have already been printed and distributed before she withdrew to take up the position at the church. Changes in the lineup of concert parties were not unusual, and there was little opportunity to inform the local committees that the artists mentioned in the brochure had been substituted. So, notices announcing Bertha's upcoming appearance with the Ladell–Fox party appeared in several newspapers in the U.S. in 1908, although she was actually working at the church in Toronto.

But while Bertha continued to sing in Toronto, both in and out of church, most conventional concerts required conventional songs, either hymns or traditional ballads. Bertha was not alone among her fellow church soloists in wanting to try new forms of song. In 1908, she joined a quartet of singers who wanted to create a vehicle to showcase some alternative secular music to relieve the steady diet of sacred music they sang every Sunday. The group, calling itself the Orpheus Quartette, was formed by an ambitious young Toronto singer and teacher, Arthur Blight (1874–1928). It comprised Bertha as the soprano (and, at twenty-one, the youngest of the four), Elizabeth Campbell singing contralto, R.A. Shaw as the tenor, and Blight as the bass–baritone. All four were regular church soloists who worked in the biggest Toronto churches and appeared regularly in concerts around the city. R.A. Shaw sang at the Metropolitan Methodist Church with Bertha. Campbell was at Bertha's previous church, Sherbourne Street Methodist Church, while Blight was attached to the Bloor Street Presbyterian Church. Campbell and Blight were also well-known singing teachers.

In March 1908, the Orpheus Quartette appeared together in public for the first time. This first appearance was an ensemble production of a cycle of 'art songs' held in the hall of the Conservatory of Music. Art songs are poetry set to music, usually in a classical style, which is designed to capture the mood of the verse. Art songs would become a major supplement to Bertha's operatic repertoire in future years, but at this point in her career, singing art songs was quite a departure from the church music that had dominated her singing experience.

This first concert of art songs provides a glimpse of the social forces that shaped the musical economy around Bertha. The concert was sponsored by a group of fourteen 'patronesses' who represented a microcosm of the Toronto ruling class that determined what music a prominent church soloist like Bertha could—and could not—perform in public. Almost all were mature women in their prime, mostly in their forties and fifties, and all could be found in *The Society Blue Book of Toronto*, the social directory of Toronto's 4,000 elite families. Most were born and bred in Ontario, making them one or more generations removed from the hard-scrabbling immigrants who had built up the wealth that these women benefited from. They probably seemed at times rather pretentious; they gave their large city houses names like 'Holwood' and 'Llawhaden,' and they vacationed in summer homes with names like 'Kawandeg' and 'Glen Oak' that were far from the heat of the city, in the Muskokas and even the Kawarthas. They lived at exclusive addresses like Jarvis Street, Queen's Park, and St. George Street, where they were served by live-in servants. Nevertheless, they probably poured the tea themselves from their well-polished silver teapots into their dainty porcelain cups when they 'received' other society women on their regular open house days.

The down-to-earth Crawfords were never listed in Toronto's *Blue Book*. Many families on Palmerston were, but these families all lived in the big detached houses on Palmerston Boulevard north of College Street—never in the more modest duplexes like the Crawfords' home on Palmerston Avenue south of College. The Crawford sisters did have individual listings in the *Toronto City Directory* (Bertha as a singer and Lucia as a stenographer), but those listings described their employability and were in direct contrast to the entries in the *Blue Book*, which specified which day of the week the society wife would be at home to 'receive.' On the other hand, Arthur Blight and his wife did take a listing in the *Blue Book* and were contemporaries and good friends with John Craig Eaton, who had recently inherited the helm of the Eaton's store and catalogue business empire. Mrs. Flora Eaton, who particularly enjoyed music and the arts, was the youngest of the patronesses and a voice student of Arthur Blight. Her musical friendship with the Blights may have been behind this first Orpheus Quartette concert. A generation younger than the other patronesses, Flora had recently become a fan of opera, and in this she probably differed from her older colleagues on the committee.

Through their sponsorship of events like the Orpheus Quartette concert, these society matrons set the tone for what was acceptable for musical performance in polite society. They had a powerful influence, and their musical taste rarely ran to European opera. They were all Protestants—mostly Methodists and Presbyterians in this group—and their lives were infused with what they viewed as staunch Protestant values. They had a respect for hard work, although their own work was all for club and charity activities like this concert, never salaried work. And they were Victorians to the core, believing in self-control, dignity, and thrift (not that their own standard of living demanded it). These self-appointed leaders of Toronto society could never have imagined that they had anything in common with the tragic women so often portrayed in Italian and French opera. Certainly they would have had no sympathy for courtesans or entertainers who are undone by episodes of passionate love, like Nelda in *Pagliacci*, Floria Tosca in *Tosca*, or Violetta in *La Traviata*, nor indeed for innocent young women who allow themselves to be seduced and ruined, like Gilda in *Rigoletto* or Marguerite in *Faust*. Although these matrons probably would have known very little of the details of these opera stories, as few of them would have understood the Italian or French singing even if they had ventured out to see one of the opera companies that came on tour to Toronto. No, grand opera was simply not to their taste.

The Orpheus Quartette concert was much closer to what the *Blue Book* ladies liked, even if the second half was devoted to relatively avant-garde art songs with the potential to expand the ladies' musical experience. The program at the Conservatory opened before a sold-out crowd with Bertha and Blight singing the duet "I Feel Thy Angel Spirit" by Gustav Graben-Hoffmann, followed by the tenor Shaw singing a solo, "Dorris," accompanied by violin and cello. Campbell contributed two solos of her own—"Eldorado" and "Only a Rose"—before Dr. Frederic Nicolai, a cellist, played three instrumental pieces. Perhaps as a concession to the unavoidable popularity of opera, Bertha was allowed to show off her coloratura work in an Italian aria. She sang Rosina's "Grand Valse" from *The Barber of Seville*—but the aria would not have raised many eyebrows since, unlike the tragic opera heroines, Rosina is an essentially virtuous (although still flirtatious) comedic heroine. Bertha's "clever singing" was heralded the next day in *The Globe* as a "triumph." The first part of the concert closed with Blight performing Hatton's musical version of "The Wreck of the Hesperus," a solo version of Longfellow's poem set to music.

In the second part of the evening, which was devoted to art songs, the group presented the "Daisy Chain" cycle of twelve songs lasting for about three-quarters of an hour. While musically avant-garde, the subject of the songs remained on very safe ground. The cycle consisted of a selection of English children's poems written by Robert Louis Stevenson and Laurence Alma-Tadema and set to music by Liza Lehmann only a few years before. Typical of Lehmann's orchestration, the cycle was set for a quartet of different voices, and the songs alternated between duets, trios, and quartets. Considering that this was the quartet's first performance together, the reviewer from *The Globe* noted that the "singing was marked by much beauty of tone, although there seemed to be a lack of balance in the ensemble at times. Nevertheless, the quartette sang with earnestness of expression and intelligent phrasing . . ." No doubt the lady patronesses retired satisfied to their well-kept homes, charmed by the high quality of the performances and unchallenged by any undue 'operatic' emotion. On the other hand, the prescient reporter from *Saturday Night* magazine went home to write that Bertha was a "clever young singer [who] has an excellent voice of lyric quality and reveals ability which eminently fits her for the operatic field."

The quartet appeared together as a group at least two more times—in August 1908, at the summer home of one of the patronesses in Peterborough, and in January 1909, at a ladies night at a Toronto branch of the Masons. However, while Bertha often appeared with various members outside the quartet in the next few years, it does not appear that the Orpheus Quartette continued as a formal group for more than a year. Bertha would have to look elsewhere for new musical challenges.

Bertha could continue to sing art songs, but she was unlikely to get any more musical challenges in operettas given that she had an image to keep up as a Metropolitan Methodist Church soloist. After the success of her appearance in *The Pirates of Penzance* in 1907, she must have been disappointed that she could not join her friends when Schuch led them in a production of Gilbert and Sullivan's *Iolanthe* on the stage of Massey Hall in December 1908. The Masseys were also great patrons of the Metropolitan Methodist Church, and their conservative attitudes towards opera, theatre, and play-acting likely would have kept a church soloist of Bertha's stature from participating in such a performance on the Massey Hall stage. Indeed, back in 1880, when members of the Metropolitan Methodist Church choir had appeared in a production of the Gilbert and Sullivan operetta *H.M.S. Pinafore*, they had been expelled from the choir for linking the church's name with a suspect secular production. Giving up the chance to sing in musical theatre was the price that Bertha would have to pay for keeping her position as a prominent church soloist.

So, despite the prestige of singing at the Metropolitan Methodist Church, the benefit of Wheeldon's direction, and the good pay, after two years of singing with the choir, Bertha was again ready for a change. Maybe she was missing the nightly adrenaline rush that comes with direct interaction with an audience, or perhaps her expectations had been raised by the comments in *Saturday Night*. Regardless, she was apparently impatient with her life in Toronto, and perhaps nostalgic about her time on tour in 1907, for, in 1909, she negotiated with the church for a leave of absence and headed out on her first cross-Canada tour.

Entr'acte –
A Satisfactory Picture

October, 1909. Aylett's Photography Studio, 1118 Queen Street West, Toronto, Ontario, Canada. Bertha watches as Charles Aylett puts his head under the camera's hood to adjust his focus on her. She smiles confidently as she waits. She has no interest in posing like one of those society women with their calculated reserve, gazing off to one side as if engaged in some esoteric reverie. Now that she has met a few of those women, she knows that they don't have anything more—or anything less—going on in their heads than she does. And she isn't worried about copying the many artists whom Aylett photographs, either. Whether or not they look straight at the camera, they usually assume a studied formality, intent on presenting their professional pursuits in the most serious and dignified light. No, Bertha isn't going to hide the fact that she is quite pleased with herself.

Bertha is enjoying her session with the society photographer. This is a pleasant confirmation that she has got her way, and she rather likes getting her way. Mr. Graham, the concert manager from Manitoba, suggested that Mr. Aylett should take her photo for the brochure and poster for the upcoming tour of Western Canada, now that everyone has agreed that she can go. These pictures will cement the reality that she really is going out to sing across the whole country, to the Pacific Ocean and back.

She thinks back to the discussion on the front porch on Palmerston Avenue. Mr. Graham had come to meet her parents in August. He'd brought with him Hugh Ruthven MacDonald, a highly respected baritone whom the Crawfords had heard singing oratorio on several occasions. They sat outside to capture some cooler air after the hot summer day. Lucia brought out a tray of lemonade as Mrs. Crawford exchanged pleasantries with Mr. MacDonald. Bertha, watching as he sat back and wiped the sweat off his shining forehead with a silk handkerchief, found herself thinking that the heat must be a trial for such a large man. But then again, his size seems essential to his deep resonant voice. On the other hand, the tall thin Graham seemed relaxed about the weather. He allowed that the dearth of bugs in Toronto, compared with his home in Manitoba, made summer in the city relatively pleasant. It was all small talk. They were politely working their way to the big question.

Graham cleared his throat. "What do you think about allowing your daughter to come on tour with Hugh's concert party this winter, Mr. Crawford? We think that a pretty girl like Bertha, with such a sweet voice, will really bring in the crowds."

Bertha blushed at the compliment, but she knew her father wouldn't be surprised by his offer. He and Bertha had talked about it already. Ruthven MacDonald and his wife were a very solid Ontario couple who were devoted to each other and always travelled together on tour. Bertha had already persuaded her father that if she was going to head off across the country, she couldn't be in any better care than with Mrs. MacDonald. Raised in the Salvation Army, Mrs. MacDonald wouldn't stand for any improprieties on road or rail. And the proposed elocutionist, Grace Merry, was related by marriage to Mrs. Carter Merry, who was, after all, related to the Masseys and listed in the *Blue Book*. You couldn't get more respectable than that.

But Bertha's real concern wasn't respectability. She had to admit to her father that she was chafing at the bit to see more of the world and to sing in front of more responsive audiences than she found at church every week. She couldn't be satisfied with just her choir work, however prestigious the church was.

Her father had seemed to understand. He, too, remembered the draw of a cheering crowd. "You certainly do like to hear that applause, don't you, lassie?"

Of course, that wasn't quite the way they had presented it to Mr. Wheeldon when they'd visited him in his office at the church a few days before Graham and MacDonald's visit. John Crawford couldn't suggest that singing in Wheeldon's choir was in any way an inadequate assignment.

"It's a great honour for my daughter to sing under your direction, Mr. Wheeldon," John had started. "But my daughter is of an age where she wants to test her wings."

Wheeldon had to agree that Bertha seemed restless, so he had offered a deal. "I can see that your heart isn't always one hundred percent with the choir, Bertha. If I give you a leave of absence for this tour, will you commit to come back and sing for the rest of next year with us? I'm not ready to start training up a new soloist yet."

And Bertha had promised to do that. So she is going to have her cake and eat it, too. She can keep her title as the leading church soprano in the city while getting out and meeting audiences across the country at the same time.

With that thought in mind, she turns to face Mr. Aylett. With her hand on her hip and her shoulders squared, she smiles.

CHAPTER FIVE –
Riding the Rails,
1909–1911

Touring across Canada in 1909 obviously appealed to Bertha's sense of adventure and ambition.

From November 1909 until March 1910, Bertha chased new experiences and a changing environment by touring with the H. Ruthven MacDonald Concert Party all the way to the Pacific and back.

As she travelled west on tour, Bertha would have found audiences made up of people like her Uncle Andrew and his family. Western Canada in the first decade of the twentieth century was the place where enterprising Canadians and new immigrants went to make or remake their fortunes. Along the new railways, small communities sprang up out of nowhere. After long days of hard work building something out of nothing, the populations of these vibrant little communities were happy to have some kind of entertainment for an evening. The bigger towns and cities across Canada had professional theatres where full-time managers would contract with big name performers and theatrical companies to provide entertainment. But if small communities—particularly those young communities that had only been populated for a few years—wanted to see professional performances, then they had to rely on the initiative of committees of volunteers from service organizations like the International Order of Foresters (IOOF) or the Young Men's Christian Association (YMCA) to arrange for a concert party tour to come to their town.

Profit margins on the tours that Bertha travelled with were probably narrow. In small communities in western Canada at the end of the decade, tickets to a show typically sold for between $0.50 and $1.00, and each show generated perhaps $100 to $150 which had to be split between the local committee and the tour management. The local committee arranged the venue, provided the piano, and advertised the show, and in return they probably kept twenty-five to thirty percent of the income from the concert. With hotel rooms running at $1.00 to $2.00 a night, and train fares between towns costing $1.00 to $1.50 a person, the touring party had to move every night or second night to find new audiences to keep the money coming in.

Bertha benefited from the innovative approach taken by the tour's concert manager, or 'impresario,' Wallace Graham (1870–1938). At the time, Canadian theatre circuits were mostly dominated by American and British acts. But Graham was a Canadian impresario who built his career by promoting Canadian talent for Canadian audiences—especially audiences in rapidly growing western Canada. The orphaned son of a printer, Graham was a decidedly working-class factory labourer in 1900. But in the early years of the new century, he separated from his wife and left his daughter behind in Ontario to make the move to western Canada to reinvent himself. In Manitoba, he began to make his living on the stage as an elocutionist and off the stage teaching elocution. At six feet two inches tall, with blue eyes and wavy brown hair, Graham was a striking figure on the stage who needed no "ranting or barn storming" to captivate an audience. He commanded respect with a quiet, dignified style that was underpinned by his large resonant voice and coloured by his effective use of pauses.

Building on his personal experience as a touring artist, Graham soon ventured into managing other performers, specializing in concert parties. As early as 1906, he was organizing tours across the Prairies and out to the West Coast. By 1910, he was heralded in *Musical Canada* as the "popular western impresario" who had "placed the concert business of the west on a higher plane." He had displaced American Chautauqua talent with higher-quality Canadian and British artists, and he enjoyed "the esteem and confidence of committees everywhere." Indeed, Bertha was lucky to be one of the Canadian artists promoted by Wallace Graham.

The brochure and poster that Graham produced to promote Bertha's 1909–1910 concert party tour are the only pieces of publicity material that survive from Bertha's life. It is fascinating to see, even this early in her career, that her story was being moulded to fit the standard script of the rising singing star of her day. The description of Bertha, which takes up a full page of the four-page document, slips in and out of hyperbole, although the basic facts are correct. It states that, like the great opera stars of her day, she has risen to prominence while still young. Her natural voice is remarkable, her range a full three octaves. She has acquired a varied repertoire and exceptional technique. She is already recognized by the top musical establishment, for she holds the "premier church choir position in Canada" (not just in Toronto). And she has met with approval far and wide, with carefully selected quotations from six newspaper reviews revealing that she has appeared with great success across Ontario and in big cities in the United States (Chicago and Atlanta). The brochure closes with the rather astonishing assertion that she is "the greatest soprano that has ever toured the West." It is a fine piece of myth-building, and it presages how she would be presented to the Canadian public in later years.

WITH THE **H. Ruthven MacDonald Concert Party**

Miss Bertha May Crawford
Soprano
Soloist Metropolitan Methodist Church, Toronto

Bertha was the poster girl for the H. Ruthven MacDonald Concert Party when it toured across Canada in 1909 and 1910.

For all the brochure's emphasis on Bertha's talents, she was not the headliner of this concert party. The success of the tour actually depended on the reputation of a much more established singer, the well-known Canadian baritone Hugh Ruthven MacDonald (1865–1949). Bertha had shared the stage with MacDonald as early as 1906, in a Massey Hall concert put on by the 48th Highland Regiment, so she was familiar with him and his reputation. At forty-five years old in 1910, H. Ruthven MacDonald was renowned for the "splendid carrying power" of his voice and his "full, mellow, organ-like tones." He was described as "a large man in every sense of the word," so he must have presented quite a contrast on stage with Bertha's slim stature. His booming voice also would have contrasted with her "voice of a bird"—a reference to her well-developed coloratura technique.

An indomitable touring baritone, Hugh Ruthven MacDonald and his accompanist wife Eleanor took Bertha across Canada in 1909 and 1910, introducing her to audiences in small communities all over western Canada.

Like many people Bertha worked with in Toronto, MacDonald was a man who'd worked his way out of a more mundane life by becoming a professional musician. Originally trained as a cabinetmaker like his father before him, by his mid-twenties MacDonald had a job singing bass baritone and leading the choir in a church in Chatham, Ontario. In 1901, he was earning an annual salary of $700 as choirmaster at a Methodist church in London, Ontario, which made him one of the better-paid people in his community. Early in the new century, MacDonald moved to Toronto, where he lived for the rest of his life, giving voice lessons and performing in churches, at local recitals, and on concert tours across Canada and the United States. MacDonald's accompanist on tour was his wife of over twenty years, Eleanor (1864–1919), whose musical roots stemmed from her early years in the Salvation Army.

Travelling with the MacDonalds, Bertha would have learned a huge amount from their extensive touring experience, such as how to pace a concert program and how to adapt to keep the attention of different audiences. MacDonald was an indomitable performer, and, in the summer of 1910, following his winter tour with Bertha, he contracted with the Redpath Vawter Chautauqua circuit to sing in sixty-six cities over sixty-six days. But perhaps the most important skills Bertha would have refined would have been the techniques for making a connection with the audience. Indeed, MacDonald was a renowned crowd-pleaser. For her part, Bertha became increasingly noted for her ability to engage with her audience and generate a warm response as her career progressed, and MacDonald was probably one of her role models.

Bertha's concerts with the H. Ruthven MacDonald Concert Party followed a standard program. Mindful that their audience contained many recent immigrants, the party members favoured ballads with an English, Scottish, or Irish heritage. The party typically planned to perform about a dozen items, although, as the entertainers were generous with their encores, the final number was probably closer to twenty. MacDonald would sing songs like the tragic Scottish story, "The Sands O' Dee," or the humorous traditional Irish song, "Father O'Flynn." He also included robust love songs that showed off his booming baritone, like Solman's "If I Had a Thousand Lives To Live." Together with Bertha, he might sing a duet like the old Scottish ballad, "The Hunting Tower." In the same Celtic vein, Bertha would sing Franco Leoni's Gaelic love song, "Coolan Dhu," or Henry Bishop's popular coloratura aria for sopranos based on Shakespearian verse, "Lo! Hear the Gentle Lark." To give the show a classical interlude, MacDonald would display his oratorio skills with one of Handel's arias, like "Ruddier than the Cherry," and Bertha would show off her operatic aspirations with "Grand Valse" from *The Barber of Seville*. The reader would introduce some humour with stories like *Mrs. Bateson's Tea Party*, and pathos with pieces like *The Two Dannies* or *The Sign of the Cross*. Indeed, the program of solos and duets interspersed with readings was especially designed to please small-town audiences. Working through a similar program every night, the party wended its way west along the railways, crossing Manitoba, Saskatchewan, Alberta, and British Columbia before returning across southern Alberta on its way back home.

Bertha's family and colleagues may have initially thought that touring across Canada in the winter of 1909–1910 would satisfy her desire to perform before a more responsive audience than the Metropolitan Methodist Church congregation, and perhaps might even cure her itchy feet. She came home with many positive reviews, like one from *The Manitoba Free Press* which said that Bertha "was the bright star of the evening. While but quite young, she has a fairly powerful voice with a big compass, her upper notes being as clear as a lark's." Perhaps she was temporarily satisfied as she went back to singing with the church choir for the summer of 1910, but that did not last.

In October 1910, she resigned permanently from her church soloist position to join the H. Ruthven MacDonald Concert Party on her second cross-Canada tour. The party started out from Winnipeg on October 31, and again it traversed Manitoba, Saskatchewan, and Alberta through the winter before finding its way to Victoria, on British Columbia's Pacific Coast, on May 15, 1911. Building on its reputation from the previous year, the concert tour was again a success. At the beginning of the tour, *The Manitoba Free Press* noted improvements in Bertha's technique since the previous year, writing, "... Little Miss Bertha May Crawford, the soprano with the voice of a bird both as regards flexibility and sweetness, delighted her audience by her artistic singing.... Her coloratura work is deserving of the highest praise while her pianissimos are delightful. Her singing of 'Coolan Dhu' was the gem of the programme." And in January 1911, the reporter from *The Lethbridge Herald* thought Bertha had "... a soprano voice of good compass, and she well sustained the flute-like trill in Bishop's ['Lo! Hear] the Gentle Lark.'" Reviews like these would have encouraged Bertha to think that she had made the right choice in trading in her church position for more time on the rails.

Indeed, by that point, Bertha must have admitted that her experiences on tour had only whetted her appetite for more theatrical work. While nobody can know precisely what factors motivated Bertha, the fact that she had resigned her church position suggests that she had already decided that she was going to move on to advanced singing studies in London. And in 1910, she and her supporters—particularly her father—would have had a new reason to think that, with the right training, she might even have a future in singing opera in Canada: the establishment of a new Canadian opera company. Inspired by several years of effort to establish permanent opera companies in New York, Philadelphia, Boston, and Chicago (activities that were closely followed in the musical journals and newspapers that Bertha would have read in Canada), the Montréal Opera Company was inaugurated in Montréal, Québec on October 31, 1910. With the exception of a brief interval in the 1890s when there had been a French opera society in Montréal, this was the first and only professional opera company in Canada before 1950.

The new company was underwritten by a Montréal businessman and philanthropist, Frank Stephen Meighen (1870–1946), who wanted to provide the wider Canadian public with a taste of grand opera at reasonable prices, and also to provide Canadian artists—artists like Bertha—with the opportunity to develop an opera career in Canada. Meighen was an Ontario boy, born in Perth in 1870, who became heir to a huge fortune built on banking, railways, land, and grain processing. While he was considered a very astute businessman, the passion of his life was the arts, and his opera company became his most costly hobby. His new opera company would far eclipse the amateur productions of Gilbert and Sullivan's satirical English operettas that Bertha was used to participating in. Indeed, Meighen's vision was to put on full-scale professional productions of Italian and French operas in their original languages. For singers like Bertha, the idea of a career singing opera in Canada had quite suddenly turned from a distant pipedream into an immediate possibility.

Unfortunately, almost immediately Meighen found (as Bertha might have told him) that there were powerful forces working against his opera project. The company's opening season in Montréal ran for eight weeks, through November and December 1910, with six performances a week. The shows were very well received, and the company came close to breaking even, but problems arose as soon as it took its productions on the road to Québec City, Ottawa, Rochester, and Toronto. First, the Bishop of Québec insisted that the operas *Manon* and *Tosca* were too immoral for Catholic audiences, and he issued a pronouncement against attending the operas to be read in all his churches. Even though these two operas were removed from the schedule, the company had much smaller audiences than anticipated in Québec City. Worse yet, the effects of the Bishop's prejudices spilled over into Ontario. As the Toronto publicity agent for the company, Hector Charlesworth, recalled it, Toronto's "private 'sneak' censorship" leapt into action, and "[l]etters poured into the police authorities pointing out that if the Montréal Opera Company was too terrible for a Catholic community, it certainly should be suppressed in a really Christian and God-fearing city like Toronto." In the end, the Toronto performances were not formally censored, although the police were dispatched to the theatre to evaluate whether action should be taken. However, some Toronto patrons were deterred from attending, and the company finished its first season with a much larger deficit than it had hoped for.

Notwithstanding the early financial setbacks of the Montréal Opera Company, it is clear that in the spring of 1911, Bertha could have had the expectation that, if she studied opera, there would be a professional Canadian opera company where she might apply her training. But the conventional wisdom remained that North American training could never be enough to launch a career in opera. A professional singer had to get training in Europe if he or she wanted to be taken seriously in Canada. To be sure, an important turning point in the biographies of aspiring American prima donnas in this era is their departure for Europe. That departure is usually facilitated by the encouragement and support of patrons who also supported opera companies in the big American cities like New York, Chicago, and Boston. But despite the appearance of a major Canadian opera patron in Montréal, the shortage of supportive opera patrons in Toronto was a limitation for many Ontario singers. This is not to say that singers from Toronto did not already go to Europe to train. A steady stream did, but few had the support necessary for a long period of study.

When Bertha began her training in Europe, it appears that she relied solely on her own and her father's money. Certainly, there is no evidence that she was supported by any patron outside her family when she left for London, and it is possible that she didn't need one. While it is dangerous to succumb to ethnic stereotypes, perhaps Bertha had inherited that cliché Scots characteristic of thrift. But although she may have carefully accumulated savings from her tours and concert appearances, it is highly unlikely that she alone could have saved enough for a year or two of study abroad. More likely, although the evidence is only circumstantial, it seems that around 1911, John Crawford advantageously cashed in on some earlier investments. Certainly, he was putting money into his brick block commercial building in Elmvale as late as the spring of 1911. Indeed, it seems that the family was in a position to spend a lot of money that year.

In 1911 or 1912, the Crawford family moved out of their duplex on Palmerston Avenue and bought (or built) a new single family home on the corner of Parkside Drive and Grenadier Street, facing into High Park. The house was to remain in the family until the late 1970s. This handsome new home had three storeys and bay windows on two sides, and it was probably twice the size of the Palmerston Avenue house. Around the same time, John stopped working from home and opened a tailoring shop on Gerrard Street East. The new home and the separate workspace made a confident statement that John and his family had arrived in the middle class. But the final proof of his success—and the realization of his immigrant dream—would be his ability to invest in Bertha's dream and send her to London to train as a professional singer.

In June 1911, Bertha sailed from Montréal for England to commence the formal training in opera singing that would change the direction of her career permanently. We can only guess what her feelings were as she set out on this journey. Was she ambivalent about her decision to leave the security of the church soloist's job for an entirely uncertain venture in opera? Would she have preferred to stay in Canada had the right teacher been available? Or did she relish the adventure and the chance to cross the ocean? Was she thinking about chancing the crowded marketplace of European opera? Or did she— and her father—think that she would come straight home after a couple of years in London? Was she caught up in an optimistic dream, or did she have a practical plan?

As it was, Bertha launched herself into the world of classical opera fed by the dreams of the previous generation and the possibility of following in the footsteps of the great opera stars like Albani. No doubt she was already looking forward to a triumphant homecoming and picturing herself riding in on the kind of success that only a European stage could offer. However, the entertainment world was on the edge of a period of huge change that Bertha could never have foreseen. Only a year before Bertha travelled east across the

Atlantic to pursue her dream of a celebrity career as an opera singer, another Torontonian of Bertha's generation, eighteen-year-old actress Gladys Marie Smith, headed west across America to Los Angeles to continue her acting career in the new moving pictures. Within ten years, as the silent movie star Mary Pickford, she would rocket past all the great female opera stars to become the highest-paid female entertainer and the most famous woman in the world. And she didn't even have to talk, let alone sing. Whether or not Bertha could be successful in opera, the position of the prima donna at the top of the entertainment hierarchy was about to be toppled.

Entr'acte –
Sailing into Uncharted Waters

June 10, 1911. R.M.S. Virginian, Allen Line Wharf, Montréal, Québec, Canada. Bertha's footsteps echo metallically as she trots up the staircase to the promenade deck. She has watched the porter deliver her trunks to the baggage master and put her hand baggage directly into her stateroom. The steward will keep it securely locked until the ship pulls out. Now she needs to find her father and sister. There isn't much time before they will have to go back on shore.

She comes out through the swinging doors into the wide enclosed walkway that runs for a few hundred feet along this side of the deck. Lucia and her father are looking out the open windows at the crowded dock below. Horse-drawn cabbies jockey for position. Muscular stevedores shout in unfamiliar languages. Nets full of steamer trunks and bags of mail swing up beside the ship and disappear into the hold. Chains dangling from cranes clang in noisy dissonance. A slightly skunky odour wafts up from a fetid backwater trapped behind the wharf.

Bertha hesitates. Already John and Lucia seem a little distant to her, standing there in their regular shore clothes, ready to take the familiar Canadian train back to Toronto this afternoon. And Bertha—in her fashionable new dress with its long pleated skirt of fine ivory cotton that just skims the deck, and its modest neckline above rows of Irish crocheted lace that run from elbow to elbow across her front—will sail in style down the St. Lawrence towards the Atlantic tonight.

She comes up beside her father, suddenly wanting to reach out to the man who has been the rock beneath her up to this point. "Is it like you remember, Daddy?" she asks, knowing it has been forty years since he started his life's adventure by crossing this ocean.

"No, it certainly is not," he says. "We came over in steerage, as you well know. Although I think if you venture down to that level today, you won't find anything like the rough conditions we had—not on a modern liner like this. Not that they will let you down there, anyway. They don't like the first-class passengers mixing it up below decks. This *is* a British ship, after all." He sighs.

Bertha has heard him talk all her life about how happy he is that he left behind the class snobbery of Britain when he came to Canada. She wonders where she is going to fit in over there. She's not the factory worker's child that her father was, but she's not an English lady, either—at least not yet.

"Now, where have you put that letter of credit?" John asks. The bank's letter represents a lot of money to be carrying around, and he is going to feel a lot better when he knows it is deposited in an English bank.

Bertha pats her handbag, held tight at her side. "I'm supposed to put it into the purser's safekeeping after we get underway. Don't worry, Daddy, I won't forget."

Bertha turns to her older sister. Lucia has been working steadily as a stenographer for several years now, and she still lives at home with their parents. It's a conventional life, and Lucia likes it. Security. Stability. Bertha is very fond of her sister, however set in her ways Lucia is, but it bothers her that Lucia doesn't seem to understand why Bertha wants to make this journey. All Lucia ever asks about is how Bertha will find a good Canadian husband on the other side of the ocean.

But Lucia is making an effort to sound supportive today. "Did you meet your cabin mates?"

Bertha drops the more serious tone she reserves for her father, and a note of excitement slips out. "They are the Irwin sisters from Peterborough, and they are on their first ocean trip, too. They seem very nice and we are almost the same age. I think we may explore the ship together this evening."

The rest of the conversation circles around the practicalities of a transatlantic journey—reserving seats at a table, booking a deck chair, sending a cable upon arrival. They have gleaned the basics from a travel guide and sundry advice from friends who have made the trip 'across the pond.' None of them wants to talk about the real reason they are here: Bertha is leaving to study in Europe for two or three years at least. That is a fact too big for open acknowledgment.

Bertha feels sorry that her mother isn't there with them. Maud said her goodbyes at the train station in Toronto. Bertha watched her grow smaller as the train pulled away, until her mother eventually slipped out of sight. She wonders why her mother wouldn't want to come to the docks. She thinks about something Maud said back home in the kitchen. "Once you get a taste of that big musical world in Europe, Bertha May, I don't think Toronto is going to hold much interest for you anymore."

Bertha had tried to put these worries to rest. "Don't be silly, Ma. Of course I'll be happy when I come back home." And she certainly meant it, at the time.

Now her father is looking at her with pride. He is as enthusiastic as she is about this journey. He had surprised her with his decision when she came home from the H. Ruthven MacDonald Concert Party tour in May. He had seen the new opera company from Montréal in January, when Bertha was far away in Alberta. John and Lucia had bought tickets for the Saturday night performance of *Carmen* at the Princess Theatre. The house was almost full.

"Oh, you should have seen it, Bertha!" Back in their front parlour, he had been quite carried away as he'd told her about it. "Halfway through the first act I really felt it. That is what you really should be doing. It's what you are really good at. Och, lassie, the passion and drama of it! All that energy building up to triumph and tragedy in the last scene. And then that moment of silence before the applause and the cheers... It was as captivating as a tight horse race!"

Bertha had only smiled and wondered how her father could have missed that feeling earlier when they'd seen all those other touring opera companies.

But John knows his daughter. "You're ever so clever when you sing those frilly ditties about birds and flowers and the wind in the night. But singing in those recitals, it's like you're dancing with your hands tied behind your back.

I've been letting you run as a pacer, when I ought to have cut the traces and let you loose at a full gallop. And to do that, we know you have to have proper studies in London and some experience on an English stage. And then maybe you'll come home a star . . ." They had laughed together at this final fantastical thought.

The ship's whistle sounds, and a steward calls out, "All ashore that are going ashore!"

The final parting is short and awkward.

"You'll write?"

"Of course, Daddy," Bertha promises, although she has never been much of a correspondent.

The three of them exchange quick kisses, and then Lucia and John exit down the gangway with the parents of Bertha's cabin mates, Mr. and Mrs. Irwin. Bertha and the Irwin girls emerge on the upper deck and wave their neatly gloved hands at their parents as the ship shudders and draws away from the wharf.

Bertha makes polite conversation. "How long will you be on holiday?"

"Oh, we're staying in England until October." The Irwin sisters are trying to sound confident. "And what about you? When will you be returning home?"

Bertha looks back at her father's shrinking figure. "I'm not sure."

CHAPTER SIX –
Crossing the Atlantic,
1911–1912

As a girl with a taste for glamour, Bertha would enjoy her time in the British Empire's capital, London.

JANE COOPER

When Bertha arrived in London at the beginning of the summer of 1911, at the age of twenty-four, she was following a well-trodden path. There was an established tradition of Canadians travelling to the Imperial capital to study, and during Bertha's time in London at least five other Canadian girls were taking lessons with the same singing teachers. So while Bertha must have felt considerable trepidation getting off the ship alone in a new country, she did not land without friends or contacts. At the very least she must have carried some letters of introduction from her long-time English choirmaster, Herbert Wheeldon. In addition, she already personally knew at least one man in London, Thomas Herbert Weatherly (1877–1961), a choir director whom she had first sung with in a 1907 concert in Toronto.

When she arrived in London, Bertha probably spent some time with Weatherly and his wife Lili in their home at 5 Launceston Place in Kensington. Did they meet her off the boat train from Liverpool? Did Bertha live with them when she first arrived in London? Later, in the early 1920s, Bertha listed Weatherly as her 'nearest friend or relative' in England on an immigration form, and she was still in touch with Lili in the late 1920s. Weatherly was an organist like Wheeldon, and he had briefly immigrated to Canada at the same time as Wheeldon, but he had returned to London after only a year. If Bertha did not live in the Weatherlys' home from 1911 to 1912, then she certainly came to know the couple well during her time studying in London, and on some level they probably acted as chaperones for the unaccompanied young student.

Typically, foreign music students like Bertha found a room in one of London's many boarding houses. Gladys Banks (1893–1953) was another youthful Canadian singer who arrived in London in the same month as Bertha, and she lived with the Harts at 8 St. Stephen's Crescent, Bayswater, in the kind of boarding house where Bertha may have lived. Many of the five-storey houses on this short curved terrace were rooming establishments catering to young women who had migrated to London to work or study. At number eight, the Harts rented out rooms to four or more young female music students from the United States and Canada. The students' rent was probably essential for the Harts to meet the expenses of bringing up their own three daughters in a fourteen-room house on the income of a travelling salesman.

When young Canadian women headed off for European studies, London was probably a favoured place given the (undoubtedly exaggerated) reputation of continental cities as unsavoury environments. Indeed, while Bertha was making her study plans, *The Toronto Sunday World* launched its new year of reporting on the music scene by reprinting an American article on January 1, 1911 that presented a rather alarmist picture of the dangers of sending girls off for a musical education in continental Europe with "insufficient means and slight protection." It cautioned that "parents of young girls should no more think of sending them to continental cities unprotected than they would of putting a thrush in a serpent's cage for safety." London, on the other hand, while somewhat removed from the hearts of Italian and French opera, was English speaking and, for British subjects in particular, could be a home away from home—and even more so for the daughters of immigrants like John Crawford, who was born in the British Isles.

Bertha knew that if she was to have a chance at becoming a professional opera singer, then she needed to begin her studies with a voice production specialist who had direct experience in European opera. During her time in London, she studied with a vocal specialist, Olga De Nevosky (1869–1932), who had made her earlier career in Italian opera. De Nevosky must have had a connection in Toronto who was recommending her name to Canadians going to London, and perhaps this is how Bertha became her student.

In Madame De Nevosky, Bertha found a teacher who not only improved her technique in voice production, but who also—and more importantly— gave her the inspiration to go on to sing opera. De Nevosky had only been teaching in London for about a year when Bertha started lessons with her in the summer of 1911, but she had an established reputation on the continent. Like most teachers of operatic technique, De Nevosky was a retired opera singer herself, so she would have been the first woman whom Bertha got to know well who had really lived—although only in a modest way—the dream of the prima donna.

Reputedly of Russian descent, De Nevosky was born in Vienna in 1869 and studied Italian opera at the Milan Conservatory under the famous Italian voice teacher, Francesco Lamperti. De Nevosky developed a reputation for her work in Italian opera roles like Aida in Giuseppe Verdi's opera of the same name and Leonora in Verdi's *Il Trovatore*, but she also had success singing works by other Italians, such as Bellini, and in Wagner's German operas. She had a fairly short but cosmopolitan career on the stage that took her across Europe to opera houses in places like Turin, Sienna, Florence, Barcelona, Paris, Lemberg (Lviv), and Bucharest. She retired from the stage when she was still in her thirties and took up teaching in Paris, offering lessons in "singing and vocal aesthetics" in French, German, English, and Italian. She moved to London around 1910, making herself a particularly appealing teacher for transatlantic students who wanted the advantages of training in Italian opera without any risk of encountering the feared degeneracy of the continent. Indeed, De Nevosky must have found success teaching in London, as she remained in England for the rest of her life.

It seems that De Nevosky, with her Italian expertise and her Parisian style, lit a spark in Bertha. De Nevosky had been one of the last students that the storied Lamperti had taught before he died, and she advertised herself as a teacher who taught lessons in the Italian method she learned directly from the famous Italian instructor. Lamperti taught many prominent singers during his twenty-five years at the Milan Conservatory, but from the perspective of potential Canadian students, his most important pupil was Emma Albani. To learn the same lessons that took the most famous Canadian soprano to the peak of international operatic fame must have sounded like a promising opportunity for a young Canadian woman considering a career in opera. Albani herself was teaching in London at the time, but De Nevosky probably presented a more affordable option for girls from Toronto living on modest budgets. But beyond good price and Italian technique, it seems that De Nevosky offered something less tangible but more valuable. A journalist later described De Nevosky as looking "as if she had stepped out of the pages of a romance and had nothing to do with everyday life." After less than a year of lessons with the teacher, Bertha confessed in a letter to her family back home in Toronto that "Dear Madame so inspires me that I feel I must sing, if only for her sake."

Bertha and her friends also took some of the lessons that would lead to the opera stage from Otto (Brandeis) Morando (1872–1953), who was also experienced in Italian opera. Signor Morando appears to have been offering complementary studies in the Lamperti method in cooperation with De Nevosky. Morando was born Otto Brandeis in Prague, in what was then the

Bohemian province of the Austro–Hungarian empire. He began his studies at the Vienna Conservatory and sang in Germany and Austria before moving to Italy to study Italian opera and the Lamperti method. In Italy he assumed an Italian persona, and he was referred to as Signor Morando for the rest of his life. Morando moved to London around the same time as De Nevosky, and Bertha was among his London students during his two or three years there. In the fall of 1912 he was invited to Canada, and from 1913 to 1924 he taught at the private Canadian Academy of Music in Toronto. Photographs from his time in Toronto show a youthful-looking forty-year-old, clean shaven and bespectacled with a slight cleft in his chin and trim short hair. Morando appears to have been a very personable teacher who inspired warm memories and friendship in his students long after they had moved on to their professional careers.

Czech tenor Otto Morando was one of Bertha's singing teachers in London. Later, he would exploit his connection with Bertha to further his career in Toronto.

In 1911 and 1912, several of De Nevosky and Morando's London students were Torontonians like Bertha. Margaret George (1888–?), Madeleine Hunt, and Gladys Banks were also chasing some kind of prima donna dream, but with varying success. Bertha's old friend Margaret George came closest. Margaret had also been a student of E.W. Schuch and had sung the operetta role of Ruth in the 1907 production of *The Pirates of Penzance* with Bertha. Margaret came to London in April 1912 with her brother, Arthur George (1886–1920), who was also a voice student. Like John Crawford, the Georges' father was an up-and-coming businessman. George ran a retail and wholesale wine and liquor business on Yonge Street in Toronto. The Georges studied singing in London for about eight months before returning to Toronto. After a successful recital in Toronto in 1913, they went to Italy together for further study, and Margaret had some successful appearances in opera. However, they returned to Canada in 1915 due to the war. Margaret went on to sing opera roles in North America for a few seasons with the San Carlo Grand Opera Company, a travelling company based out of New York, while Arthur taught music. Madeleine Hunt returned to Toronto in 1913 and also took up teaching. Gladys Banks, who arrived in London the same month as Bertha, followed a different trajectory. In August 1912, she married a diamond merchant and lived the rest of her life in England. She continued her studies after her wedding and still sang professionally on occasion into the 1920s, appearing on London radio in 1923. The experiences of Bertha's fellow students show that while a well-trained singer might have found work, very few became well-known stars in opera.

Bertha may have first learned the basics of the Lamperti method from his popular instruction book published in New York.

As they studied the Italian method together in London, the Toronto girls could have read about Lamperti's approach in his treatise *The Art of Singing* (an English translation was published in New York in 1890). Lamperti emphasized first and foremost correct breathing based on good posture. Albani remembered his fundamental maxim as "the art of singing [i]s the art of breathing." Lamperti suggested that the student should practice in front of a mirror to ensure they were standing straight and did not fall into the habit of grimacing while singing. Although he was aware that the tightly laced Victorian corset distorted a woman's natural breathing, he did not go so far as to suggest that women go without foundation garments. But other more radical experts of the era were suggesting that women should sing with loose corsets or even without corsets at all.

Lamperti insisted that the best time to practice was "after the period of digestion" and never on an empty stomach, and he recommended practicing only moderately, "with a variety of exercises, always finishing before feeling tired." Albani specified that the beginner student should limit themselves to three practice sessions a day, twenty minutes each, working up to half-hour sessions for proficient students. Lamperti emphasized the importance of mental study before actually singing, so as to preserve the voice "fresh and unworn for the professional career." He also advocated singing the Solfeggio (the Do-Re-Mi system) to practice good pronunciation. And he was not in favour of humming! No doubt Bertha and her friends followed a regime very like this during their studies in London.

Building on what Schuch had begun to teach her in Toronto, much of what Bertha studied with De Nevosky and Morando would have been the techniques of *bel canto*, or coloratura singing. Coloratura passages were a common feature of Italian and French operas written in the eighteenth and early nineteenth centuries, and were characterized by birdlike trills lifting high above the staves, as well as decorative ornaments and cadenzas. Bertha, with her range from F below the staff up to high F, could manage the coloratura passages found in both lyric and dramatic coloratura opera roles, but she needed to learn more than just vocal gymnastics. A lyric soprano is expected to have a light, agile voice that ranges from middle C up to high F, and lyric opera roles require warmer tones than pure coloratura singing. A dramatic coloratura soprano usually has a range between low B and high F, and dramatic soprano opera roles call for a more theatrical style and delivery while maintaining a strong lyric song line. Bertha became most famous for roles written for lyric coloratura sopranos such as Gilda in Verdi's *Rigoletto*, Rosina in Rossini's *The Barber of Seville*, Marguerite in Gounod's *Faust*, and Juliette in *Romeo and Juliette*, also by Gounod, but she also could carry off dramatic coloratura roles like Verdi's Violetta in *La Traviata*.

However, even as Bertha arrived in London to begin her studies in opera, coloratura singing was waning in popularity. From the middle of the nineteenth century, the German composer Wagner had introduced a new style of opera that had gained popularity and changed the style of singing. Wagnerian musical dramas had little place for mere virtuosity in singing. His operas revolve around arias where the singer must dramatically portray human emotions. Inspired by this trend towards more theatrical roles, in the latter part of the nineteenth century, fewer composers created new roles designed to show off the pure vocal technique of coloratura singing. Of course, by the time Bertha died, jazz was a phenomenon, and operatic singing in general faced a decreasing audience. However, when she began her European studies, there was still a place for the coloratura singing that she excelled at.

If she was looking into the future at that point, Bertha might have been more concerned about her age. All the classic coloratura roles for prima donnas were written for young women. When Bertha began studying opera in London in 1911, she was twenty-five years old—an age where she could convincingly portray a young woman. But, while the opera world was used to the top sopranos continuing to play young roles into their middle years (and even past), for most performers there would come a time when they would not be able to compete with younger singers for these roles. And there were no roles for the coloratura voice that portrayed middle-aged or older women. Indeed, in opera tradition, the roles of older women were typically written for the mezzo soprano or contralto voice. Did Bertha consider that a career as a coloratura soprano was something of a freight train, moving inevitably along a track towards the day when age would disqualify her from the roles she specialized in? She probably knew that she could extend her career somewhat by maintaining her "slender girlish figure" for as long as possible. Indeed, in 1923, when Bertha was already thirty-six, *The Washington Times* described her as "young, slender and pretty—an ideal Gilda in appearance." Regardless of whether she dwelt on these implications when she was still a young voice student in London, Bertha must have known that she had a limited number of years ahead of her on the opera stage—and that she needed to get her start on that stage as soon as possible.

As a starting point, Bertha and her friends in London were keen to exercise their improved singing skills on some English stages. By the end of 1911, Bertha was getting concert bookings in England about once a month, which must have been a useful source of funds to subsidize her singing lessons. But more important for the long run was to build up a collection of European press notices. Getting useful notices in London was a challenge, as the critics were perceived to be capricious, and competition for the critics' attention on any one night in such a large city was fierce. Getting notices in smaller towns was easier, so it may not be a coincidence that Bertha did not restrict herself to London stages, but also took bookings outside the city.

Amongst her notices from these provincial English appearances are early examples of Bertha—or was it the press?—playing with her persona as a Canadian singer and using her nationality to create a distinct identity in a market crowded with many singers. In December 1911, she sang as a soloist with the Bromley Choral Society for a performance of Coleridge-Taylor's popular trilogy of art songs, *Scenes from the Song of Hiawatha*. Coleridge-Taylor had set to music parts of Longfellow's epic poem, *The Song of Hiawatha*. The poem, which is based on Ojibwa legends, takes place on the shores of Lake Superior, so perhaps Bertha was considered for the part because she was born not so far from the poem's locale. (Although Longfellow's romantic representation of the life of Indigenous North Americans bore little resemblance to Bertha's Canadian reality.)

In a more obvious example, over Christmas 1911, Bertha was promoted as "the great Canadian soprano" when she appeared as a soloist in a series of five concerts with the Winter Orchestra. The concerts took place in the pavilion on the Palace Pier in the seaside resort of St. Leonard's on the south coast of Sussex. Showing off some recently acquired operatic repertoire, she sang coloratura showpieces like "Caro Nome" from *Rigoletto* and "Oiseau Charmante" from *La Perle du Bresil*. The reporter from *The Hastings and St. Leonard's Observer* was pleased to note that, "judging by the enthusiastic reception . . . and the encores demanded, she must have captivated all who heard her." Despite the warm welcome, Bertha could not tarry on the coast, as she was due back in London for a New Year's Eve concert at the Metropole Hotel. And then, two weeks later, she was on stage for a concert arranged by the National Sunday League in London's Alhambra Theatre. The National Sunday League was a non-profit organization committed to offering "intellectual and elevating recreation" for the masses on Sundays (the only day off for most working people), and Bertha appeared in several of their frequent concerts.

In February 1912, she was invited back to the Sussex coast to sing at the Public Hall in Hastings. This time she was touted for her dual heritage as "the famous Scottish-Canadian soprano." Her singing accompanied a lecture by a Reverend W.E. Shaw on "Scotland and the Scots," where "[h]er sweet mellow accents in those haunting Scottish melodies were some of the finest vocalism we have heard for some time." Success on the stages of small coastal towns like Hastings and St. Leonard's could hardly be compared with an appearance on a major London stage, but nonetheless Bertha was proving that she could charm an English audience just as well as she had Canadian ones. And while the British press might have made a point of highlighting her Canadian or Scottish roots, the Canadian press was more interested in any ammunition that would build her story as an overseas sensation, regardless of the size of the stage she was on. Wasn't *The Toronto World* subtly implying that Bertha might be on track towards prima donna fame when, in March 1912, it reported (presumably fed by reports from her family) that Bertha was "meeting with great success in London, England"?

And it was true that Bertha had much more prestigious concert dates coming up, such as at the Queen's Hall in London. The Queen's Hall was a large, modern hall with excellent acoustics and room for an audience of 2,500, and it was renowned around the British Empire as the principal concert venue in London. Bertha's name headed the list of vocalists billed to appear at the Queen's Hall in two National Sunday League concerts in April and May. To sing from the stage of the Queen's Hall was an event worth writing home about, and when Bertha did, someone in her family proudly took the letter to E.R. Parkhurst, who was the editor of the monthly journal *Musical Canada* and the music critic for *The Globe*. It might have been her sister Lucia, on her way to a stenography assignment. It is harder to imagine her quiet mother fighting her way across a noisy newspaper office. But most likely it was John Crawford who wanted Bertha's Toronto colleagues to know about his clever daughter's progress and to be expecting big things from her when she came home. For he *was* sure she was coming home; he had never removed her name from his residential listing in the Toronto City Directory.

Parkhurst was a keen booster of Canadian talent and was happy to contribute to building the reputation of a Canadian making a musical splash in London. His report was effusive about Bertha's reception and her encores. And he made a point of describing how, at the end of the concert, she had been asked to sing the hymn "Nearer, My God, to Thee" to the tune used in

Canada and the United States, in sympathy with the victims of the Titanic, which had sunk only the week before the concert. He was proud to relate how a Canadian was considered a particularly appropriate person to express sorrow for the passengers who had never reached their North American destination. The idea that a Canadian could find a special place in the hearts of a foreign audience was particularly pleasing to Parkhurst and his Canadian readers.

Over in England, Bertha was already thinking about how to reach a wider audience. In the summer of 1912, a little more than a year after she had arrived in London, she attended her first (and probably last) recording session. On August 26, 1912, she went to the London studio of the Gramophone Company and made two test recordings for the HMV label. The business of recording music and selling discs had only begun in Bertha's lifetime, and commercial recordings—and the gramophone machines to play them on—had only been widely available for a little over ten years. The first Canadian record company, E. Berliner of Montréal, had only started making records in 1900. But the gramophone rapidly moved from being a novelty toy to becoming big business, and, by 1914, the Gramophone Company of England was selling four million records a year. The gramophone joined the piano as the ultimate marker of middle-class success, and a popular recording could make the singer and the record company a lot of money. So it is also possible that, at this point, Bertha was dreaming about earning something from her recordings.

Bertha's recording session was engineered by one of the first great recording engineers, Will Gaisberg (1876–1918). Will and his brother Fred were pioneer recording engineers who, ten years earlier, had been the first to record a prominent Italian operatic tenor, Enrico Caruso. Only a couple of years later, in 1904, the first million-selling record was recorded by Caruso and featured an aria from the opera *Pagliacci*. Caruso was the first artist whose rise to international fame and fortune was underpinned by a successful recording career, but plenty of opera singers were quick to follow his tracks. While Toronto was far from the centres of European singing, Bertha would have grown up familiar with the voices of the great singers of her day via the gramophone.

By the time Bertha arrived at their studio, the Gaisberg brothers had already made thousands of recordings around the world, and most of the great opera stars of the day had stepped up to their trumpet. For, in these early days of acoustic recording, there were no microphones. The singer had to perform somewhat awkwardly, standing close to the end of a long trumpet and projecting his or her voice down into its funnel. The trumpet concentrated the sound of the voice onto a taut diaphragm, and the vibrations of this diaphragm were transferred to a stylus that cut a fine groove into the coating of a revolving zinc disc. The disc was later etched with acid to make the master record or matrix, which could then be used to create huge numbers of wax copies.

Neither of Bertha's recordings was released as a record, so it may be that Bertha did not sound as good on wax as she came to sound on stage. It is unfortunate for posterity that Bertha's recording session did not result in a commercial record, as many recordings from this era still exist. After the First World War began, there were limited opportunities to make records for some years, especially in Eastern Europe. And so Bertha missed her chance to have a recording career, and, as a result, modern audiences miss the opportunity to hear her voice. In contrast, her old colleague, H. Ruthven MacDonald, had a successful recording career in Canada after the First World War, and so his voice lives on. As it was, Bertha would continue to look to the stage to reach her audience.

By the fall of 1912, twenty-six-year-old Bertha had been studying in London for eighteen months and had probably learned all she needed to know about voice production from De Nevosky and Morando. She continued to make concert appearances in small venues, such as in October 1912, when she—the "Canadian soprano"—was one of the headline acts in a concert in Wisbech, Cambridgeshire in support of the Isle of Ely Constabulary Widows and Orphans Benevolent Fund. Small concerts such as these would have been a useful source of additional money to fund her studies, but they were not what she came to Europe for. According to a letter she wrote home in the spring of 1912, she was already serious about making the leap to the much more glamourous operatic stage. Now that she had the recommended studies in London under her belt, and had proven that she could hold her own on English stages (albeit mostly minor ones), the time had come for her to decide if she was really going to move up to the next level and learn full-length Italian operas.

Entr'acte –
The Singing Lesson

*M*orning, July 7, 1912. 17 Colville Square, Kensington, London, England. Bertha looks down through the tall window from the worn but still elegant drawing room into Colville Square Garden. A number of small children are out taking their midday exercise, supervised by uniformed nannies. It is drizzling again, but not enough to dampen the spirits of a Canadian in London.

Behind Bertha, Madame De Nevosky corrects Gladys Banks on her breathing. "*Oui, oui, comme ca, mais plus fort.*"

Madame De Nevosky always speaks in French with the girls. French is not the first language of any of the four Canadian girls sharing a group lesson this morning, but it is the lingua franca they use when they meet with Madame. The girls all appreciate that they will not be taken seriously as European trained singers if they cannot make themselves understood in French, and they are happy to practice the language through their singing lessons.

Bertha was initially mortified to discover how inadequate the French she learned in Toronto was for conversation with her singing teacher from Paris. Thus, in addition to studying her music, she has been studying the language seriously, and she has improved a lot in the past year.

Madame turns to the fifth young woman, who is assisting at the piano. *"Bessie, encore s'il vous plaît."*

Bessie Mark strikes the critical note. Bessie is an American but her French is much better than the Canadians', as she started her studies with Madame when they were both living in Paris more than two years ago. Now that she lives with Madame, she speaks French every day. Bertha thinks about how lucky Bessie is to learn under the patronage of an experienced older woman like Madame.

Madame works her way around the group. Each girl listens to the corrections the others receive and hopes to outdo her friends. Bertha tries to focus on the basics of the Lamperti method. Is she standing straight? Is her mouth an open smile? Has she remembered to breathe in through her nose?

In this lesson, they are trying to perfect the *tenuta* of their voices by practicing smooth diminuendos and crescendos on one note. Bertha and Gladys have been taking lessons with Madame for a full year now. They have graduated to working a note from pianissimo up to crescendo and down to pianissimo again, and they both feel a bit superior about their progress.

Margaret George and Madeleine Hunt only began their lessons with Madame two months ago, and they are still working on the initial exercises. They are only allowed to start in their full voice and then take the note down to pianissimo. It is a slow and tedious process to practice like this, but a professional soprano is expected to be able to produce the same quality of sound in all the gradations of crescendo and diminuendo, and that kind of control doesn't come without hard work.

"Et vous, Mademoiselle Crawford?"

Bertha is startled out of a reverie. She was thinking about the Canadian girls' plans for the afternoon. Mr. Borden, the new Prime Minister of Canada, is arriving in London today. They have been reading about the impending visit for days in the papers. He has come to England to talk about 'the empire' and Canada's role in the great imperialist venture.

"What is a dreadnought, anyway?" Gladys asked only yesterday. At nineteen, she is the youngest of them—although, considering that she has managed to become engaged to a wealthy English diamond merchant, she shouldn't be the most naive.

Still, imperialism is not a subject that really interests any of the four music students. But now that the girls are so far from home, it seems like the thing to do—to go out and show their support for their country's leader during his travels. They may even get a glimpse of their famous High Commissioner, Lord Strathcona.

So, after their lesson, they plan to walk over to Paddington Station and join the crowd. And when the 3:20 train from Bristol comes in, they will wave and cheer with the best of them. Then they will probably retire for a cheap cup of tea and a bun in the station café before they make their way home to their lodgings. It is the kind of thing that none of them would have thought about doing for a moment back at home. But then, they aren't at home anymore.

Bertha doesn't spend a lot of time thinking about home these days. From time to time she will meet up with the other Toronto girls who study with the same teachers as she does. But since the day she arrived just over a year ago, she has been more interested in discovering London and meeting new people. Her lessons and practice take up several hours every day. But after that, she is free to walk along the streets, shop the markets, visit the museums and churches, and look for cheap tickets to the opera and the theatre.

And recently she has met an interesting older woman from Poland who has taken her to see the English opera at Covent Garden and has put enticing thoughts into Bertha's head about travelling to the continent to complete her opera training. Bertha hardly dares to think about what the patronage of a friend like Mrs. Słubicka could do for her career; the lessons she might learn would go so far beyond the breathing and notes that Madame is drilling her in. But how does one make a thing like that happen?

With so many new ideas and possibilities swirling around in her head, Bertha hasn't been bored or homesick for a day yet. Sometimes she feels a little guilty when her mother's letters ask why she hasn't written recently, or when her father has to ask if she has received his latest bank draft. But surely they must understand how impossible it is to keep a foot planted on both continents. For she has crossed the Atlantic now, and Canada seems to be a very long way away. She is moving forward into a new life with new ways of doing things.

Bertha turns her full attention to Madame and breathes in deeply, through her nose.

CHAPTER SEVEN –
An Italian Interlude,
1912–1913

In 1912, before she left for Italy to complete her opera training, Bertha had her portrait taken in London. In contrast with earlier portraits, she looks very demure—perhaps a sign that she was now being groomed for a more restrained professional image.

Towards the end of 1912, after a year and a half of studying singing in London, twenty-six-year-old Bertha faced what seems, in retrospect, to have been the most critical decision of her career. She could go back to Canada with a sound bout of training under her belt and a guaranteed future as a top-notch Canadian church and concert singer. Or, she could take a gamble by going on to Italy to seriously train to be a European opera singer. The first option was obviously easier, and it more or less ensured a successful conventional career. Moreover, it was also probably the choice her family would have preferred, for the alternative was much riskier and more complicated. But from Bertha's perspective, the second option would have been much more exciting. However, two practical barriers stood in the way of making that leap onto the European opera stage. Firstly, it is unlikely that she had enough money to personally cover the cost of travel, accommodations, lessons, costumes, and the sundry other expenses that are bound to arise during foreign travels. Secondly, if she travelled alone as a woman, she would have faced many dangers—at the very least to her reputation, if not in fact to her person. Therefore, it was apparent that if she was to stay in Europe and have a credible chance at an operatic career, then Bertha needed help beyond what she and her father could arrange.

It is impossible to know how actively Bertha was trying to solve these two problems, but she certainly must have thought a lot about her options as she was finishing up her studies with De Nevosky and Morando. And so, when she met Zofia Alexandra de Słubicka (neé Kosińska) (1871–1944?), she may have recognized quite quickly that a friendship with the forty-year-old Polish widow presented an unexpected opportunity for a young singer at a turning point. How and where in London the two met remains a mystery, but what is clear is that, by the end of 1912, they had become friends.

Zofia Alexandra Kosińska was a slight, plain woman, not particularly tall, with thin lips, a narrow nose, and fine, dark straight hair that she wore in bangs when she was young. She was born in Warsaw in 1871 into an aristocratic family. Her father, Julian Kosiński (1833–1914), was a member of the noble Rawicz family and held the hereditary title of Baron, and Zofia's maternal grandmother, from the de Hauke side of the family, was a Countess. While she herself was an only child, Zofia had many wealthy relatives across Europe, including well-connected cousins like the Stackelbergs, some of whom were attached to the royal court in St. Petersburg, and two Battenberg cousins who had married into the English royal family.

Zofia was raised in a cultured intellectual household. Both Zofia's father and her uncle Alexander Kosiński were Lithuanian-born, Russian-trained doctors, and her father was a renowned professor of surgery at the University of Warsaw. Her mother, Maria Theresa Salomea de Hauke (1849–1892), was an author of children's books, and her maternal aunt, Ludwika de Hauke (1884–1930), had a long and successful career in journalism as the founder and editor of the Warsaw magazine *Wieczory Rodzinne* (Family Evening). Zofia herself was probably equally well educated, and no doubt she spoke not only her native Polish, but also Russian (the language of the rulers of her country) and French (the lingua franca of intellectuals in much of Europe). She also spoke English, for, by 1912, she had spent more than a decade, on and off, in England.

In 1890, at the age of nineteen, Zofia married Josef Jan de Słubicki (1869–1898?) in Warsaw. De Słubicki was a Roman Catholic like Zofia's father, and the couple married in a Catholic church. However, like her mother before her, Zofia remained a member of the Protestant Lutheran church. Within a few years of her marriage, two events occurred that would have had a profound impact on any young wife: in 1892, she had a son, John Marys de Słubicki; and, not long afterwards, her husband died. Accordingly, before the age of thirty, Zofia had become an independently wealthy—and an independent minded—widow.

A young Zofia Słubicka (neé Kosińska) around the time she bore her son. His education in England would lead to her meeting Bertha.

There were plenty of examples of marriages between Catholic men and Lutheran women in Zofia's family (for instance, her parents), and usually the sons were raised in their fathers' Catholic religion while the daughters were brought up in their mothers' Protestant faith. Zofia, however, had her own ideas, and she was determined to raise her only son as a Protestant. And so, perhaps to sidestep Catholic pressure from her relatives, she decided, in 1899, to enroll seven-year-old John at a Church of England boarding school, St. Ronan's, in Sussex, England. Over the next twelve years, Zofia would spend a lot of time in England supervising her son's education, first at St. Ronan's, then at Westminster School in London, and finally at the University of Cambridge.

Zofia may have thought that she could keep her son closer to herself by taking him away from his Warsaw relatives and sending him to a Protestant school in England. Certainly, it is unlikely that she knowingly meant to rob him of his Polish identity in the process. However, it is hard to imagine a more effective tool of socialization than the English public school system, renowned as it was for manufacturing the 'pukka' English gentlemen who defined and ran the British Empire. In fact, there is no evidence that, after studying from ages seven to twenty-one in English boarding schools and a renowned English university, John really identified himself in any practical way as Polish. Perhaps Zofia already sensed that her son was drifting away from her when she was introduced to the young Canadian soprano sometime in 1911 or 1912. Maybe, consciously or not, she was looking for a relationship to replace an eroding bond with her son.

By the time Bertha met Zofia in London, Bertha was quite well travelled in North American terms. However, in comparison with Zofia, she was still a young and unsophisticated colonial. And although Bertha was a professionally trained singer and musician, it is likely—given that she only had a grade-eight education from a rural Ontario school—that there remained some gaping holes in her education, at least from an aristocrat's perspective. Like Mary Trent, the heroine of Sarah Jeanette Duncan's 1908 novel *Cousin Cinderella: A Canadian Girl in London*, did London society look down their noses at Bertha's Canadian ways? Did Zofia see Bertha as a kind of 'diamond in the rough' when they first met? Did Zofia imagine that, if she supported Bertha to obtain further opera studies in Italy while at the same time personally giving Bertha the polish (and perhaps also the connections) that she would need, then the young Canadian might be able to really carry off a professional singing career in Europe?

Perhaps Zofia's interest in Bertha began as a kind of 'Pygmalion' project, with Zofia personally supervising challenges like raising the standard of Bertha's French, coaching her in elegant manners, and guiding her through an appropriate reading list—in short, easing Bertha through a subtle form of finishing school that paralleled her musical studies for the opera stage. Even if the process was not structured (or conscious on Zofia's part), Bertha would have inevitably absorbed, from Zofia's example, a sense of how the upper classes in Europe spoke, acted, and carried themselves.

Certainly, at the most basic level, the two women had one problem in common. From Zofia's perspective, it was not usual for a woman of her class, however wealthy and well educated, to travel and live alone. While travelling with a servant provided some propriety, independent women—particularly widows—often took on a female companion (that is, a woman who played a role not unlike a sister or a daughter) to ensure their respectability. The unmarried De Nevosky, for example, had a young American singer, Bessie Mark, as a companion living with her in London. Bertha, for her part, needed a chaperone, preferably an older woman who could act like a mother in guarding her reputation and providing advice and support. So it seems that, by the end of 1912, Bertha and Zofia had come to some kind of agreement that they would travel together to Italy. Bertha would be a companion to Zofia, and Zofia would act not only as a chaperone, but also effectively as a patron, covering many of Bertha's expenses as she studied for the opera stage. They may have seen it as just a temporary arrangement at the time, but it was a decision that would shape the rest of Bertha's life.

And so, at the end of 1912, Bertha's adventure really began as she left the familiar English-speaking world of London and crossed the English Channel to France with her new companion, Zofia. From there, they travelled by train to the Italian city of Milan, where the two women found respectable lodgings as guests in a Catholic convent. Milan was the old home of Francesco Lamperti, and so it was an excellent place to look for a teacher who followed Lamperti's methods and could coach Bertha in the classic coloratura opera roles. After all, if Bertha really had decided to be an opera singer by this point in time, she could not wait until she got an engagement to begin learning her roles. When a theatre company puts on a play today, it is not uncommon to hire actors and actresses who have not played the parts before; it is expected that they will learn their new roles and rehearse the new show. However, this was not the case for opera in Bertha's lifetime. Guest soloists were expected to know their parts completely when they were hired, so as to require minimal rehearsal with the new cast. So, touring singers were limited to the roles they had already mastered, and those roles could only be roles that were written for their type of voice—which, for Bertha, were the coloratura soprano roles found in particular Italian and French operas.

By the turn of the century, the opera world had begun to settle on a canon of established favourite operas that were regularly performed by most companies. Within this canon, there were only a limited number of prima donna (leading lady) roles that featured a coloratura soprano voice. Few new roles for coloratura sopranos were being written, and many of the previously popular coloratura soprano roles (e.g., Amina in Verdi's *La sonnambula,* Elivra in Bellini's *I Puritani,* and Lucia in Donizetti's *Lucia de Lammermoor*) were rarely performed during Bertha's years on the stage.

Consequently, it was inevitable that Bertha, as a coloratura soprano, would have to specialize in the classic prima donna roles like Verdi's Gilda and Violetta and Rossini's Rosina, all usually sung in Italian, and Gounod's Juliette and Marguerite, usually sung in French. She possibly also sang Nedda in Leoncavallo's *Pagliacci,* an Italian opera, but this opera was not performed often. There were some seconda donna (second lady) roles written for the coloratura voice, like Micaela in Bizet's *Carmen* or Oscar the Page in Verdi's *A Masked Ball,* but playing seconda donna was a compromise that Bertha would not make. It appears that from the start she was determined to be either a prima donna or not sing opera at all.

Over her career, Bertha often performed arias from other operas in recital, but there is no evidence that she ever learned any other complete opera roles. Limited as she was to this specialized operatic repertoire, she was destined, from the beginning of her operatic career, to work only as a guest soloist hired for a limited series of appearances in the roles she specialized in. While most opera companies would include several of these Italian and French classics in their annual programs, few would be likely to hire a full-time soloist for only a limited number of appearances. How carefully did Bertha weigh this reality as she set out to Italy to train in the *bel canto* coloratura repertoire? Did she consider a future as a travelling guest soloist to be a disadvantage, or did the prospect of a peripatetic career dovetail nicely with a love of adventure and travel?

During the early months of 1913, from her and Zofia's base in the Milan convent, Bertha went out to daily lessons with Emilia Corsi (1870–1927), an Italian soprano who had a reputation for teaching and interpreting operatic roles and who was familiar with Lamperti's approaches. It seems likely that Corsi was the teacher who taught Bertha her basic Italian repertoire of Verdi and Rossini classics. Bertha may also have studied Gounod's operas with Corsi, although, as these are French operas, she may have begun learning these parts in London with De Nevosky.

Emilia Corsi was born in Lisbon in 1870 and learned the lessons she taught to Bertha from her family of professional musicians. Her father was a reputable voice teacher, her grandfather had been a successful baritone, and her two cousins were stars on the opera stage. She was a short, buxom woman who wore her thick dark hair low over her forehead. She made her debut in Bologna singing Micaela in *Carmen* the year that Bertha was born, and she went on to a substantial career singing mainly in Portugal, Spain, and Italy. She also made some early recordings in 1906 for the Victor Record Company. She toured widely, visiting Russia as well as Cuba, Mexico, and Argentina in Latin America. After almost a quarter of a century living the prima donna dream on the stage, Emilia retired in 1910 to become a singing teacher in Milan.

Emilia Corsi, a retired Italian soprano, gave Bertha's opera training the requisite Italian touch.

The Italian approach to singing lessons was more intense than the London equivalent, with daily hour-long private lessons being the norm for new students. The goal of a student at

Bertha's level was not only to learn the music, but also to memorize the full *libretto* (words) of the opera in Italian, with an authentic accent, as well as the standard *scena* (stage instructions). Bertha probably read the elaborate *disposizione scenica*, which were published in book form for all the famous Italian operas and which described in detail the costumes, properties, and scenery to be used, exactly which part of the stage the action should take place on, and all the entrances, movements, and exits for the characters. The opera copyright holders expected all productions to conform to these prescribed *messa in scena*, and a singer needed to learn all of this before she could take on a new role. Learning this standardized approach to opera production must have entailed very intense study for Bertha, but once she had mastered the music, *libretto*, and *scena* for a particular opera, she could be confident that she could perform that opera with any new company with very little rehearsal.

After only a few months of study in Italy, at the age of twenty-six, Bertha secured her first engagement to sing a full Italian opera in the opera house of the small lakeside town of Salo. With excitement, she cabled home to her family from Milan in February 1913 to announce that she would be making her European opera debut in May in a prima donna role that gave her an opportunity to put to the test all her coloratura training. Her family passed on the news, and advance notices appeared in both *The Globe* and *The Toronto Daily Star*. How Bertha got this debut performance in Italy remains an open question. It was common for teachers to help arrange a debut for their students, and Corsi certainly knew various agents and impresarios. Nonetheless, there was ongoing controversy in the Canadian musical press about the reality that some North American vocal students needed more than a simple introduction to secure an engagement, and in fact achieved their Italian debuts by paying a fee to an impresario. This was less common in the smaller provincial theatres like Salo, so it is possible that Bertha got her first assignment purely on her merits. However, as many impresarios demanded compensation for taking a gamble on an untried foreign student, it may be that part of Zofia's support of Bertha during this time included paying a few hundred lira to arrange Bertha's debut.[1] Practical voice students viewed these payments as a necessary investment to

---

1   100–300 Italian lira was roughly equal to 130–360 Canadian dollars in 1913, or more than six months' salary for an Ontario school teacher.

ensure a hearing before a knowledgeable audience and reputable reviewers. The demands of the Italian market would have brought home to Bertha, if she had not already grasped this reality, that—self-serving reminiscences of retired prima donnas not withstanding—it took more than talent to get onto the stage. Compromises would have to be made, and sometimes they involved money—money that she would have had to accept from her patron, Zofia, at least until Bertha's own earnings were more secure.

Ironically, in her debut role in European opera, Bertha was playing exactly the kind of character that the conservative society matrons back in Toronto would have considered suspect. Bertha sang her first opera in the part of Nedda in Leoncavallo's opera *Pagliacci*, a tragedy about a troupe of travelling actors that is built around the theatrical device of a play within a play. The overall plot certainly would have justified the Toronto society matrons' low expectation of the theatrical world. They would have considered Nedda a disreputable character for a respectable single young woman to portray, for Nedda is a married woman who is engaged in an affair with a fellow actor. As such, she is the very embodiment of the immorality that was purported to attend the woman who pursues a life on the stage, where the portrayal of characters with dubious morals slides across into the actress's real life. Of course, like many characters in classical tragedies, Nedda ends up dead at the end of the opera (in this case, at the hands of her jealous husband).

We do not know what the Italian papers wrote about Bertha's Salo debut, but perhaps just as important from Bertha's perspective was the reaction of the Toronto press, for, at this point, there is no reason to think that Bertha was not planning to return to Canada fairly soon. Indeed, wasn't the point of getting European experience to capitalize upon it on a Canadian stage? *The Toronto Sunday World* reported that, on the night of Bertha's debut in *Pagliacci*, she received enthusiastic applause, repeated calls for encores, and numerous baskets of flowers, as well as the jewellery that opera singers often received in addition to (or in lieu of) payment: a gold locket inscribed with the date of the debut from the theatre directors and a pearl pendant from the impresario. Although it had no reporter in Italy, *The Toronto Sunday World* determined that her debut had been a "phenomenal success" and described her as a prima donna with a voice of "rare beauty." Bertha and her family must have felt that her ten years of study had now paid off. She had sung in European opera, and the press had crowned her a prima donna. She was beginning to live the dream—and all of Toronto would know it.

However, when read closely, it becomes clear that the point of *The Toronto Sunday World* article was not so much to announce Bertha's success as the success of one of her teachers, Signor Morando, now of the Canadian Academy of Music in Toronto. Morando is credited with suggesting that Bertha go to Italy in the first place (as though it was not her own idea), arranging for her reception and study (as though she and Zofia were not capable of making arrangements), and for predicting her great future (as if she had no inkling herself). There was no mention of Zofia or De Nevosky, let alone Toronto's own Schuch and his six-year contribution to Bertha's vocal development. Tellingly, the article runs adjacent to an advertisement for the Canadian Academy of Music. So, while the review confirms Bertha's reputation as a rising star, it is also a clever piece of marketing for the Canadian Academy of Music and its recently hired singing instructor. In that light, the credibility of the rest of the article's assertions is less certain. In fact, later in life, Bertha would tell the press that her Italian debut was in Venice (not Salo), and Morando did not make the short list of teachers she credited with her long-term success.

What is certain, however, is that Bertha had enough success with her debut to get further engagements in Italy. After her first appearance in *Pagliacci* in Salo in May 1913, Bertha sang the prima donna role of Gilda in Verdi's *Rigoletto* in Venice and at the Teatro Dal Verme in Milan. This second role in Italy, the role of Gilda, might have been considered a more decent role than the role of Nedda, although it is equally tragic. Gilda is a young, innocent daughter who is abducted and then seduced, and eventually killed in error, at the instigation of her own father. The role includes the famous aria "Caro Nome," which Bertha would go on to sing frequently as a concert staple and encore piece during her career. *Rigoletto* also includes several father–daughter duets, which must have evoked some poignancy for Bertha, who had sung many duets with John Crawford in her youth.

Following her appearances in Venice and Milan, Bertha was hired for a tour of some smaller opera houses in Italy. Presumably, Zofia continued to travel with Bertha, most likely along with a professional theatre dresser hired to support Bertha during the tour. Indeed, Zofia had no reason to return to England at this point. In May 1913, while she was caught up in her new project of chaperoning Bertha, Zofia's son John had dropped out of Cambridge without completing his degree. More surprisingly, he then left England for Halifax, indicating on the ship's manifest that he intended to spend at least six months farming in Calgary, Alberta.

With her son slipping far from her reach, Zofia probably took extra comfort in Bertha's company. In any case, Zofia would not have wanted to miss the opportunity to see Bertha put into practice the lessons she had learned both in the professional singing studio and, more informally, in Zofia's company. As they travelled the country, they both may have begun to envisage a longer career for Bertha in Italy. Rather than playing on her Canadian identity, as she had done in London, Bertha actually began to hide it by assuming an Italian stage name, 'Berta de Giovanni'—literally, 'Bertha, daughter of John.' Here she was following the example of the Canadian prima donna Emma Lajeunesse, who took on the Italian name of Albani for her debut in Italy, and the tenor from Guelph, Edward Johnson (1878–1959), who had rechristened himself Edoardo di Giovanni for his Italian debut just the year before. But although Albani went by her Italian stage name for the rest of her life, Bertha abandoned the 'de Giovanni' when she left Italy a few months later. However, she continued to spell Bertha without the 'h' for the rest of her career in Europe, perhaps consciously wanting to signal a dual identity by combining a European-sounding first name with her very Canadian family name.

Back in Canada, Bertha's family followed her progress through her letters and waited for her to make the inevitable triumphant return. But changes were happening for them all. While Bertha was gaily travelling around Italy, her siblings were beginning to settle down and think about marriage and children. In July 1913, Bertha's younger brother was the first in the family to get married. With his father's support, he went into business, opening a corner grocery store not far from the Parkside Drive house. Lucia and Ernest Pearson, the young electrician she had met fifteen years before in Elmvale, began courting. Did the family still think that Bertha would return to Toronto and merge back into their commonplace domestic life? They were certainly using her correspondence to make sure the Canadian press was up to date with her advancing career and well prepared for her return to the Canadian stage. Did any of the Crawfords sense that she was getting drawn into a European world with which Toronto could never compete? Did Bertha herself even recognize it?

In the meantime, any dreams that Bertha and her family may have had earlier of her singing opera with a Canadian company had come crashing down. In the spring of 1913, the Montréal Opera Company succumbed to increasing deficits. The company had produced three full seasons of grand opera, with more than 300 performances in five cities, but the mounting losses were unsustainable. Colonel Meighen regretfully folded his operation after covering more than $100,000 in losses. Of course, it had never been certain that Bertha would have been able to perform the more controversial female opera roles in Toronto; the passion and honest portrayal of real women's lives found in the great opera tragedies went beyond what Toronto society considered polite entertainment. But Bertha was well advanced in her studies in Europe when it became undeniably clear that the Canadian public was not yet ready to make grand opera a financially viable prospect. In fact, Canada would not have another permanent opera company until 1950, thirteen years after Bertha's death.

Did Bertha ever consider a future singing with an American travelling opera company, like those she must have seen on their way through Toronto over the previous decade? After all, her friend and fellow student, Margaret George, had some success singing with one. Or did those companies, with their pared-down casts and battered sets, seem rather tawdry to Bertha after Zofia had taken her to the great opera houses of London and Milan? Did they look more like a fallback position for the singer who had failed to reach the standard of a first-rate opera company? Or worse, like the final stand for the 'has been'? For surely it was rare that singing with a second-rate travelling company would launch a singer upwards towards better roles. So, settling for a place with an American travelling company may have seemed to Bertha like an admission that she would never have a place in the top tier of prima donnas. Perhaps it was these fears that kept Bertha from ever performing with one of those travelling companies. Regardless, for the time being, Bertha was singing prima donna roles in Italy, and she was unlikely to abandon that opportunity to return to an uncertain singing market in North America.

But then quite a different prospect arose. In the fall of 1913, Zofia learned that her eighty-year-old father's health was in decline, and she realized that she must return home to Warsaw. Rather than abandoning Bertha in Italy at this early stage of her opera career, it seems that Zofia offered to take Bertha back with her to Warsaw—and no doubt Zofia would have pointed out that the fine Warsaw Great Theatre (*Teatr Weilki*) was just beginning its fall opera season and would be hiring imported Italian opera soloists to enhance its local company. And so, after less than a year in Italy, Bertha was on her way east into the Russian Empire.

Entr'acte –
Backstage at the Opera

11:45 pm, September, 1913. A municipal opera house, northern Italy. Bertha is quite the sight as she throws open the door of the drab little dressing room. Having just finished a performance of *Rigoletto*, she is *en travesti*, wearing Gilda's final costume of the third act in which she is disguised as a young man. Off the stage, the dark, thigh-length tunic and the long black tights of a sixteenth-century courtier that looked so dramatic to the audience suddenly appear both scandalous and a bit ridiculous. She snatches off her floppy velvet cap, with its long feathered plume, and plops it on a scruffy upholstered chair near the door. The blonde ringlets of her wig tumble onto the short cape that is draped across her shoulders, and then the cape, too, is flung onto the chair. Bertha's face is mostly chalked white, as are the backs of her hands—a stark contrast with her darkened eye sockets, pink cheeks, and red lips. From the distance of the theatre seats, and under the bright house lights, she looked the part of a beautiful yet betrayed young woman. But close up, lit by the glare of the twenty electric bulbs surrounding the dressing room mirror, she seems to be wearing a ghastly mask.

A stagehand leans in to cram a large basket of fresh flowers against the cracked plaster wall. The door closes behind him, muffling the distant reverberations of hundreds of feet making their way down the theatre stairs to the lobby exit. Flopping onto the old chair in front of the cluttered toilet table, Bertha is indifferent to the grubby condition of the room, dilapidated by a long succession of visiting singers. Her only thought is to gauge her patron's reaction to the evening's performance. She turns to the older woman, who is still sitting in the armchair where Bertha left her after the intermission. Zofia looks up from the paper she is holding.

"How many curtain calls?" Zofia asks, as if she had not been proudly counting the number of times she heard the applause rise and fall.

"I think we took eight. These small-town audiences are so generous!" Bertha is clearly elated from the 'bravas' still ringing in her ears. "Who would have thought that dying on stage would leave you feeling so alive?" She laughs, turning to the mirror.

At the mention of death, Zofia drops her eyes again to the paper.

Stella, the professional theatre dresser recommended to Bertha by her Italian teacher, comes up behind the exhausted performer. She lifts off the wig and balances it on a stand at the end of the table. Bertha's natural hair is revealed as a rumpled coil that begins to slowly unravel from where it has been pressed and matted close to her head. Stella pulls the hair tightly back and, reaching for a large curved comb, pins the hair out of the way above Bertha's forehead. She hands Bertha a can of fresh butter.

Much to her surprise, Bertha has learned that there is no better medium to remove theatrical paint and powder than butter. She dips her fingers in the tin and spreads a generous layer across her face, massaging it into her skin. When all the paint has dissolved into a swirly greasy mess, she turns to the washstand, where Stella has ensured that there is ample hot water and gentle soap available. As Bertha lathers, Stella stands by to hold back any hair that falls loose. Then, as Bertha rises, her face still dripping, Stella hands her a clean towel.

With her face and hands restored to their natural pink complexion, Bertha can now take off the rest of her costume without soiling it with grease paint. As Bertha changes into her street clothes, Stella takes up the discarded elements of the costume and folds them carefully into a wicker hamper that she will carry back with them to the hotel.

Bertha turns to Zofia, who is frowning at the paper. When Zofia looks up, her face is distracted. Bertha cannot read her expression. She raises her eyebrows in question, a smile still dancing around her lips.

"I've had a cable from my aunt," Zofia says at last. "My father is not well. I think the time has come for me to go home to Warsaw. I've already been away for much longer than I had ever planned."

Indeed, it has been more than two years since Zofia arrived in London for a visit, never imagining that her journey would lead to something as improbable as chaperoning a young Canadian singer on a tour of provincial Italian opera houses.

Bertha catches her breath in surprise. This tour is coming to a close, but she had thought she might find more work in Italy without too much trouble. But she can't do that without Zofia's support—and not just her material support. Zofia is so good at keeping Bertha's spirits level when that huge burst of confidence that follows the applause always threatens to slide between performances. Bertha sits still, wondering where this conversation is going.

"You know, as I've told you before, we have a very good opera company in Warsaw. And the opera house is much bigger than these places we have been these last weeks." Zofia seems to weigh her words carefully as she speaks. "In Warsaw, the new opera season will be starting this month, and they always hire international soloists for the Italian operas. And I can introduce you to influential people there."

Finally it dawns on Bertha that Zofia thinks there could be opera work for her in Warsaw and is offering to take her there. This is not an idea that Bertha has thought about before. Her plan was to get experience singing in *Italy*.

"But I've never heard of a Canadian singing in Warsaw," she blurts out before she can catch herself.

"That is because there haven't been any. Not that I can remember. But I think that might be to your advantage," Zofia says slowly.

Bertha can see that Zofia must have been thinking through the practicalities, in the quiet of the shabby little dressing room, while Bertha was strutting around the big stage, dazzling the audience with her high-flying notes.

Bertha fastens the row of hooks on her shirtwaist as she evaluates this sudden change of plans. She has relied on Zofia to guide her career for almost a year, and Zofia's judgement has not been wrong yet. After all, Zofia got them to Italy, secured an excellent teacher, helped Bertha get her debut, and supported her through this tour. Bertha's debt to her patron is no small thing. And Zofia seems to have decided that she will not abandon Bertha now, although she is in no way obligated to go on helping.

Bertha stands up after buttoning her street boots and accepts the shawl that Stella is holding out. "Well, that could be a new challenge—to be the first Canadian to sing opera in Warsaw!" she says.

And this time, she can plainly read the look of relief crossing Zofia's face.

CHAPTER EIGHT –
A Year in Warsaw,
1913–1914

Bertha's mother, her sister Lucia, and her father on the porch of the Crawfords' new home on Parkside Drive in Toronto. They thought Bertha would rejoin them soon, as they listed her name in the Toronto City Directory under this address.

Bertha was already twenty-seven in the fall of 1913, when she first travelled to Warsaw, and she would have been aware that if she was going to get recognition as an up-and-coming opera star, she needed to build on her initial momentum and quickly step up to more prestigious stages. The fact that Bertha, in later years, tended to gloss over her time in Italy suggests that she mainly sang in quite minor opera houses there. In contrast, the Warsaw Great Theatre was the most prestigious theatre in the western provinces of the Russian Empire, and it was a venue name that would resonate with novelty in Canada and elsewhere. And so Bertha was probably quite optimistic as she accompanied the well-connected Zofia back to her home in Warsaw. Indeed, *Saturday Night* would later describe Bertha's move to Warsaw as "the event which would shape her history for more than seven momentous years."

While it may sound simpler to say that Zofia took Bertha home to Poland, it is more accurate to say that she took Bertha home to the Polish province of the Russian Empire. In 1913, there was no independent country of Poland as there is now (and as there had been before). For more than a century, since 1795, the land that had once made up the Polish Kingdom had been divided between three empires: the Russian, the German, and the Austro–Hungarian. Warsaw fell under the Russian Empire. The people of Warsaw, which was the third largest city in the Russian Empire, still held a memory that their city had once been the vibrant capital of an independent country. But in 1913, Warsaw was the seat of the Russian military and civil administration for just one of the many provinces within the Tsar's vast empire.

For a Canadian like Bertha, the city of Warsaw must have presented an intriguing combination of old-world culture and modern utilities. The city had a population of more than 800,000 when Bertha arrived in 1913, which made it bigger than the biggest Canadian city, Montréal, and almost twice the size of Toronto at the time. Like Toronto, Warsaw had experienced a recent population boom and had doubled in size since 1900. Although Warsaw was dominated by Polish Catholics, more than a third of the population was made up of Polish Jews—a significant proportion of whom were Hasidic Jews, with their distinctive long black coats, broad-brimmed hats, and long curls hanging before their ears. There was also an important minority of Russians who belonged to the Orthodox Church, but Protestants like Bertha were almost invisible.

Bertha probably found the older parts of Warsaw crowded. The city had a much denser core than sprawling Canadian cities like Toronto, with many buildings packed into the Warsaw city limits, which had been tightly defined by defensive earthworks built around the city in the late 1700s. In the city core, uninterrupted rows of multi-storey brick buildings lined the streets, the details of their façades highlighted with ornate plaster mouldings. Unlike the new cities and towns of Ontario, which were laid out by surveyors in a consistent grid pattern, Warsaw's streets had evolved over the centuries, and many of them—although picturesque—were narrow, winding, and poorly suited to modern traffic.

Zofia's home was probably in the central, more modern part of Warsaw, where the services were as good, if not better, than what Bertha was familiar with in Toronto. The central streets of Warsaw were all paved, although many with uneven fieldstone, which resulted in a bumpy ride and probably encouraged the use of the municipal tram system. Indeed, more than 300 electric tramcars carried people smoothly and efficiently on rails laid along the main arteries. Since the 1880s, the central part of the city had been served by modern water pipes and sewers, although less than sixty percent of the city's buildings were connected by 1914. The gas system was much older, having been in use since 1856, and more than a third of the buildings were connected to the newer electric grid—including, of course, the Warsaw Great Theatre— and more than 30,000 households had telephones.

It was probably around this time that Bertha acquired her first dogs, although she might have brought them with her from Italy. The pampered, yappy lapdog was something of a cliché trophy for the archetypical prima donna, but Bertha seems to have genuinely been a dog lover. From this period onwards, Bertha always had at least two small dogs, and she took them along wherever she travelled. Walking her dogs in Warsaw, Bertha would have enjoyed the simulacrum of tamed nature in the city's large and well-established parks, where she might exercise her pets on gravelled paths, around fountains and sculptures, and along shady green walkways. Through the centre of the city, the real forces of nature could be found in the Vistula River, which wound along a shifting course and periodically slipped its banks to flood low-lying neighbourhoods. The dogs certainly would have enjoyed its riverside paths.

Although Bertha may have initially explored the city's byways as a visiting dog walker, she would have soon realized what Zofia well knew: that Warsaw offered some excellent opportunities for a professional musician. Ironically, to the benefit of a visiting artist like Bertha, the century of Russian political domination over Warsaw and the Polish lands had been a period of growth for the fine and performing arts. In response to the loss of political power, the educated Polish population directed their nationalist passions towards cultural and intellectual life, and the arts became an outlet for frustrated energies, particularly in the cities. Buoyed up by the attendance of both the Russian and Polish residents of Warsaw, the quality and quantity of artistic performances—including musical performances—rose, and significant permanent facilities were established.

Of the six major government theatres built in Warsaw during the previous century, the most important (from the perspective of Bertha's career) was the Warsaw Great Theatre. Already a venerable eighty years old in 1913, it had opened in 1833 with a performance of Rossini's *The Barber of Seville*, an opera in which Bertha would often appear a century later. The theatre was built to house three artistic companies that were already well established in the Warsaw arts world—one for opera, another for ballet, and a third for theatre. Almost 200 metres wide at the front, the central core of the building was almost six storeys high and was flanked by two large three-storey wings. The central neoclassical façade was dominated by two tiers of massive stone columns with a stately portico protecting the main entrance. Of course, performers like Bertha would have come in the quieter entrances at the back, where the staff came and went. Opening onto the Wierzbowa Street side, the theatre's side doors led into the smaller performance halls, the artists' dressing rooms, the rehearsal rooms and ballet studios, the snack bar, and the ticket window.

The Warsaw Great Theatre complex was imposing. It was several times bigger than Massey Hall, where Bertha had so often sung, and slightly bigger than Queen's Park in Toronto. In front of the building, Theatre Square swarmed with the activity of the audience going in and out, as well as carriages and cabs, fountains splashing, and the rumble of electric tramcars. On the opposite side of the theatre, along Nowo Senatorska Street, many of the artists kept apartments. Behind the theatre, facing onto Trebacka Street and taking up much of the rest of the block, was the five-storey administration building of the government theatres, built in 1905. Indeed, the whole complex was like a small, self-contained principality in the centre of Warsaw, and it constituted a bastion of the Polish language and culture during the years of Russian rule.

The main opera hall where Bertha made her Polish debut was at the centre of the building. It was a place where all classes of society in Warsaw went to see and be seen, and it reflected the steep stratification of Warsaw society. Only about 800 of the 1,200 seats had a reasonable view, while the remaining 400 cheap seats were really only good for listening. The boxes in the ground- and first-floor galleries were priced for the pockets of the hereditary aristocracy and other wealthy Varshavians. The auditorium would remain lit during the performance, and the better off in the audience took advantage to show off the latest fashions from Paris. They favoured the theatre as a place to meet people and catch up on business. They might sometimes strike up a new romance under the guise of sympathizing with the romantic turns on the stage. They might even listen to the music.

The Warsaw Great Theatre was the most important opera house in the Polish province of the Russian Empire.

Bertha's audiences in the Warsaw Great Theatre included people from all classes. The inexpensive seats in the upper gallery would have been crowded with craftsmen, apprentices, and students. Priests might even turn up, albeit in secular guise. Attending the theatre was technically forbidden for them, but some went anyway. The cheapest seats were the unnumbered places in the top balcony, colloquially known as 'the heavens,' where the seats were for 'swallows.' Up near the ceiling, students might take advantage of the relaxed atmosphere to gossip, flirt, and snack on nuts, gingerbread, and caramel. Ironically, it was often these poor students, listening from up above, who determined the success of a performance, as they had the least compunction about loudly expressing their opinions if they did not think much of a show. Sometimes they even formed vociferous *claques* of supporters to cheer on their favourite stars—and to boo those they disliked.

Did Bertha and Zofia arrive in Warsaw in the fall of 1913 already knowing that Bertha would make an opera debut in only a few weeks? Almost every fall, Warsaw opera lovers like Zofia looked forward to the arrival of an Italian impresario who brought a small company of Italian soloists to spice up the local opera season. The Italians would take on the leading roles in the Italian operas staged at the Warsaw Great Theatre, while the supporting cast, the chorus, and the orchestra would be made up of Poles. In the fall of 1913, at least five stars from Italy were appearing with the opera company in Warsaw. Three of them were tenors: Giovanni Genzardi (1881–1972), an Italian; Romano Ciaroff-Ciarini (1878–1964), who was really a Russian singing under an Italian name; and Leon Geitler (1884–1933), who hailed from Prague in the Austrian Empire. In addition, there was the Italian soprano Ersilde Cervi-Caroli (1883–1964), as well as the baritone Riccardo Stracciari (1875–1955). Perhaps with Zofia's help, Bertha may have made contact with the impresario of this small company while Bertha and Zofia were still in Italy. Alternately, Bertha may have been introduced—either by Zofia or by one of Zofia's friends in Warsaw—directly to the Musical Director for Italian Opera at the Warsaw Great Theatre, the Italian Pietro Cimini (1874–1971). Either way, before she had been in Warsaw a month, Bertha had an engagement to debut with the opera on December 2, 1913.

Bertha debuted in Warsaw in 1913, singing Gilda in Rigoletto opposite the Italian baritone Riccardo Stracciari in the title role.

Bertha signed her contract to work for the Warsaw Great Theatre Opera Company with the directorate of the Warsaw Government Theatres. The Warsaw Great Theatre, along with the other major theatres in Warsaw, was managed by the directorate, a government body established in 1810 and under the control of an official appointed by the Tsar. The Russian administration—a typical imperial power—was conscious of the need to exercise control over the nationalist passions of the Poles and their expressions through the arts. The directorate hired—and fired—all of the staff and performers for the theatres it managed (directors, actors, singers, musicians, dancers, set designers, etc.), who worked as government employees serving at the pleasure of the Russian government. All performances were subject to the Tsar's censor, and theatre performances in particular were heavily controlled. Very few Polish-language plays were permitted, but Polish-language operas were approved more often. However, fortunately for Bertha, less controversial Italian and French operas were also performed regularly.

For years before Bertha arrived, the Warsaw Opera Company already had a reputation as a welcoming stage for Italian opera, and Warsaw had strong cultural relations with Italian impresarios and opera centres like Milan. These relations were only strengthened when it hired an experienced Italian conductor from Milan, Pietro Cimini, as its Musical Director of Italian Opera in 1910. Cimini was responsible for all the production details of a large repertoire of Italian and French operas, including finding appropriate guest artists like Bertha. In December 1913, Cimini was the most experienced opera director that Bertha had worked with yet, and she would have benefited from his advanced approach. Born in Capri in 1874, Cimini originally trained to play the violin in Bologna; by the turn of the century, he was playing first violin with the orchestra at the storied Milan opera house, La Scala. Working at La Scala under the famous conductor Arturo Toscanini, Cimini absorbed the new ethos of artistic direction in the opera. Toscanini's approach was to bring together the hitherto disparate details of the performance—the soloists, chorus, orchestra, costumes, acting, sets, and lighting—to form a coherent and complete work of art. Cimini brought this approach with him to the Warsaw Opera Company, and he would have expected a young guest artist like Bertha to conform to his direction.

Bertha would have felt the pressure of Cimini's reputation for meticulous preparation and attention to detail in his work. He was a small man, with thick wavy hair and brown eyes, and *The Los Angeles Times* later described him as "a man of serious purpose and high ideals" who "invariably sacrificed himself to perfection." In later years, he admitted that he hadn't really learned good manners until his years working in Russia, and in his Warsaw days he had not yet fully tamed his melodramatic Italian style. But he was also known for his sense of humour and democratic outlook.

Cimini probably thought a new Canadian guest soloist like Bertha would have enough novelty to sell a lot of tickets and would make an interesting contrast with the more established male stars she appeared with in Warsaw. Regardless, Bertha certainly benefitted from Cimini's casting choices. Looking back on her career years later, Bertha never mentioned the men she sang opposite in Italy, which suggests that they were not major stars who could advance her career. However, she certainly did mention the stars she first sang with in Warsaw, and their stature confirms the impression that singing at the Warsaw Great Theatre was a step up for her career.

In her debut performances at the Warsaw Great Theatre on December 2 and 19, 1913, Bertha played the young Gilda opposite Riccardo Stracciari as the father figure of Rigoletto. At thirty-eight years old, Stracciari was hardly old enough to be Bertha's father, but he had been specializing in the role for some years already. Under a tasselled multi-pointed cap, and with an artificial hump under his colourful cape, he created a convincing older hunch-backed court jester. Stracciari probably knew Cimini from his time singing at La

Scala in 1904. He had also sung in London, New York, South America, and Russia, and his speciality was always Italian opera, particularly *Rigoletto* and *The Barber of Seville*. In retrospect, he was considered one of the finest Italian baritones of the century, so it was something of a coup for Bertha to secure an engagement with a star of his standing this early in her career.

Performing in a city like Warsaw, where there was such a long tradition of high-quality classical music performances, meant appearing before a very different breed of music critics compared to the self-taught men who wrote about music in the Toronto newspapers. For instance, the deeply experienced Alexander Polinski (1845–1916), who covered opera for the Polish-language *Kurjer Warszawski* (Warsaw Courier), was a professor at the Warsaw Music Institute and the author of seven learned books on Polish music history. So Bertha must have been very encouraged when, the day after her Warsaw debut in *Rigoletto*, Polinski wrote that she had a very beautiful voice which was already very well developed technically, and that, "all in all, she presented herself as a serious candidate to be a great singer." With a respected critic saying that about her debut Warsaw performance, Bertha would have had good grounds to feel that she had arrived in a city where she might feel at home.

And indeed, Bertha was immediately taken into the local musical community when, two days later, the Warsaw Theatre Directorate invited her to sing alongside some of the most famous musical artists in the city in a benefit concert at the Warsaw Philharmonic Hall. Bertha opened the concert, singing an aria from Bellini's *La Sonnambula* to enthusiastic applause. Polinski's fellow critic at the *Kurjer Warszawski* (Warsaw Courier), Adam Dobrowolski (1860–1921), wrote that she made "a very favourable impression" and was "an outstanding talent." When she joined a similarly star-studded cast in a charity concert a week later, on December 10, to sing one of Violetta's arias from Verdi's *La Traviata*, as well as Dvorak's "Humoresque," Dobrowolski said she "shone in her interpretation" and "conquered the whole audience." Within a month of arriving in Warsaw, Bertha had caught the full attention of two of the most senior music critics in the country—and had captured the hearts of the local audience in Warsaw as well. Zofia would have been pleased, if not also relieved, as it must have been quite a gamble to introduce Bertha as her protégé when the Canadian still had rather limited experience.

Intent on increasing her experience, at the end of December, Bertha made a second pair of guest appearances at the Warsaw Great Theatre, this time singing opposite another of the visiting tenors, Romano Ciaroff-Ciarini, in two performances of *Romeo and Juliette*. Ciaroff-Ciarini, whose real name was Gurovich, was born in Odessa in the Russian Empire. He had spent much of his career singing in the Russian provinces and had only been appearing in Italy since 1912. The critic Polinski was again impressed with Bertha, saying that she was more graceful in this role and made a very good impression, singing sweetly in the lyrical parts (like Juliette's famous balcony scene) and yet expressing herself powerfully in the dramatic scenes. After at least one more charity concert at the beginning of March 1914, in the third week of March she shared performances of *Rigoletto* and *Romeo and Juliette* with Dmitri Smirnov (1881–1944), one of the most prestigious co-stars she ever sang opera with.

Smirnov, who was born in Moscow, was a handsome Russian tenor only five years older than Bertha. Smirnov spent some of his formative years singing with the avant-garde private opera company run by Savva Mamontov, a Russian industrialist and patron of the arts. Smirnov went on to have successes in the Imperial Theatres in St. Petersburg and Moscow, singing in both Russian and Italian operas. By 1914, he had travelled widely, singing in Paris and at the Metropolitan Opera in New York, as well as touring in South America. He also had a busy recording career. Fortunately for Bertha's career, Smirnov appears to have squeezed his guest appearances in Warsaw in 1914 between engagements in Russia, New York, and London.

Bertha's opportunity to appear opposite this big Russian star might easily have been derailed, however. On March 24, 1914, between Bertha's performances of *Rigoletto* on March 23 and *Romeo and Juliette* on March 25, Zofia's father died. Zofia must have appreciated Bertha's moral support during such a difficult moment, and Bertha probably felt that the least she could do, after all of Zofia's support for her career, was to stand by her patron during this difficult time. However, demonstrating mature professional concentration, Bertha did not allow any personal stress to show through on the stage. The critic from the Russian-language *Warshavskij Dnievnik* (Warsaw Daily) lauded Bertha's Juliette for producing "the most favourable impression both in the duets with this amazing partner and in the solos" and for Bertha's "artistic interpretation of the task, the soft femininity of her expression and, in general, her serious preparation for the part."

Why these reviews from Warsaw did not get repeated in the Toronto papers is something of a mystery. After the initial reports of her Italian debut, Bertha's family does not appear to have fed any more information to the Canadian press about her follow-up Italian appearances or her debut performances in Warsaw in 1913 and 1914. Were they waiting for even better reviews? Or was Bertha beginning to think that it didn't matter what the Canadian papers wrote about her in the short run, as she would not be going home for some time? In any case, it seems that in Canada, the record on Bertha's progress was silent for more than a year, from mid-1913 to early 1915. As it was, the Crawford family in Toronto was caught up with more immediate concerns. On January 29, 1914, in Port Arthur (Thunder Bay), Ontario, Lucia—who was now thirty years old—had married Ernest Pearson, the electrician she had first met fifteen years before. Henceforth, the two sisters' lives would proceed on very different paths.

In the meantime, Bertha was using her exposure during the 1913–1914 opera season in Warsaw to develop useful contacts that had the potential to help her realize a longer singing career in Poland. There is no evidence that Bertha was supported by a professional manager or music agent at this stage, although presumably Zofia provided Bertha with useful advice and informally introduced her to friends and connections in the music business. In any case, the overall trajectory of Bertha's career suggests that she herself was savvy at making—and taking advantage of—the useful connections that came her way. She seems to have been personable as well as professional, as she was repeatedly hired to work by the same people over the years she worked in Poland. She must have built a reputation for being able to deliver consistent performances at a reliable standard, and for being pleasant to work with, or it is unlikely that her career would have lasted as long as it did. The new young director of Polish opera at the Warsaw Great Theatre, Adam Dolzycki (1886–1972), was one acquaintance she made at this time who would serve her well in the future. More connections who continued to be useful to Bertha over the years were the conductor at the Philharmonic, Jozef Oziminski (1877–1945), and the Philharmonic's resident accompanist, the piano professor Dr. Ludwik Urstein (1871–1939), known in Warsaw as the 'king of accompanists.' Bertha met

Oziminski and Urstein during at least three charity concerts in the Warsaw Philharmonic Hall during her first months in Warsaw.

Bertha later told the Canadian newspapers that she hadn't intended to stay in the Russian Empire for long; perhaps she'd initially thought that Zofia's father would recover. In any event, it seems clear that she had expected to return to Italy. However, she met with such encouragement from the Warsaw audiences that she decided to stay longer. She had at least two other engagements in March 1914 in addition to her opera appearances. Perhaps she was also hired for small unadvertised recitals or private concerts later in the year. Her reviews in the Warsaw papers definitely confirm that she was popular with local audiences, but her friendship with Zofia must have also been an important reason why she stayed on in Warsaw. On the one hand, Bertha had no reason to worry about where to live or how to pay the bills if she was staying with Zofia. On the other hand, she may have felt responsible for helping her patron through her grief. After all, Zofia's son John remained far away in Canada. And so, through the spring and early summer of 1914, staying in Warsaw continued to make more sense to Bertha than returning to Italy or Canada.

But whatever Bertha's earlier reasons for staying on in Warsaw, by August 1914, political events overtook her, and she found she couldn't go back the way she had come even if she wanted to. Did Bertha see the First World War coming? How much attention did artists in the opera world pay to such political threats? The war was widely anticipated, and the dangers of increasing militarism across Europe were prominently discussed in the newspapers. However, many predictions underestimated the scale and length of the coming war. There was much talk that, if it were even to start, it would be over by Christmas. As it was, when the war broke out across Europe in August 1914, Bertha found herself behind the Russian front line and cut off from Italy by the belligerent states of Germany and Austro-Hungary. And when Canada joined with Britain, France, and Russia in declaring war on Germany, Bertha found that she had unwittingly taken sides, whether she wanted to or not. Zofia's son John had no hesitation about where he stood. He joined a Canadian regiment in Montréal less than a week after the declaration of war.

The fall of 1914 became a roller coaster ride for the population of Warsaw. Fighting on the Eastern Front began on August 17, 1914, when Russian troops took the offensive and invaded the German province of East Prussia, only a hundred miles north of Warsaw. Within three weeks, the Germans had driven the invaders out of East Prussia and had inflicted a disastrous defeat on the Russian army. By early September, fears of a German attack on Warsaw were real, and concern was rising among the population. Then, in mid-September, the Russians had a major victory south of Warsaw over one of Germany's allies, the Austrians, in Galicia.

Back in Canada, Bertha's family must have been alarmed by the rapidly deteriorating situation in Eastern Europe. The Toronto papers made front-page news out of the oscillating fortunes of the people of Warsaw. The status of Warsaw as a fortress city made it an attractive target for the Germans from the outbreak of the war, and Bertha and Zofia—like everyone else in Warsaw—spent September and October in a continual state of uncertainty. The Russian administration had little confidence that the Polish people would rise to the defence of the empire, and they made poor preparations to prevent the Germans from reaching Warsaw. As Bertha told it in 1921, "We did not know what morning we would waken to find the Germans in possession of the city. Bombs were dropped by German airplanes and the general suspense was terrible."

To reinforce the Austrians, the Germans moved some of their forces south from East Prussia, and from September 28, Bertha would have been hearing increasingly alarming rumours about a German advance on Warsaw. By October 9, the Germans had reached the Vistula River south of Warsaw, and by October 12, they were only twelve miles from the city. The sound of the German guns shook the windows across the city, and the streets were filled with wounded Russian soldiers. As Bertha recalled in 1921, "as the German hordes advanced on Poland, it became dreadful in the capital. Guns, guns all day, and all night bombs dropping in the street. Oh it was terrible." However, on October 17, just when the people of Warsaw were giving up hope, the Germans started to withdraw. By November 1, they were back where they started, almost a hundred miles from the city. But by November 12, the Germans had pressed forward again, advancing fifty miles towards the city of Lodz, south of Warsaw. On December 6, Lodz fell to the Germans.

The leaders of Polish society, including Zofia and her aristocratic class, were now caught in an impossible dilemma. Should they continue to align themselves with the Russians, whom they had always resented as oppressive colonial overlords? Or should they look towards the Germans in the hope that a German imperial government would be more sympathetic to the Polish national cause? Should they abandon their families, friends, and property to evacuate into the relative safety of Russia, or should they stay in Warsaw and take their chances under a German occupation? And could this war perhaps even open a space for the resurrection of an independent Polish state? At this stage, there were all kinds of hopes and fears, and no one could accurately predict the outcome. Many of the Polish artists who were employees of the Russian state, such as Adam Dolzycki, felt they had no choice but to evacuate deep into Russia.

Whether or not Zofia preferred to take her chances under the Germans, she had the added dilemma that she was now responsible for Bertha. And while an occupying German force might be lenient with the local Polish population, the risk was real that they would arrest citizens of enemy states, even Canadian artists. And so, after a few months of dithering, Zofia took Bertha a thousand kilometres northeast of Warsaw, to the safety of Petrograd, in the late fall of 1914. By the time the Germans took Warsaw a year into the war, about 100,000 people had likewise left the city, most of them fleeing to Russia. Joining this refugee trail, Bertha became totally dependent on Zofia—not only for money and career advice, but also for the very safety of her person.

Entr'acte –
A Brush with Fame

February 9, 1915. Backstage in the New Auditorium, People's House, Petrograd,[2] *Russia.* Two stagehands are snickering. They are watching something behind the scenery, out of Bertha's sight. There is scuffling and a yelp. One of the men catches Bertha's eye and grins, but his remark is directed to the tall, imposing man standing on the other side of the stage.

"Feodor Ivanovich, it looks like your dog has a taste for foreign flesh, no?"

A small Boston terrier sprints out from behind the painted flat and runs up to Shalyapin, who absentmindedly bends down to pat the dog's head. A few seconds later, Bertha's two Griffon Belge dogs emerge somewhat sheepishly, a little ruffled and confused. Bertha doesn't understand the stagehand's Russian, but she can catch a ribald undertone in any language. She blushes and fumbles in the deep pocket of her fur coat to find the dogs' leashes. Beside her, Zofia directs a sharp comment in Russian at the men, who erase the smirks from their faces like a pair of reprimanded schoolboys.

---

2   The city of St. Petersburg, Russia, was called Petrograd between 1914 and 1924, and Leningrad from 1924 until 1991, when it reverted to St. Petersburg.

Trying to calm her flustered nerves, Bertha looks across the stage upon which she will make her Russian opera debut tomorrow night in *Rigoletto*. She takes in the sight of the most famous opera star in Russia, the bass Feodor Ivanovich Shalyapin. Dressed in a crisp modern suit and tie, with his short blonde hair carefully combed back, he looks nothing like any of the dramatic historical characters he is renowned for portraying on stage. He leans down from his dominating height towards a man whose head sticks up out of the floor-level prompter's box. Surrounded by attentive members of his cast, Shalyapin dictates instructions about tonight's performance. Although only in his early forties, he is already a singer of huge experience, and he knows exactly how he wants his performances to be staged. A man whose artistic dedication matches his great energy, Shalyapin aims to shape every performance to the highest standard. Bertha is not the only person standing in awe of this man today. She wonders how many years it will take before she can summon up his composure so close to a major performance.

Tonight, Shalyapin will sing in Dargomyzhsky's version of the fairy tale *Rusalka*. Bertha and Zofia will not miss the opportunity to be in the audience for this performance. Shalyapin is renowned for his ability to completely transform himself for each of the parts in his extensive repertoire. Bertha finds it easy to imagine how such a striking and confident man can be convincing as a king or a tsar—or, indeed, as the devil himself. But tonight's incarnation as a humble mad miller is more difficult to envisage, and Bertha anticipates the show with interest.

Bertha is very aware that to debut in the Russian capital as a guest artist on the same stage, in front of the same audiences on alternating nights, as a star of Shalyapin's stature is an unprecedented opportunity for her career. She knows she is lucky to have been offered this chance. She turns as a bureaucrat, wearing the decorated uniform of a Major-General, comes up behind her.

"Shall I introduce you to our great Shalyapin, Bertochka?"

Major-General Cherepanov knows everyone who is anyone in the theatrical world in Petrograd, and he has become a very useful friend. Bertha is charmed that Cherepanov has managed to change her very Canadian name into a Russian diminutive, but she can sense Zofia begin to bristle at her side.

"Of course Miss Crawford and I would appreciate the honour," Zofia says, stepping smoothly between the older man and her young charge. She firmly takes hold of Bertha's arm.

Cherepanov will not be easily deterred by a chaperone's presence. "And then perhaps I can take you to lunch?"

"That would be most kind," replies Zofia for them both, in a tone that somehow suggests just the opposite.

The stagehands smirk again as the steel-haired officer escorts the young singer and her guardian across the stage, the two lapdogs at their heels.

CHAPTER NINE –

A 'Canadian Nightingale' Takes Flight, 1915

Миссъ Берта Кровфордъ.

An increasingly sophisticated Bertha wore the latest fashions and hairstyle for this portrait, which appeared in the program for a recital in Petrograd in early 1915.

*I*t was no coincidence that, of all the Russian cities they might have fled to, Zofia took Bertha to Petrograd. Petrograd was the capital of Russia, and the Tsar and his family lived in the small community of Tsarskoe Selo just outside the city. Fortuitously, Zofia had two cousins who were attached to the Tsar's court. One of them, Nickolai Karlovich Stackelberg (1862–1942), was master of ceremonies at court and probably a handy contact. But perhaps more useful from a musical perspective was his elder brother, Konstantin Karlovich Stackelberg (1848–1925), who was the honorary director of the Tsar's Court Orchestra—and, as such, was in a very good position to introduce Bertha into the musical world of the Russian capital.

Baron Konstantin Stackelberg's father was an Estonian Baron while his mother (Zofia's great-aunt) was a Polish Countess. Baron Stackelberg was born in 1848 near Petrograd, where his wealthy family had estates covering 21,000 acres. Educated in the exclusive Corp of Pages military academy, he was a talented musician who not only played the piano and cello but also composed music. He helped found a society of amateur music lovers, and he played a leadership role in the Evangelical Lutheran Church in Petrograd. However, like his five brothers, he made his career in the military, serving in the Horse Guards, and, by 1907, he had risen to the rank of Lieutenant-General. Along the way, in 1882, he was given responsibility for the Court Choir, which included an ensemble of instrumentalists. Working from this base, he spent twenty-five years building a Court Orchestra, which became the first professional symphony orchestra in Petrograd. Starting with a mandate to perform for the Tsar's court, Stackelberg built the Court Orchestra into a highly respected musical ensemble that regularly gave performances for the public in Petrograd and worked with top Russian and international conductors.

By the time Zofia and Bertha arrived in Petrograd in late 1914, Stackelberg and his wife, Baroness Kaulbars (an intimate friend of the Tsarina), were living in an apartment at 4 Malaya Konyushennaya Street, just a stone's throw across the Griboyedov Canal from the venerable Mikhailovsky Theatre. Living with them were their two daughters, Dagmar and Helena, who were only a few years younger than Bertha. It is not certain that Bertha stayed at this address; however, a few months later, she was photographed exercising her dogs in front of St. Isaac's Cathedral, which is within walking distance from Malaya Konyushennaya—so she definitely became familiar with the Stackelberg's neighbourhood.

Baron Konstantin Stackelberg, Zofia's cousin, was the Director of the Tsar's Court Orchestra and a very useful contact for a Canadian musician newly arrived in Petrograd.

Initially, Bertha must have been impressed—and perhaps even overwhelmed—by the grandeur of central Petrograd. The city, which had more than two million people in 1914, sits astride the broad Neva River, with the city's core divided by many canals. The central thoroughfare, the lengthy Nevsky Prospect, was fronted by expensive stores, elegant hotels, and chic cafes, and the side streets were lined with huge pastel-coloured palaces, multi-storey buildings, and magnificent gilt-domed churches. Of course, Petrograd also had the great Imperial Theatres: the Alexandrinsky, the Mariinsky, and the Mikhailovsky. But there were no small houses and individual shop fronts on the modest scale such as those built by middle-class Canadians back home. Indeed, as Bertha would have quickly seen, Russia had a very different social structure than Canada. Russia was not a country with a large middle class, and the few who had achieved that status rented apartments in large buildings belonging to the rich. There was little space for the middle class or workers to put down a personal footprint in the centre of the city. Central Petrograd was dominated by big households, and a minority of nobles, served by large staffs of servants and retainers far beneath them, held all the wealth and power.

The contrasts of Petrograd society cannot have escaped Bertha. Petrograd, in early 1915, was the capital of a country engaged in a disastrous war. The Russian armies had begun a prolonged retreat across large sectors of the Eastern Front, and the losses were catastrophic. But the city was physically and psychologically a long way away from the fighting. Of course, Bertha could have seen evidence of the war in Petrograd if she looked for it: soldiers recuperating from their wounds in the parks; bulletins detailing the progress of the war hanging at street corners; pictures of the leaders of the Allied States displayed in shop windows; nurses in their white uniforms and veils making their way to one of the many private hospitals in the city; and Cossack soldiers swaggering along the pavements. But in 1915, much of the business of the city went on as usual. The restaurants were packed, the stores were full of goods (at least for those who could pay the rising prices), and the theatres were crowded.

In fact, Bertha would have quickly learned that the biggest theatre crowds in Petrograd gathered not at one of the august Imperial Theatres, but at the modern, municipally owned Emperor Nicholas II People's House. The huge, red brick, glass-domed building had been built in 1900 in Petrograd's Alexandrovsky Park with the support of the Emperor. It contained a theatre, a large dining hall, and an immense, well-lit, and heated opera auditorium that seated 2,800 people. In theory, the prices were set low enough that working people could afford the meals and tickets to the entertainments. However, the building was located far from the working peoples' quarters, and so it was seen by some as a wasted good intention. In practice, the majority of opera patrons at the People's House were better-off people who came to the more expensive weeknight shows to take advantage of lower prices and more accessible tickets than they would find across the Neva River at the exclusive Imperial Mariinsky Theatre. Regardless, from a performer's perspective, the People's House was the second-most prestigious stage (after the Mariinsky) for opera in the capital of Russia, and it was a magnet for all the big opera stars in the country.

Bertha's adventure on the stage of the People's House is probably the best example we have of the value of a chaperone like Zofia at this point in Bertha's career. How Bertha came to meet the bureaucrat in charge of the People's House theatre, Afanasi Vasilevich Cherepanov (1858–1917?), is not known, but perhaps Baron Stackelberg gave her an initial introduction. Cherepanov was born in 1858, the same year as Bertha's father, and, like John Crawford, he was an ambitious man. But in contrast with the dynamic Ontario free market where Crawford prospered, the Russian social ladder that Cherepanov climbed was strictly delimited by government regulation. As a state employee with aspirations, Cherepanov had to rise up through the government service Table of Ranks, where each of the fourteen ranks carried its own clearly defined responsibilities and privileges. Those who worked their way far enough up the ranks might eventually earn a place in the nobility and even hand that status on to their children.

Cherepanov was not born into the nobility like Stackelberg; similar to Bertha, he came from the merchant class. He left his home in the Vologoda province, west of Petrograd, to study at the St. Petersburg Commercial College, but he launched his climb towards nobility by joining the army in 1879 as a twenty-one-year-old ensign in St. Petersburg's Semenovsky Regiment. Nine years later, he married a merchant's daughter, Antonina Kolchina. The match may have begun with love, but as Antonina was the sister-in-law of one of Cherepanov's fellow officers, the marriage was probably also a good career move. No doubt calculating the impression it would make, Cherepanov took care to invite a senior Colonel to be godfather when their first son, Vladimir, was baptised in 1894. But however carefully his married life began, by the time he met Bertha in 1915, Cherepanov had been living apart from his wife for several years.

Cherepanov had worked his way steadily upwards, collecting the ranks and medals that were essential to a rising officer's career. In 1905, he was appointed Vice Chairman of the St. Petersburg Municipal Committee for the Guardianship of Public Sobriety. The Guardianship of Public Sobriety was a uniquely Russian temperance organization: a government organization funded from the proceeds of the state vodka monopoly. The St. Petersburg Municipal Committee was convinced that boredom and illiteracy were behind the problem drinking that was so common among the working classes, so they funded diversions like tea rooms, libraries, mobile kitchens, and clinics and hospitals. However, the vast majority of their investment went into popular theatre designed to distract and entertain the masses, and their flagship theatre was the Emperor Nicholas II People's House.

As Vice Chairman of the committee that owned the Emperor Nicholas II People's House, Cherepanov was in an excellent position to help Bertha. In 1915, his office was located in the same building as the theatre, and he had the position and power to dictate to the Director of the Opera which guest soloists to hire. In January 1915, only two months after arriving in Russia, Bertha contracted for eleven appearances as a guest artist with the People's House Opera Company to play the prima donna role in performances of *Rigoletto, Romeo and Juliette, La Traviata,* and *The Barber of Seville*. She then parlayed this exposure into additional appearances in at least nine charity concerts and recitals alongside the biggest stars of the day in opera, theatre, and ballet. Bertha owed Cherepanov a lot for starting her on an unusually rapid rise to celebrity in Petrograd in the first few months of 1915. But, as Zofia would have been well aware, there were risks associated with Bertha accepting the support of a powerful and unattached older man.

Did Zofia have to enlighten Bertha about the kind of man Cherepanov was when they first met him? By the time she debuted on the stage of the People's House in early February 1915, there were rumours that linked Bertha and Cherepanov circulating among the opera cognoscenti. The night before Bertha appeared in *Romeo and Juliette*, Petrograd opera devotee Olga Michailovna Gardner wrote in her diary that Cherepanov had forced Nikolai Figner (1857–1918), the Director of the Opera Company, to employ Bertha because Cherepanov was in love with her. Did Olga think that Bertha had used her feminine charms rather than her singing voice to get her contract? And what would the audience think if they also suspected the same? Certainly Zofia could not have been pleased, and, as a good chaperone, she probably made sure that Bertha did not get caught alone with this man.

Cherepanov, of course, had little to lose from such rumours. Indeed, he probably considered it a mark of his status to have a beautiful young performer at his disposal. Cherepanov moved in a world where it was common for high-ranking officers and bureaucrats to indulge in liaisons with ballet dancers, actresses, and singers. As the perceptive contemporary travel writer, the Englishman John Foster Fraser, noted at a 1915 Petrograd luncheon he attended, "A well-known general arrives, and with him is a dainty frou-frou'd French actress with a reputation—it is only in Russia that such things are done so openly."

Bertha, on the other hand, did not need any aura of scandal. In fact, she needed to tread very carefully given the lax moral environment of war-time Petrograd, where the rich and privileged were caught up in an epidemic of decadence, gambling, and drug use—and where, as the Russian author Alexei

Tolstoy later described it, "Young girls were ashamed of their innocence and married couples of their fidelity to each other." No doubt Bertha was relieved to have Zofia available to accompany her to rehearsals and performances. But she could not afford to offend Cherepanov, and she may even have felt obligated to accept at least some of his attentions.

Whatever other interests Cherepanov may have had in Bertha, it appears that he recognized early on that she could be a useful asset to him in his long-running feud with the Director of his opera company, Nikolai Figner. When Cherepanov and his management team hired Figner, the famous Russian tenor, four years earlier to direct the opera company at the People's House, it should have been the final triumph for the tenor. Figner had not always been considered a great singer; indeed, during his early studies at the St. Petersburg Conservatory, his teachers had dismissed his vocal talent. But, after studying in Italy, he launched an international singing career at the age of twenty-five and became a star tenor in the 1880s. A handsome man who sported a dark Shakespearian moustache and beard, Figner toured in Italy, Spain, and South America before settling back in Russia. He must have felt some vindication for the misjudgement of his early teachers when he was appointed as the opera director and lead tenor at the People's House in 1910. He was certainly very proud of the position.

From the time Figner had been hired to work with the People's House Opera Company, he and Cherepanov had been at odds. Figner had little respect for bureaucrats who interfered with his artistic work. With all the pride of a successful but ageing stage star, Figner took up the position of the righteous artist, while Cherepanov struggled to assert himself as the ultimate bureaucratic authority. By 1915, Cherepanov seems to have been involved in various intrigues to have Figner replaced in his job. Unfortunately for Bertha, in her second appearance at the People's House, she briefly became a pawn between these two powerful men in their two-way struggle to be the top dog at the People's House.

Figner was advertised to sing in *Romeo and Juliette* opposite Bertha in her second performance at the People's House on February 14, 1915, and it is quite possible that he was under pressure from Cherepanov to appear. Figner was already fifty-eight years old in 1915, and although he still appeared in concerts, he hadn't given an opera performance since 1913. Perhaps Cherepanov hoped the fading talents of the ageing Figner would be shown up if Figner performed opposite Cherepanov's lively and youthful new protégé, Bertha. Cherepanov's exact plan will never be known. However, Figner's wife and her friends feared the worst—that a noisy *claque* of opera patrons was being organized to mock Figner's performance—and the women persuaded him not to appear. Reluctantly, Figner acquiesced. As it turned out, Bertha sang opposite another member of the company, and apparently she sang well. Perhaps she was not even aware of any machinations in the background. Figner continued in his job for a few more months, but, by the middle of July 1915, he was finally forced out of the theatre.

Whether or not she knew about the rumours of scandal, Bertha would not have given up this contract. The prestige of singing with Figner's company cannot be underestimated. Bertha had been vaulted onto the same stage, albeit not on the same nights, as Feodor Ivanovich Shalyapin (1873–1938), the most famous opera singer in Russia and a genuine international star. In her first two weeks under contract with the People's House, she appeared on its stage four times, on alternating nights with Shalyapin. There is no evidence that Bertha actually sang opera opposite the famous Russian bass, but she must have observed his performances on her nights off, and she certainly met him and may even have shared the stage with him at a charity concert. Regardless, in her first weeks performing in Russia, Bertha certainly picked up momentum by surfing in the wake of this Russian juggernaut. For example, *Teatr I Isskustva* (Theatre and the Arts) tacked on very favourable comments about Bertha at the end of their review of Shalyapin's performances, noting that her "general manner of performing is gracious, noble, and proves the presence of good taste and great musicality. She was a great success with the audience."

As Bertha negotiated the complicated backstage politics of the People's House Opera Company, she could have taken inspiration from Shalyapin's well-known life story, which proved that a true star rises above the biggest challenges through a serious commitment to art. Shalyapin came from a much more modest background than Bertha, but by the time they met in 1915, he had risen to be the superstar of the Russian opera stage. Born a peasant in a distant provincial town, he began singing in his local Russian Orthodox church. He caught his passion for the stage from touring theatre and opera troupes that were not so different from the touring performers that Bertha would have seen in rural Ontario. After only one year of formal singing lessons, he signed a contract, at the age of twenty-two, with the Imperial Theatre Directorate as a soloist with St. Petersburg's Mariinsky Opera Company, the most important opera company in the country. Despite the prestige of this position, Shalyapin soon became frustrated with the power that the bureaucrats at the Directorate held over their artists, and he left for the artistic freedom of Sergei Mamontov's Moscow Private Opera. Here he really began the experimental work that would make him famous for the ability to combine his lush bass voice with dramatic makeup, carefully constructed costumes, and realistic acting.

Bertha debuted in Petrograd in 1915 on the same stage, in the same week, and in front of the same audiences as Russia's foremost opera star, Feodor Shalyapin. Here he is in costume as the mad miller in the opera Ruslaka.

Shalyapin created some of the most memorable dramatic characterizations seen on the stage in his time. He was most celebrated for dramatic roles in newer Russian operas, but he sang more than fifty roles during his lifetime, including all of the Italian classics. His first international contract was with La Scala in Milan in 1901, and between his extensive engagements in Russia, he travelled to New York, London, and Paris before the First World War. After the war broke out, he was unable to travel internationally, but he continued to work at a furious pace in both Moscow and Petrograd, singing in opera and concerts, participating in many charity performances, and sponsoring a hospital for wounded soldiers in each city. When Bertha crossed paths with Shalyapin in Petrograd, and later in Moscow, she must have taken note of how hard he worked. Looking at his example, did she ask herself whether the popularized dream of the prima donna—and the apparently effortless life of the established star—underplayed the role of constant effort in creating lasting success?

As it was, Bertha found a different entré to success that was particularly suited to her situation—and one that even a great Russian star like Shalyapin could not compete with. Fortunately for her, there was a strong surge of public gratitude towards the British in the early years of the war. Great crowds had surrounded the British embassy in Petrograd when Britain had come into the war on the side of the Russians the previous August, and this pro-British sentiment seems to have worked in Bertha's favour. Reviewers who saw her in Italian operas forgave her lack of Italian style precisely because she embodied the qualities of a different ally. For instance, her depiction of the broken-hearted Gilda in *Rigoletto* in February 1915 showed an "Anglo-Saxon coldness but the acting experience and somewhat sweet simplicity and naturalness sharply distinguishes her from the Italian Gildas and makes us sympathize with the image created by her." And her characterization of the sharp-witted and flirtatious ingénue, Rosina, in *The Barber of Seville* in March of that same year was "something reminiscent of Dickens' characters: a soft and tender coquettishness is seen through the veil of sweet girlish heartiness and mildness. It is the Rosina of Northern countries..." It sounds like Bertha's Canadian style of charming an audience was as effective in Russia as it had been elsewhere.

In fact, from her first performance in Petrograd, Bertha was noted as much for her nationality as for her singing voice. The reviewer for *Obozrenie Teatrov* (Theatrical Review) thought her debut as an English woman singing in Italian on a Russian stage was highly symbolic of the great alliance that was fighting the war together. When she sang a lullaby in Russian at her next performance, the reviewer was touched, saying "the Russian words being performed by this English-American nightingale sounded like a genuine symbol of our union with the English people." To be sure, the Russian newspapers were rather vague about whether Bertha was English, Canadian, or American, and Bertha herself seems to have adopted a pragmatic approach to her national identity during her time in Petrograd. On posters for her solo concerts, for which she must have had a say in the wording, she is advertised as "an American from

Canada," presumably to accommodate her Russian audience's more generic understanding of transatlantic geography.

However, some reviewers understood quite well where Bertha came from, as it was during this period that the sobriquet 'Canadian Nightingale' was first attached to her. With this nickname, which she kept for the rest of her career, the Russian press promoted Bertha to the class of such storied sopranos of the previous century as Jenny Lind (1820–1887), who is still remembered as 'the Swedish Nightingale.' Of course, Bertha was not the only Canadian making a name for herself in Russia. Mary Pickford's movies had begun to be screened across Russia several years before Bertha arrived, although publicity materials made no mention of Mary's Canadian roots, and she was commonly referred to as 'America's Sweetheart.'

By the middle of March 1915, twenty-eight-year-old Bertha had achieved remarkable success on Petrograd stages and was receiving the kind of recognition reserved for a true prima donna. When she sang opposite the ageing but still famous baritone Oscar Isaevich Kamionskiy (1869–1917) in *La Traviata* in March, flowers—which were under moral prohibition due to the war—rained down from cheering students in the top balcony. And then, in the final death scene, the enthusiastic students came down to stand in front of the orchestra to "be flamingly furious in honour of the dying and again resurrected Traviata." Of course, one might ask how much of this excessive adoration was really spontaneous. Was it orchestrated by some powerful influence in the background? Could Cherepanov have been showing his appreciation for Bertha in more subtle ways—ways that even a careful chaperone like Zofia could not object to?

In any case, Bertha had earned the approval with her "voice, amazing in its clearness and ripeness with again, rare trillos and fiorituras and sustained breath." The reviewer from *Obozrenie Teatrov* (Theatrical Review) reported that "the audience was totally unanimous in their delightful appreciation of the new opera star which sparkled so unexpectedly in the Petrograd sky." Bertha must have wondered if reviews like this meant she had permanently captured the kind of stardom that she had dreamed of back in Toronto. Could she hold on to dreamlike nights like this?

As it was, she was riding on a wave of popularity that left her generous with her time and reputation. As an artist representing a major ally, Bertha seems to have been particularly sought after to sing in charity concerts, and she accepted this additional exposure a number of times. From the outbreak of the conflict, the Russian people had enthusiastically taken on fundraising to support the war effort, filling vital gaps where the government had made few official provisions. These efforts were made all the more necessary by the prohibition on alcohol sales, which the Tsar had instigated during the initial mobilization of the army and then made permanent. Prohibition was a noble move that certainly led to a more sober and efficient army, but the lack of state liquor sales reduced the government's revenues by more than a quarter, and at a time when the costs of running the war were huge. What is more, several million Poles and Belorussians had been displaced by the fighting on the Eastern Front; many lost everything as a direct result of the scorched-earth policy of the retreating Russian army, which wanted to leave nothing of value for the advancing Germans. Farms and crops were burned, and the peasant population was forcibly evacuated deep into Russia, where those who survived arrived to a very uncertain reception. Charities stepped in to take primary responsibility for what meagre support was available for these refugees, and charitable organizations set up the majority of hospital facilities for the wounded soldiers.

The music and theatre community that Bertha joined took their responsibility to do their patriotic part for this war effort seriously, and the scale of their charitable activity during the war was unprecedented. The programs for these patriotic fundraising concerts seem to have been a kind of spontaneous variety show, depending on who amongst the long list of advertised talent actually showed up. One theme that seems to have been common was a desire to celebrate Russia's place in the alliance, so it was useful when the music and the performers could personify particular Allies. Bertha regularly represented the English, while one or more actors from the Mikhailovsky Theatre's French Drama Troupe would be there to represent the French. It is no stretch to imagine that Bertha's sympathy for the plight of the refugees—natural in someone who was a refugee herself and who might even have been destitute without Zofia's protection—was in large part at the heart of her participation in these performances.

But while Bertha was no doubt sincere in her desire to help the victims of the war, she can hardly have been unaware of the opportunities that these charity events presented, not only in terms of making contacts that would be useful for her future career, but also in regards to displaying her talents in front of leading members of the theatre world and the press. Many charity concerts were arranged by the top artists of the Imperial Theatres, and several of the concerts in which Bertha sang included large star-studded casts. Through participating in these concerts, Bertha met some of the top opera singers, ballet dancers, and actors from the Imperial Theatres, and even famous painters and diplomats. She shared the stage at charity concerts with singers from the Mariinsky Opera Company, including the bass P.Z. Andreev, the baritone I.V. Tartakov, and—ironically—Nikolai Figner and his wife, Rene. She met dainty ballerinas from the Mariinsky troupe, such as E.V. Lopukhova, E.M. Lukom, and L.N. Egorova, as well as the dynamic choreographer Mikhail Fokine and his wife, the dancer Vera Fokina. She trod the boards alongside the ageing (but still beloved) Russian actress, M.G. Savina, and members of the French Drama Troupe from the Mikhailovsky Theatre, including Paul Robert and Henrietta Roger. And, after the show was over, quite likely she was introduced to guests such as the British Ambassador Sir George Buchanan and the French Ambassador Maurice Paleologue. When she and Zofia returned to their lodgings in the early morning hours after another dazzling gala evening among her fellow stars, did Bertha sit back and contemplate how far she had come from the world of her childhood in Elmvale? Did she feel like she had finally achieved the status of a top prima donna?

In the spring of 1915, Bertha was featured in Petrograd charity concerts alongside top Russian opera stars, such as I.V. Tartakov, here dressed as Figaro for The Barber of Seville.

Eventually, it was one of these charity appearances that brought her to that pinnacle of the prima donna's career: the meeting with royalty. On March 29, 1915, Bertha sang at a charity event in the Mariinsky Palace for the Committee for Providing Relief to Victims of the War Emergency—a committee officially sponsored by the Tsar's second daughter, the seventeen-year-old Grand Duchess Tatiana Nikolaevna, to help address the mounting refugee crisis. A week later, Bertha was called to the great Winter Palace, along with other artists who had assisted the charity, for the presentation of awards by the Grand Duchess herself. It was a simple ceremony, and Bertha was one of more than a dozen artists present as she took her place amid a group of prominent Russian musicians, painters, ballerinas, and actors. They were presented with new decorations created for the committee. Each woman received a small enamelled silver brooch in the shape of a crest with a blue 'T' for Tatiana imposed over an 'N' for her father, the Tsar Nicholas. On the back of Bertha's her name and the date were engraved.

In principle, Bertha must have been excited to have achieved the ultimate marker of prima donna success—the encounter with royalty. But did the actual event live up to her expectations? Of course, it cannot have been as impressive as Emma Albani's backstage introduction to Tatiana's grandfather, when, as Albani highlighted in her biography, Tsar Alexander II "kindly complimented" her voice and singing and later sent "a very valuable diamond ornament." Bertha's presentation was probably very brief, and, at a formal event like this, it is unlikely that the artists would have had any conversation with the Grand Duchess herself. Tatiana was, by most accounts, a reserved and retiring young woman who carried out her duties with dignity, and it is very unlikely that she lingered to mingle. Most probably she returned directly to the palace at Tsarskoe Selo, where her family lived in seclusion from Petrograd society. Still, Bertha recognized the publicity value of this encounter, and she wrote home describing the event and her award in detail. She also seems to have kept the decoration into the 1920s.

Bertha had little time to sit back and savour the excitement of her invitation to the Winter Palace, however. That same week, she was on stage at the Mikhailovsky Theatre for another concert in support of Polish refugees. In parallel, she was also helping with fundraising for a few of the thousands of private hospitals that were vital in providing treatment for the huge numbers of wounded soldiers. Her performance was lauded as the highlight of the evening at an April 11 concert at the Vladimir Palace to raise funds for the Grand Duchess Maria Pavlovna's hospital charity. Then there were three more opera dates at the People's House in mid-April. On top of that, on April 28, she was at the Petrograd Conservatory as the lead singer for a ballet evening that raised money for the hospital that the Conservatory sponsored.

While Stackelberg and Cherepanov certainly would have helped to open these doors for Bertha with their musical connections, she would not have been recognized as a star in these opera and charity concerts if she had not been coached to the highest standard in a broadened repertoire. As it was, in 1915 and 1916, she got that coaching from another Russian, Alexei Vladimirovich Taskin (1871–1942). A sensitive and sympathetic musician, Taskin was a slight man in his forties, who wore a small moustache above his full lips and swept his short hair back from a high forehead. Born in a small town deep in Siberia, he was enrolled at the Mining Institute in St. Petersburg when he met Nikolai Figner, who persuaded Taskin to follow his true passion and study music. Taskin went on to write more than 400 songs during his life, but his bread and butter was earned as a vocal coach, preparing singers for new roles and playing their piano accompaniments during concerts and recitals. He also played the role of concert manager from time to time. He worked with some of the greatest artists of the era, including Shalyapin and Sobinov, but from 1902 through 1913, he had mainly worked with a mezzo-soprano operetta star, Anastasia Vyaltseva. After Vyaltseva died in 1913, he began looking for another artist whom he could coach and manage. In 1915, he found that artist in Bertha, with whom he worked for at least eighteen months.

A vocal coach like Taskin plays a different role from a singing teacher. Where the singing teacher focuses on voice production, the vocal coach helps the artist to interpret and shade the musical phrases in a song. Furthermore, Taskin had a reputation as an excellent teacher of diction and pronunciation—essential skills if Bertha were to sing credibly in Russian. In fact, Taskin was probably the coach who helped Bertha to prepare the Russian lullaby by Lermontov that she sang during her Petrograd debut of *The Barber of Seville*. It was only her second performance in Petrograd, but the reviews said "Miss Crawford sings in Russian amazingly, almost without an accent." Bertha had worked with many accompanists in the past, but it is unlikely that she had worked with someone of Taskin's calibre before. He was noted for his ability to bring out the genuine intentions, desires, and emotions of the vocalist with his subtle playing. "The softer the accompanist strikes [the keys]," he explained to an interviewer, "the less he drowns out the voice of the singer, and the better the production of the intended vocal effect."

Bertha first performed in public with Taskin at the March 29 charity concert; later that spring, she appeared with him again in three rather more intimate recitals. Working with Taskin in the spring of 1915, Bertha debuted a number of songs, including arias from French operas like *Dinorah* and *Mignon*, as well as showpieces like "The Nightingale" by Alyabyev. This Russian song was a popular choice for the singing lesson scene in *The Barber of Seville*, and the Italian soprano Adelina Patti had famously added her own cadenza to ornament the simple melody. Taskin worked with Bertha to master Patti's showy coloratura part, and they advertised it as a highlight at two of the recitals that Bertha put on with the help of Taskin in April and May.

The program for the May 8 recital emphasized Bertha's credentials as a singer of Italian and French opera, and it let her sing arias from operas that were not being given as full performances at the time. But she also showed that she had broadened her repertoire to include Russian favourites. The program began with a violin piece by V.A. Zavetnovski, a soloist from Stackelberg's Court Orchestra. Bertha came on second, singing an Italian aria from Meyerbeyer's opera *Dinorah*. She was followed by a tenor from the Theatre of Music and Drama, P.S. Raichev, singing an Italian aria from Donizetti's opera *L'Elisir d'Amore*. Bertha returned to sing the aria "Polonaise" in French from Thomas's opera *Mignon*, and then joined in a trio version of Gounod's "Ave Maria" with Taskin and Zavitnovski. After an intermission, Bertha returned to sing a French duet with Raichev from Gounod's version of the opera *Faust*. Zavetnovski played Henri Wieniawski's "Romance in D Minor" for violin and piano, and Raichev followed with two lyrical Russian songs: Tchaikovsky's "Again, As Before, Alone" and Rachmaninov's "Do Not Sing, My Beauty." Bertha took the final set of the evening, opening with an Italian aria from Bellini's *La Sonnambula* and then finishing with Alyabyev's "The Nightingale," including Patti's cadenza, accompanied by Taskin and a flautist, A.I. Semenov, who was also a soloist with Stackelberg's Court Orchestra. The whole program ran about three and a half hours and finished at midnight. Taskin must have been pleased with his new protégé, for he saved the concert program, which featured a portrait of Bertha, for the rest of his life.

Swept up as Bertha was with all the attention she was getting from Petrograd audiences, it was clear that Bertha and Zofia had already planned to leave Petrograd, as her May 8 recital was billed as a 'farewell concert.' But in contrast to the previous year, when news of her Warsaw debut was absent from the Toronto newspapers, Bertha definitely wanted to make the most out of her 1915 Petrograd experience by sharing with the Canadian public that she was now an internationally recognized prima donna. She sent home several reports, enclosing clippings from Russian newspapers (with translations that Zofia likely helped her with). Once again, her family took the news of Bertha's success to the leading Toronto music critics. In May 1915, Bertha's old supporter Parkhurst passed on to readers of *The Globe* that Bertha was "winning honours in Petrograd" and included flattering quotes from *Novoye Vremya* (New Age) and *Petrogradskii kurer* (Petrograd Courier) that put Bertha in "the first class of world-renowned singers." In this way, Bertha was portrayed as a rising star in one of the world's great imperial capitals.

The family also took Bertha's letters to *Saturday Night*, where another important Toronto music critic, Hector Charlesworth (1872–1945), was an editor. Charlesworth was a self-educated liberal cosmopolitan who felt he had a mission to counter parochialism and help Canadians be less provincial by educating them on the efforts of Canadian artists. He was an early supporter of cultural nationalism, and he took pride in the success of Canadians overseas. In June 1915, *Saturday Night* featured Bertha in a special section of its "Music and Drama" column, describing the "great success in opera of a young Canadian soprano" who had "more engagements than she can accept," for "naturally, Miss Crawford, being a Canadian, is much sought after in Petrograd." As proof of her prima donna status, Charlesworth gave all the particulars of Bertha's meeting with the royal Grand Duchess and the presentation at the Winter Palace—details that had been taken from Bertha's letters home to her family about the event. Charlesworth then closed with quotations from a *Novoye Vremya* (New Age) review of one of Bertha's charity concerts, which claimed "At the present time, it is possible fully to compare her only with one, viz. [Adelina] Patti," and "We anticipate for her the career of a star of the first magnitude." In July, E.R. Parkhurst highlighted "Bertha Crawford's Success" in his journal, *Musical Canada*, quoting the same text—only this time translated into French, as if to emphasize the international provenance of the praise. Indeed, anyone who followed music in Toronto would have become aware that Bertha had had a major success in Petrograd that spring.

But while Bertha was enjoying her taste of life as a prima donna in Petrograd, Zofia must have been closely following the news of the changing situation in her home city of Warsaw. A seven-day campaign in January, during which the Germans attacked north of Warsaw, had achieved little, and by April it was clear that the Germans had failed again. By May, the war on the Polish front had stuttered to a temporary stalemate. Despite the fighting and the heavy military rail traffic, some passenger trains continued to run between Petrograd and Warsaw, and some people thought that the front lines had stabilized and that the risk to Warsaw had receded. In fact, the Russian press was under pressure to put the best light on the war effort. In his May column, the Warsaw correspondent for *Russkaya Muzykal'naya Gazeta* (Russian Musical Gazette) took pains to stress how normal the musical season was in Warsaw and how the recent "extraordinary events of war" were no longer considered interesting. Moreover, he reported that the new director of the Warsaw Opera, Aleksander Rajchman, was welcoming excellent guest singers from outside the city.

And so, during the lull in the fighting, Zofia and Bertha packed their trunks and, not forgetting Bertha's two dogs, made the return journey to Warsaw. No doubt Zofia's priority would have been family obligations, and it may have been at this time that she commissioned the striking bronze cross that continues to mark her father's grave. For her part, Bertha probably hoped she could leverage her Petrograd stage success into some return appearances before the Polish audiences that had received her so warmly the previous year. In any case, Bertha had little option but to follow Zofia, as she was dependent upon her patron's support, both moral and financial. Moreover, if Bertha separated from Zofia at this point, even temporarily, there was a high risk that they would be unable to reconnect in the unsettled conditions of the war.

By the time Bertha and Zofia arrived together in Warsaw, the opera season was drawing to a close, and there is no record that Bertha found any paid work. But on June 20, 1915, she did appear with the Warsaw Opera Company in a benefit concert opposite Nino de Perya in the Summer Theatre in the

Saski Gardens in Warsaw. The 1,000-seat wooden Summer Theatre was built in 1870 in the middle of the oldest public park in Warsaw, and it hosted an annual series of summer performances until 1939. Nino de Perya, an Italian tenor born in Palermo, had made his debut in *La Traviata* and sang mostly in Italy. However, nearly ten years earlier, he had toured the U.S. and Canada with a small opera company put together by the composer and impresario, Ruggero Leoncavallo. It is quite possible that Bertha first heard Perya sing when his company performed in Massey Hall in October 1906.

At this 1915 appearance, Bertha sang the part of Violetta in *La Traviata*, with de Perya appearing as Alfredo. *La Traviata* is a Verdi opera about a doomed love affair between Violetta, a Parisian courtesan, and Alfredo, the son of a respectable family. Under pressure from Alfredo's father, Violetta does the honourable thing and leaves Alfredo. Ultimately, they have a passionate reunion, but only at the end of her life as she is dying of tuberculosis. The role of Violetta calls for a flexible coloratura voice and is a more intense role than Gilda in *Rigoletto*, giving the singer more time on stage and requiring the portrayal of a wider range of emotions. It is a more demanding role to sing, but many sopranos have found Violetta a more rounded and satisfying character to play. Bertha's performance was well received in Warsaw, and the *Kurjer Warszawski* (Warsaw Courier) called her portrayal of Violetta "exquisite" and said she had "a voice of crystal purity, like a diamond flashing fires and colours."

But while Bertha's sparkling tones were bringing down the curtain in the Summer Theatre, the German army was about to raise the curtain on a new production in the theatre of war. On July 13, the Germans launched another major attack towards Warsaw. Within a few days, the Russian army was falling back towards the city, and the population of Warsaw was in despair. The Germans began dropping bombs on the city from the air, bringing the war close to the civilians who had thought they were a safe distance from the fighting lines. Moreover, rumours were spreading in the streets that the Germans would soon cut the railroad to Petrograd.

Bertha and Zofia must have felt an awful sense of déjà vu—although this time their situation was much worse, as it soon became clear that the Russians really were going to give up the city. The Russian army began evacuating Polish peasants from the land west of Warsaw, driving them back from the front, and long columns of desperate families filed through the city, dragging what possessions and livestock they could with them. Behind them, the Russian army made sure they left nothing but smouldering timbers and charred stubble to greet the Germans. On the evening of July 17, 1915, the Russians announced they would be evacuating the civil administration from Warsaw. Henceforth, the city would be no place for citizens of the Allied countries, signalling an abrupt end to Bertha and Zofia's brief summer sojourn in Warsaw.

Entr'acte –
A Narrow Escape

9:00 am, mid-July, 1915. Stare Powązki Cemetery, Warsaw. Bertha lifts the black umbrella over Zofia's head as the older woman reaches up to hang a wreath on her father's memorial. The stylized three-metre bronze crucifix is fashioned to look like a living tree growing out of its plain stone base, and it has a short stump of a bronze branch midway up the trunk for mourners to hang their garlands of greenery or flowers. Of course, secured around the branch-like bar of the cross, there is also a bronze wreath, designed to remain as a permanent testament to the life of Dr. Kosinski well into the future centuries.

Bertha had been fascinated by the discussion between Zofia and the artist about how to create a monument that combined her father's simple character, his deep faith, and his love of nature. The result, installed just a few weeks ago, is nothing like the other slabs of stone and the carved angels and Madonnas that are so closely packed in their thousands over the many acres of this huge city cemetery. Bertha supposes that, in the end, this poignant memorial says as much about Zofia's determination to leave her personal stamp on this grave as it does about her father's character.

The two women stand for a moment of silence. It may be summer, but Bertha is shivering. It is raining, but the rumbling that intrudes from the distance is not thunder—it is the sound of artillery. The German army is only seventeen miles from Warsaw now, forcing the Russian army steadily back towards the city. And the Germans will get here this time, Bertha is sure.

It feels much different now than it did the first time, when the Germans had come so close to Warsaw in October of the previous year. True, Bertha had been unsettled then, too. But there had been a relative sense of adventure in hopping on the train to Petrograd. She doesn't feel any sense of adventure now, just a nervous knot in the pit of her stomach and a strong desire to be gone.

It had seemed like a fine idea to accompany Zofia back to Warsaw two months ago. Similarly, performing in the Summer Theatre in the Saski Gardens had been a lovely opportunity. But how quickly things have changed! Within days, the Russians will most likely give up the city, and after that, it will no longer be a place where an Allied citizen can feel safe.

Bertha takes Zofia's arm as the two women turn to find their way back to the cemetery gates. Zofia's normally stern visage looks particularly piqued today, her long narrow nose pink in the cold and her straight lips pressed firmly together. Bertha knows that this decision to leave Warsaw again has been fraught for her patron.

Bertha took no part in the family debates of the past week, not understanding the Polish anyway. But she is aware that Zofia's aunts and uncles have all been hotly debating whether it would be better to stay in a German-occupied Warsaw and protect their property, or to seek peace deeper in Russia. But Zofia has been adamant that she has no choice—she will take Bertha back to the safety of Petrograd. And for that, Bertha can only be grateful, although she has no idea how she will recompense her patron for everything she has already done, let alone what she is about to do.

As the two women walk back to Zofia's apartment, they filter through dense crowds. Warsaw's streets are congested with a massive stream of peasant carts heading across the city towards the east, their rough wooden wheels creaking and groaning. Pathetic piles of household goods are stacked high, and stony-faced grandmothers and frightened children precariously perch on top while the adults trudge alongside in resignation. Frightened farm animals scramble between the wheels. They have left behind nothing but smoking fields and ashes for the Germans.

Bertha's mind is blank when she imagines where these peasants will go. She is certain she won't find them in the first-class train compartment that Zofia has managed to reserve for tonight. However serious this turn of events, Bertha can't envisage it upsetting the deeply entrenched Russian hierarchy. But her experience of the world doesn't extend to accommodate the reality that these peasant refugees will be packed into boxcars like livestock, then shipped, dead or alive, thousands of miles into the depths of the Russian steppes. Nonetheless, she can see now what a tiny impact the charity concerts that she had been so proud of will have in helping more than a million refugees.

When they reach the apartment, the two women go straight to their rooms to finish packing their trunks. This is not the time for pondering problems far beyond their control. When they are safely on the train, there will be plenty of time for Bertha to think about how she can repay Zofia for the sacrifice she is making—leaving her family and property with no idea of when or how she can return, all to ensure Bertha's safety.

CHAPTER TEN –
Adrift in a Storm of Change,
1915–1918

Bertha returned to Russia in the summer of 1915 hoping to capitalize on her success earlier in the year and earn a living.

When Bertha and Zofia boarded the train from Warsaw to Petrograd in July 1915, they both officially became refugees. On August 5, the Germans took control of Warsaw, preventing any possibility of Bertha and Zofia returning to Western Europe for the next three years. With Zofia now officially cut off from her home, and quite possibly her income as well, there was new pressure on Bertha to try to parlay her few months of success in the spring into a more substantial career in wartime Russia. To be sure, Zofia's finances were probably constrained now that all Warsaw property and banks were in German hands, and Bertha could hardly start asking her father for money, especially after boasting about her spring success. At the same time, in the back of Bertha's mind must have lurked the threat that, if she did not secure more substantial appearances in the coming opera season, she risked becoming another one of those operatic shooting stars who had one brilliant season and then disappeared from the scene.

Enterprising entrepreneurs produced postcards of the Russian Army's July 1915 retreat from Warsaw, to sell to Poles and Germans. By then Bertha was already safely back in Petrograd.

Did Bertha consider parting ways with Zofia at this point and going back to Canada? She must have thought about it. There was a circuitous but well-travelled northern route out of embattled Eastern Europe—one that took people across Finland and through Sweden to England and beyond. But with the sinking of the British passenger ship RMS Lusitania in May 1915, travelling by ship in the waters surrounding the British Isles looked more and more dangerous. Furthermore, Bertha must have felt some sense of commitment to Zofia, who had taken good care of her for more than three years and who had invested her time and money in building Bertha's career. Lastly, and perhaps most importantly, Bertha may have already heard from her family that the war was making it increasingly difficult for musicians to make a living in Toronto, as more and more Canadian entertainment took the form of unpaid charity concerts like the ones Bertha was already doing in Russia. In contrast, in 1915, Russia still offered a huge market for classically trained musicians like Bertha. And Bertha now had a number of musical friends in Petrograd, including Taskin, with whom she could continue to work in order to expand her repertoire of songs in Russian as well as in other languages. So Bertha must have hoped that, if she stayed on in Russia with Zofia as her chaperone and sometime patron, she might capitalize on the momentum of her successful appearances in the spring. With the right engagements in the fall, she might solidify her tentative position as a prima donna in Russia—and contribute to paying both of their bills at the same time.

Almost immediately, Bertha went back to work with Taskin to expand her concert repertoire. In September 1915, she aired her improving skills in Russian at the final concert of the summer series put on by the orchestra at the Pavlovski Vauxhall. The Pavlovski Vauxhall was a similar venue to the Saski Gardens in Warsaw—that is, there was a summer theatre in a park with a pavilion that was made of wood and lacked insulation or heat—which hosted concerts from May to September, when the big city theatres were closed for the season. The Vauxhall Pavilion was located at a railway station terminus on the edge of a great 500-hectare royal park south of the city. The auditorium had originally been built by the railway owners to draw summer traffic to their railway line. A hotel complex with restaurants and park pavilions offered a refreshing retreat during the hot summer months; here, the city's better off could escape the heat with dining, billiards, music, and dancing. By 1915, the season of summer concerts at the Vauxhall Pavilion had been running for about seventy-five years and attracted the top musical talent in the city.

Petrograd's *Novoye Vremya* (New Age) was enthusiastic about Bertha's performance of opera arias and lyrical songs there, noting in particular how she sang a Gretchaninov lullaby in Russian: "Miss Crawford speaks Russian much better than half a year ago. Her speech is almost without reproach, only she is a little tense, not yet completely free to articulate naturally." Bertha's work with Taskin was paying off.

Bertha's productive relationship with the Russian vocal coach and accompanist A.V. Taskin continued through 1915 and 1916.

However, when the Petrograd People's House opened its new opera season in the fall of 1915, Bertha was not one of the guest artists, which suggests that Cherepanov had lost whatever interest he'd had in her in the spring. So, in mid-October, with no immediate opera work in the offing for Bertha, Taskin organized a charity recital for his protégé so she could debut more of the new Russian material she had been studying with him. Like their concerts together in the spring, they used the Small Hall at the Petrograd Conservatory, a popular smaller venue for serious musical performances. The room, with its ornate moulded plaster work, gilded trim, and painted ceiling, provided an elegant but intimate concert experience and was acoustically ideal for performances by soloists and small ensembles. Bertha sang arias from Rimsky-Korsakov's opera, "The Snow Maiden," and two lyrical songs by Sergei Rachmaninov, "How Fair Is This Spot" and "I Fell in Love, to My Sorrow." Rimsky-Korsakov had only died in 1908, and Rachmaninov was still very much alive, so, with Taskin's help, Bertha was venturing into contemporary Russian music to complement her more traditional Italian opera repertoire. No doubt Bertha would have appreciated some money from such an appearance, but the proceeds of this concert were dedicated to the Committee of the Marble Palace, another of the many charities run by a member of the Tsar's extended family—this one in support of a hospital and convalescent home for wounded soldiers. Now, a year into the war, it was becoming increasingly difficult to stage a concert purely for the benefit of the artists.

Bertha earned little or nothing from this recital, but around the end of October, she got a lucky break that had the potential to lead to a prestigious and profitable engagement. The owner of the largest private opera in the country, Sergei Ivanovich Zimin, arrived in Petrograd in search of talent to enliven the opera season at his theatre in Moscow, almost 700 kilometres to the southeast. The son of a rich merchant, Zimin was a theatre enthusiast who had spent much of the previous fifteen years following in the footsteps of Savva Mamontov and building a pioneering private opera company outside the confines of the State Theatre Directorate. Committed to putting on innovative productions that kept up with the latest international trends, Zimin was always looking for interesting guest artists, and someone must have recommended Bertha for an audition. At the end of the month, *Obozrenie Teatrov* (Theatrical Review) reported that Bertha had secured a three-night test run with Zimin to sing in performances of *Rigoletto*, *The Barber of Seville*, and *La Traviata*, with a decision about further work with his opera company to be made after these performances.

Bertha must have had a lot of hope riding on this opportunity with Zimin. If she could secure a longer contract with Zimin's Moscow Opera, then her reputation as a prima donna would be cemented. During the 1915–1916 opera season, Zimin's company had thirty-two operas in its repertoire and was planning to put on 255 shows—considerably more than the 175 opera performances that the famous state-supported Imperial Bolshoi Theatre would stage in Moscow that year. About half of the composers represented that season on Zimin's stage were Russian, but the Italian operas that Bertha knew well were also very popular. *La Traviata* was scheduled to be staged sixteen times over the winter, while *The Barber of Seville* and *Rigoletto* were included seven and three times, respectively. If she was good enough, there would be plenty of opportunities to sing—and to earn money to support herself (and possibly Zofia) while doing so.

Bertha's three guest appearances in Moscow occurred at the height of the new opera season, and, coincidentally, her performances at Zimin's Moscow theatre were again bracketed by guest appearances by Shalyapin. But unlike in the spring, when Bertha had seemed to benefit from performing at the

People's House in the same week as Shalyapin, the contrast between her performances and those of the famous bass did not serve her well in her fall appearances with Zimin's company. Indeed, the most popular visiting guest singers at Zimin's theatre that year were the duelling stars of the Russian opera stage: the bass Shalyapin, who sang twenty-six times, while the equally popular tenor Leonid Sobinov (1872–1934) sang fifteen times (although, of course, never in the same performance). Both were indefatigable performers who appeared many times in both Moscow and Petrograd during the season. In comparison, Bertha's three guest appearances at best would have made a very minor impression on the Moscow audiences.

Still, Bertha's hopes would have been high that she would again be regarded as the prima donna of the day, as her photo was carried on the covers of both of Moscow's daily theatre magazines on the morning of her Moscow debut. But what a letdown when she understood that the reviewers who followed opera in Moscow showed none of the enthusiasm she had received in Petrograd. The following day, damning with faint praise, *Novesti Sesona* (News of the Season) found Bertha's voice on her debut night neither powerful nor especially beautiful, but "well trained." It was not a virtuoso performance, but it was "correct" and "satisfying." The reviewer from *Teatr* (Theatre) also said that she was not a virtuoso and had a "miniature voice" that well matched her "miniature appearance;" she met the requirements, yes, but in comparison with the brilliance of the Italian singers, he found her reserved and cold. Perhaps part of the problem was that she sang in Italian, while the Russian cast probably sang in Russian.

In any case, she did not get further work with Zimin's company. Bertha must have been very disappointed that she was not able to make more of this opportunity. While she was always proud to talk about her time at the People's House in Petrograd, she never mentioned her performances with Moscow's Zimin Opera to the newspapers when she came back to Canada. Hiccups on the road to success had no place in the steady upward trajectory that a true prima donna was supposed to follow. Still, even when she was facing such a disappointing setback in her career, she does not appear to have considered cutting ties with Zofia and returning to Canada.

Instead, with opera contracts in Petrograd and Moscow apparently out of reach for the moment, Bertha looked farther afield to find more welcoming audiences in the vast provinces of Russia. Did she think that the audiences in the smaller towns of the Russian Empire might have some commonalities with the people in small-town Canada? Perhaps she thought those audiences would be more easily impressed by her having had engagements in major cities like Warsaw, Petrograd, and Moscow, regardless of how many—or how few—nights they lasted. As she would undoubtedly be the only Canadian working these circuits in the middle of the war, perhaps she estimated that her novelty value would be high. Or did she just have itchy feet? As it was, she must have found a manager or agent who thought she would be able to sell tickets in the provinces, for soon she was on the road again.

In the early months of 1916, Bertha and Zofia embarked on a short tour to meet new audiences in Finland. This northern province of the Russian Empire was just a few hours' train ride west of Petrograd. It may be that Zofia had relatives in Finland—or, more likely, that her relatives from Petrograd had a property in Finland, perhaps a country house or *dacha*. The Finnish rural landscape, particularly the 'cottage country' nearest to Petrograd, was much like Ontario's Muskokas region, and it probably felt more like Canada to Bertha than any of the many other parts of Russia she visited. In the winter, the dense pine forests and small lakes were blanketed under a clean, peaceful layer of snow, and the skiing and sleigh rides would have brought Bertha back to memories of her childhood in Elmvale. The Finns were predominantly Lutheran, a Protestant sect much closer to Bertha's roots as a Presbyterian than the official Eastern Orthodox Church of Russia. Just as significant, in the cities of Finland in particular, there was a keen interest in modern music and an appreciation for high-quality singing. In March 1916, Bertha and Zofia reached the Finnish industrial city of Tampere, where Bertha was scheduled for a solo recital—probably one of several engagements she had in the country. Tampere, the second largest city in Finland, was the farthest north that Bertha had ever been. Sitting at nearly the same latitude as the Yukon goldfields, Tampere is located between two large lakes, and, in 1916, it was already a busy industrial city, with many factories taking advantage of the locally generated hydroelectricity. It was a modern city that was embracing change—something that almost defined Bertha's life at this point.

Perhaps the lukewarm reviews Bertha received in Moscow persuaded her to re-evaluate her narrow career focus on Italian opera, at least temporarily.

Or perhaps it was the Finnish audience's enthusiasm for their most famous composer, Sibelius, and his ability to evoke his passion for the Finnish natural landscape through his music that encouraged Bertha to try something new. Certainly, the smaller cities of Finland would have offered a safe place to experiment with a new repertoire in front of audiences who might be more open minded and forgiving than those in the Russian capital cities. As it was, Bertha used her provincial engagements in places like Tampere to test out new songs that were to become a major part of her repertoire—songs that would help reinforce her identity as a North American singer before European audiences.

From early 1916, around the time of her Tampere appearance, Bertha began performing modern 'art songs' by an American, Charles Wakefield Cadman. Cadman was one of a group of American songwriters who looked to Indigenous sources to inspire an authentic North American musical style. Following anthropological fieldwork among some American Indians, he borrowed Native American melodies and themes and incorporated them into a collection of art songs. Cadman's set of four "Indian Songs" were published in 1909 and had been popularized by one of America's most famous prima donnas, Lillian Nordica, who recorded them for Columbia Phonograph Co. in 1910. So it is possible that Bertha first heard the songs on the gramophone, although she could just as well have heard Nordica sing them in person in London in 1912. Taking a page out of Nordica's song book, Bertha used Cadman's "Indian Songs" to assert her North American roots while demonstrating a more sensitive artistic singing style that contrasted well with the showy coloratura work of the Italian opera arias.

Bertha's Tampere concert featured a mixture of classic Italian arias and Cadman's "Indian Songs." Her accompanist for the Tampere concert was the Finnish musician and composer, Kosti Vehanen (1887–1957), who had a reputation as a sensitive and skillful pianist and who put Bertha's singing in a most complementary light. Following the Tampere recital, a reviewer from *Tammerfors Nyheter* (Tampere News) waxed poetic about her singing, her clear bell-like tones, and the "cascade of notes like a shower of silver." And while he enjoyed her performance of the obligatory Italian arias, he was more impressed with her performance of the four Cadman songs and felt that Bertha had penetrated deeply into the inner core of these melodies and "wrapped them in art." It seemed that her experiment with a new musical art form was paying off—and the reviews from Finland would have been a comforting antidote after her unfortunate reception in Moscow.

Despite her success in Finland, Bertha's sojourn in the north seems to have been short lived, as she and Zofia were back in Petrograd for Easter 1916. On April 1, 1916, again with the support of Taskin, Bertha appeared in a charity concert at A.S. Suvorin's private theatre in aid of the hospital run by the Psycho-Neurological Institute. The Institute addressed the increasing problem of soldiers with psychological wounds, then called 'shell shock.' While it was once again an unpaid performance, Bertha must have enjoyed sharing the stage with the internationally famous dancers Mikhail Fokine and Vera Fokina, as well as other prominent Russian actors and singers from the Imperial Theatres and the Moscow Art Theatre.

Bertha might have felt differently about singing for a theatre full of young men in uniform—or hospital pyjamas—if she had known that she now had a brother in uniform on the other side of the Atlantic. Like Zofia's son John had done in 1914, seventeen-year-old Lorne Crawford joined the Canadian Expeditionary Force in February 1916. He was bound for the trenches of the Western Front in France, where John had been fighting since September 1915. What a change it would have been for Bertha to envisage: Lorne, who had still been in school when she had left Canada five years before, now a soldier. But later reports suggest that Bertha would not receive news of his enlistment for some time yet. In fact, while she had been exchanging letters with her family up to the beginning of 1916, she was about to slip completely out of touch.

Initially, communications became more difficult because Bertha again left Petrograd for the provinces. In April 1916, not long after the Petrograd charity concert, Bertha joined a concert party on a tour of twenty-five towns through southern Russia into the Caucasus region. Bertha was probably invited to join the tour by her voice coach, Taskin, who was the tour's manager and accompanist as well as a performer of his own compositions. Or she may have been introduced to the concert party headliner, the well-known dramatic actor Robert Adelheim (1860–1934), at an engagement in Petrograd. Robert Adelheim was one half of the Adelheim Brothers acting team, which often included his brother Raphael. The sons of a Jewish doctor, the brothers grew up in a cultured multi-lingual Moscow family; they studied acting in Vienna and singing in Italy, and they worked on the stage in Germany. Over a forty-year career in Russia, they had built up a reputation as serious and disciplined dramatic actors. They are particularly remembered for making long tours of the provinces, where they brought the best of the classic tragedies to appreciative audiences in smaller communities. In early 1916, Robert was planning a tour to the Caucasus region without his brother, and he was looking for suitable artists to make up a concert party. Along with Taskin and Bertha, he included Alfred Barker (1895–1949), a twenty-one-year-old English virtuoso violinist whom Adelheim had met during a private afternoon concert they'd given for the Tsar's family at Tsarskoe Selo. A lyrical mezzo-soprano, E.A. Vlasova, was the fifth performer. Zofia presumably continued to play the chaperone, and Bertha's little dogs completed the troupe.

Did Bertha feel that it was a comedown to take second billing to Adelheim after singing prima donna roles in Petrograd? Or was she pragmatic about the benefits of working with an actor of Adelheim's stature and grateful for the exposure that touring with him would provide? Surely, she must also have appreciated the income. It was becoming clear that the only engagements she could secure in Petrograd at that point in the war were unpaid charity events. But she probably also relished the adventure and the chance to see more of Russia, a country where "every little town has an opera house where the best music is heard." She would not have been afraid of long train journeys, having completed extended tours across Canada and the U.S. when she was much younger. She also may have been drawn by the knowledge that the provincial audiences would be more receptive and rewarding than those in Moscow had been. As she later put it, "in Canada people do not realize the numbers or the musical enthusiasm of the minor Russian cities . . ." and "the Russians love music with an intense appreciation." Touring could give her career the continued momentum that she was not getting in the big cities, with the added satisfaction of connecting with truly appreciative audiences—not to mention a potential paycheck.

Although the Russian army was fighting farther to the south against the Ottoman Empire (in what is now Turkey), the northern Caucasus region was not only quiet, but still considered a prime holiday destination. So the tour must have felt a bit like a vacation, particularly for Zofia, whose responsibilities as a chaperone would have left her plenty of time to enjoy the sights. The Caucasus region is 2,500 kilometres south of Petrograd, and, like the concert party tours Bertha had made in Canada, this tour followed the route of the railway. After zigzagging east along the Vladikavkaz Railway through the northern Caucasus to the Caspian Sea, the group headed west along the Transcaucasia Railway through the Georgian capital of Tiflis (Tbilisi), and possibly as far as the Black Sea. While enjoying the scenery of green rolling hills and distant snow-capped mountains, the party would also get some impression of the great diversity of the empire's population. In the Caucasus, Bertha could have encountered the famous free Cossacks, the loyal soldier-farmers of the empire. But she might also have met Muslim Chechens, Dagestanis, and Azeris, always chafing under the control of their overtly Christian Emperor. And close by, there would have been the Christian Georgians and Armenians, who held to their distinct versions of Orthodoxy and pursued age-old tribal feuds. However, the concert party's audiences were probably predominantly Russian tourists staying in the European-style spas promoted by the railway companies.

Bertha and the troupe reached the northern Caucasus in time for a May 13 concert in Rostov-na-Don. A week later, on May 21 and 22, they played in the spa towns of Kislvodsk and Piatigorsk, located in the fashionable holiday region around Mineralnye Voda. The four small towns of Piatigorsk, Kislvodsk, Essentuki, and Zheleznovodsk, all clustered in the foothills of the Caucasus Mountains, were at the heart of an area of state-managed hot springs that supported popular sanatoria and hotels. Despite the privations of the war (or perhaps because of them), the spas were a favourite escape of the wealthy and the arts community from Petrograd, and Bertha would have met various guests there whom she already knew. The northerners went there to escape summer in the city and to bathe in or drink the waters of whichever spring was considered most beneficial to their condition. And, when their day of taking the waters was done, they looked forward to a relaxing evening of music and entertainment.

But while Bertha might have succumbed to a temporary illusion that she was on holiday at the resort, the program for the concert demonstrates how completely her career was now subsumed into the war effort. Advertised as "A Tragic Concert," Adelheim's parts in particular were a moving commentary about the ongoing war. Meanwhile, the musicians and their music represented major Allies on the Russian side, which may have been why Adelheim thought

Bertha would be a good fit for the party. Act One opened with the Englishman Barker playing "Praeludium and Allegro," a sombre piece by Pugnani-Kreisler. Adelheim followed with three dramatic recitations: the poem "My Friend" by Semyon Nadson; a prose piece called "Two Hordes" by the Petrograd writer Lydia Avilov; and a piece Adelheim had written himself about Russian soldiers, called "Fallen Heroes." Taskin provided an appropriate musical accompaniment. Then Bertha made her first entrance to sing two classic Italian arias from Donizetti's *Lucia de Lammermoor* and Rossini's *The Barber of Seville*. The act closed with another patriotic piece written and performed by Adelheim, "A letter to [Kaiser] Wilhelm II."

The second act opened with Bertha's second set in which she sang three modern art songs: one of Cadman's "Indian Songs;" a lullaby by the Czech Anton Dvorak (in French); and "The Nightingale" in Russian by Alexander Alyabyev. Barker and Taskin came next, performing "Nocturne (Opus 72)" by the Polish composer Frederic Chopin and "La Capricieuse" by the Englishman Edward Elgar, both in arrangements for violin and piano. Vlasova followed with three Russian lyrical songs written by Taskin, with the composer at the piano. Finally, the show closed with Adelheim, who was also a seasoned singer, performing selected lyrical songs. The troupe must have met with great success, for, in later years, Bertha mentioned this tour as one of her big achievements during her time in Russia.

Bertha made a useful contribution to the Russian tragedian Robert Adelheim's concert theme. Through her singing, she personified the British, French, and Italian Allies who were supporting Russia in the First World War.

After the tour of the Caucasus, Bertha and Zofia travelled west more than 1,000 kilometres across Ukraine to the Black Sea port of Odessa. Bertha's old colleague from the Warsaw opera, Pietro Cimini, was spending the war years in Odessa, and he may have helped to arrange the invitation she had at the end of June 1916 to sing in the magnificent municipal Odessa Opera House. The city of Odessa was established in the early 1700s to improve the connections between Russia and Europe. By 1916, it was the fourth largest city in the Russian Empire, with its broad shady avenues lined with elegant classical façades. European shipping to the Odessa port was cut off during the war, when the Turks closed the entrance to the Black Sea. However, the industrial city remained a hub of wartime activity in southern Russia while still remaining a safe distance from the fighting. The ornate 1880s Odessa Opera House was the premier opera venue on the Russian Black Sea, and it was regularly visited by all the major stars when they were on tour. The opportunity to add an appearance in the Odessa Opera House to her profile must have convinced Bertha that it was worth diverting across Ukraine from the Caucasus to reach the city.

Bertha was invited to sing in Odessa for the Serbian Premier, Nickola Pashitch, who had been sent by the exiled Serbian King Peter to present regimental banners to a new Serbian regiment. In the early months of 1916, a volunteer army division of 12,000 Serbian exiles was being formed in Odessa. They would serve as part of the Russian army in the fight to regain their country, which had been overrun by the Austrians, Germans, and Bulgarians in October 1915. The mayor of Odessa arranged an entertainment in the theatre for the Premier, local Consuls of the Allies, and some of the soldiers, with Bertha as a main attraction. Yet again, it is likely that Bertha was favoured because she could personify one of the key Allies while she sang before the assembled diplomats and politicians.

During the first half of 1916, Bertha travelled at least 7,500 kilometres by train through numerous Russian provinces in pursuit of audiences that would respond to her singing. The last Canadian report of Bertha's work in Russia, which E.R. Parkhurst printed in the August 1916 issue of *Musical Canada*, mentions the concert in Odessa and quotes the Petrograd *Birzovia Vedomosti* (Stock Exchange News) as saying "the Canadian nightingale...Miss Crawford may be reckoned as one of the [Russian] public's beloved." Did Zofia help Bertha to translate these clippings as they whiled away the hours between railway stations? Did Bertha post them off to Canada from the next major town, dreaming of a glorious return to her home country when the war was over? Although, surely, she must have realized that such a trip was still very far in the future. In September, the two women continued 2,000 kilometres north from Odessa, through Petrograd, and back to Finland to take advantage of the success that Bertha had found in this northern province earlier in the year. On September 21, Bertha appeared with the Helsinki Philharmonic Orchestra, singing arias from *The Barber of Seville* under the baton of the Finnish conductor, Robert Kajanus, and again a week later with conductor Karl Ekman. As Helsinki's *Dagen Press* (Daily Press) reported, "she delighted the audience," suggesting that Bertha succeeded in reaching out across the footlights in yet another provincial capital.

However, after the summer of 1916, Bertha's letters—if she wrote at all—stopped reaching Canada. The Canadian public would know little about Bertha's life for almost three years, and as time went on, her family became increasingly concerned. From what Bertha told Canadian reporters several years later, it would seem that her work on the stage continued unabated during the war. But Bertha was not isolated from the deteriorating political and social situation in Russia as 1916 drew to a close. No one was immune from the developing food and fuel shortages, not even upper-class Zofia and her young protégé. Bertha later spoke to a Canadian reporter with respect for the enthusiasm of the Russian audiences even when they were "cold and hungry;" she also told of how she had sung wearing her fur coat in unheated theatres, and how, during the latter years of the war, "the problem of getting decent food was a sore one." And Bertha could hardly have missed the scandal surrounding the Russian monk Rasputin, who held enormous sway over the Empress due to his apparent ability to reduce the suffering of her son, the Tsarevich, who had haemophilia. Bertha told Kingston, Ontario's *The Daily British Whig* that she had once met Rasputin at a dinner party in Petrograd, and that he was "horrible, horrible!" It is entirely possible that Bertha and Zofia did encounter Rasputin at some point, as the powerful monk was patronized by various society women in Petrograd and could be found at surprisingly elevated dinner tables in late 1916. However, Rasputin's interference in Russian politics was a major exacerbating factor in the slide towards revolution, and his assassination in December 1916 did little to halt the descent towards chaos.

A brief reference in a small Finnish newspaper in January 1917 suggests that Bertha appeared again in Tampere. It is possible that she and Zofia had spent the better part of the fall of 1916 in Finland, as it seems that they were based there for much of the coming year. Helsinki was an easy train journey from Petrograd, so Bertha would still be available if engagements came up there. And in the meantime, it was probably cheaper for the two women to live outside the capital, whether in a relative's country *dacha* or in a modest pension in the city of Helsinki. Cheaper and safer, that is.

It was probably fortunate for Bertha that she was in Helsinki in February 1917, when the first stage of the Russian Revolution began. The surprising news of the Emperor's abdication, along with the violent mutiny that ensued among the ships of the Baltic fleet in the Helsinki port, were probably the first concrete signs for Bertha that a major political force had been unleashed. This so-called February Revolution led to the creation of Kerensky's Provisional Government, which took over control of the central administration. Revolutionary committees and councils sprang up almost immediately in businesses and local governments across the country. The old rulers lost their titles, their positions, and their jobs, and many, including Baron Stackelberg, left the country. No doubt Bertha and Zofia rapidly realized that the spring of 1917 was not an opportune time for a foreigner like Bertha—or an aristocrat like Zofia—to return to Petrograd.

Instead, the two women took the somewhat surprising decision to join another concert party tour, this one journeying 10,000 kilometres across Russia to the Pacific Ocean port of Vladivostok. Of course, the income would have been useful, but they likely had other reasons for choosing an extended tour at this time. Perhaps life farther afield from central Russia looked more comfortable, for as the revolution progressed, the food production and distribution systems in the big cities slowly came undone; however, in the provinces that were farther removed from the politically volatile capital, food was still arriving in the markets. And in the provinces, despite the political turmoil, audiences were keen for diversion, and concert party tours were as welcome as before. It is not clear who else was in the party that Bertha joined. Like the previous year, she was probably a supporting artist travelling with a bigger name. We do know that Taskin was not part of the group, although he also toured into Siberia in 1917. In fact, quite a few Petrograd and Moscow artists thought a Siberian tour was a good antidote to the revolution that year.

The Toronto Star Weekly later suggested that Bertha's party had initially hoped to tour all the way to Japan. Indeed, the previous year, a Russian concert party had gone to Japan on a charity fundraising tour, stopping in seven major Russian towns along the eastern section of the Trans-Siberian Railway, then venturing west into Manchuria to the Chinese city of Harbin before backtracking to cross the Sea of Japan. The positive reports of that group's reception in Japan certainly could have encouraged other groups to repeat the tour. Moreover, Bertha may have also thought that if she reached the Pacific Coast, she might be able to get a ship directly to Canada and take Zofia—the mother of a soldier in the Canadian army—with her. In fact, Zofia's son John had become a naturalized British subject in February 1917, although it is unlikely that Zofia knew this yet.

For all of Bertha's experience with touring by train, she can't have found travelling on the Trans-Siberian Railway in the first year of the Russian Revolution a simple—nor a particularly comfortable—undertaking, even with the company of Zofia and the dogs. The trains were slow, rarely moving more than twenty kilometres an hour. And where an express train had taken eleven days before the war, the journey now could take weeks. The trains were also incredibly crowded. The majority of the country's rolling stock had long ago gone to the Eastern Front to supply the army, and a considerable amount of that had been destroyed or captured in the fighting. Only a bare minimum of carriages was left for passenger traffic within the empire. In the rundown passenger cars that remained, people fought to get into a compartment. As the journey progressed, more and more riders (and more and more garbage) crammed into the corridors, onto the platforms between the cars, and even onto the roofs. Increasingly, even the better heeled passengers like Bertha and Zofia travelled in boxcars.

Bertha and Zofia's fellow travellers would have been a cosmopolitan lot: young revolutionaries being sent out by the Provisional Government to replace the Emperor's old bureaucrats in the provinces; entrepreneurs jumping into the shuttle trade with China and Japan, making the most of the suddenly lax regulation of the economy; soldiers theoretically going 'on leave' to their villages, but unlikely to return to the front; bourgeois refugees—not unlike Zofia—fleeing the radical politics of the capitals in the direction of a passenger ship across the Pacific; foreign 'experts' spying on the revolution for

European powers (and even for small countries like Canada); and entertainers like Bertha, hoping to find a wider audience in the cities and towns along the railway in Siberia. Everyone held forth on their political opinions, making speeches, debating the past and the future, and arguing about change. The journey was long, but it probably wasn't dull.

When Bertha's party reached the Pacific port city of Vladivostok, a city of 150,000, it probably wasn't what they expected. Like most Russian cities in the middle of 1917, Vladivostok was ruled by a Committee of Workers' and Soldiers' Deputies, which was vaguely loyal to the Provisional Government far away in Petrograd, but mainly subservient to a local Executive Committee. The Committee was dominated by the Socialist Revolutionary Party, but included a number of members of the ambitious Bolshevik Party, foreshadowing the change towards more radical politics that would come in a few months. There were 50,000 soldiers in the city; they had not deserted, but their military discipline had crumbled, and the officers who remained—now elected by their subordinates—were treated with the minimum of respect by the ordinary soldiers. Finding a safe place to stay was difficult and expensive.

How much interest did this population have in the kind of classical music that Bertha could provide? The city was witness to a huge flow of refugees, whose diametrically opposed outlooks would define the civil war that was to come a few months later. The trainloads of middle-class people who arrived from the west were already worn down with cynicism about the revolution, which had undermined their way of life. If they could not re-establish an Imperial stability, then their desire was to leave Russia on one of the steamers that arrived in the harbour twice a week. From the east, these same ships brought in cargoes of passionate idealists—returning Russian political exiles anxious to join in the revolution they had waited so long for. And among them, small teams of humanitarian aid workers from organizations like the American Red Cross and the YMCA, hoping to reduce the suffering of the millions of refugees, displaced and hungry, across the country. In the streets and theatres of Vladivostok, these groups mingled with the stoic local population and the restless soldiers in an uneasy confusion. It was not really the place for a party of refined musicians.

It is not clear how long Bertha's concert party stayed in Vladivostok, but, try as they might, they could not find a passage on any ship to Japan. If Bertha had hoped to cross the Pacific to Vancouver, it would have been even more difficult to get a ticket. With no tickets to be had, it certainly cannot have made sense for them to stay long in the city after they had exhausted the local audience's interest. So, in the end, they retraced the 10,000-kilometre journey back across the country, and, by October 1917, Bertha and Zofia were back in Finland, this time staying in the relative security and comfort of a pension run by the Soederstroems at 5 Annegaten Street in central Helsinki.

With the Russian postal service in tatters due to the revolution, Bertha could not have got a letter to Canada during her extended trip across Russia. As the silent months stretched into a year, her family grew ever more concerned, while Bertha fell ever further out of touch. She still did not know that Lorne was now on the front lines in France, nor did she know that her sister Lucia had given birth to her first daughter in early 1917. Eventually, reacting to the increasingly alarming news reports from Russia, Lorne Crawford—presumably at the behest of his parents—approached the British Foreign Office in mid-October 1917 to ask if they could find out what had happened to his silent older sister. The Foreign Office sent off a telegram to the British Ambassador in Petrograd. A message came back from the British Consul in Helsinki saying that Bertha was in Finland, still in the good care of her chaperone Zofia, and that their situation was fine. But that was about to change.

Bertha, Zofia, and the two dogs were still in Helsinki at the end of October when the Bolshevik Party, under their dynamic and radical leader Vladimir Ilyich Lenin, took power in Petrograd. This second wave of revolution, which swept rapidly across Russia, came to be known as the October Revolution. During the months that Bertha had been on tour, between the February and October revolutions, there had been much political and economic uncertainty and upheaval. But that was nothing compared to the catastrophe that occurred after the October Revolution, as huge swaths of the country descended into a violent civil war.

However, in the early days after the October Revolution, there were few indications of the war and terror that were soon to come. Initially, Bertha and Zofia felt safe enough with the situation in general to leave Helsinki for Petrograd. In November 1917, they moved to an address in one of the large eighteenth-century apartment buildings that lined the Moika River in the very centre of the city. It must have unsettled the two women to see how far Petrograd had slid downhill from the glittering capital it had been when they had arrived in late 1914. *The Daily British Whig* later described how, "after Bolshevism had taken its deadly hold on the people of eastern Europe," Bertha visited the Winter Palace in Petrograd and saw "its wonderful tapestries slashed with swords, its pictures cut from top to bottom, the whole scene of ruin and desolation." It must have been an uncomfortable awakening from her prima donna dream, which had reached such a peak during her encounter with royalty in those very rooms, to see the palace turned upside down and to know that the Tsar and his family were now under arrest.

When news of the second revolution reached Bertha's family members in Toronto, their relief at the recent telegram about Bertha's whereabouts and wellbeing must have evaporated. In the first week of February 1918, Lorne again asked for help. In January, 1918, a prominent Canadian industrialist and political organizer, Sir Albert E. Kemp (1858–1929), had just taken over the London position of the Canadian Minister of Overseas Military Forces. While Kemp was supposed to be sorting out the confused military administration of the Canadian Expeditionary Force in England, he was immediately besieged by families like the Crawfords, all wanting help with tracking down lost relatives. However, while Bertha's case was just one of many, it probably stood out for Kemp, who would have remembered hearing Bertha's young voice lifting up above the choir at the Sherbourne Street Methodist Church, where he had been a stalwart member just over ten years before. On Lorne's behalf, Kemp repeated the request to the British Foreign Office in London, asking it to contact Bertha again. This time a cable came back with the disconcerting news that she had already quit Helsinki for Petrograd and had left only a general address.

As Bertha later recalled, in those first weeks after the overthrow of the Provisional Government, she did not feel personally threatened by the Bolsheviks, as "they let artists alone, especially women like herself whom they knew had no political purposes or affiliations." Nonetheless, as Bolshevism took hold, Bertha's dream of the prima donna seemed at risk of slipping into a nightmare. While the chaos and the hunger in Petrograd got worse, arbitrary punishments began to be meted out by radicalized Workers and Soldiers Committees, and it became dangerous to be identified as bourgeois. To be sure, for all the Crawford family's factory-worker roots, Bertha had devoted her life to putting herself firmly in the ranks of the bourgeoisie. Ironically, by 1918, the meeting with royalty that had defined her ascendance to the heights of a true prima donna in 1915 had become a liability. Her decoration from Grand Duchess Tatiana could have been enough to imply dangerous Tsarist sympathies. Indeed, one contemporary English nurse who had served with the Russian army described how she kept her war decorations well out of sight after a Bolshevik decree declared all Tsarist awards "degrading and void." How much more dangerous, then, to be in the company of Zofia—a Baroness whose cousins had directly served the Tsar?

Nevertheless, as winter turned into spring, Zofia and Bertha stayed on in Petrograd. This must have been the period when, as the Canadian press later reported, Bertha "sang for the Bolsheviki," but any details of the performance are lost. Certainly, Bertha and Zofia would have had other things on their mind. Perhaps they were now hoping for liberation by the Germans. By mid-February, the Germans had advanced close enough to Petrograd to frighten the Bolsheviks into evacuating their government to Moscow. Then, on March 3, 1918, the Bolshevik government signed the Treaty of Brest-Litovsk with Germany and the other Central Powers, thereby ending Russia's participation in the war. The treaty left Poland occupied and under German protection but nominally independent. While most Russians felt the treaty was a disastrous compromise to buy peace, Polish refugees like Zofia saw the treaty as a very positive turn of events. Not only might they return home, but real independence for their country was within reach.

Frustratingly, in the short term, many of the travel routes from Petrograd back to Warsaw were blocked by local fighting and instability. Finally, a window of opportunity opened on June 12, 1918, when the Bolsheviks signed a preliminary treaty with the Ukrainian nationalists they were fighting in the south. For the moment, travel through southern Russia to Poland might be possible. Zofia and Bertha decided to cut their losses and leave when they could. On June 14, 1918, *Obozrenie Teatrov* (Theatrical Review) reported that "The famous American singer, Miss Bertha Crawford, is leaving Petrograd after four years here."

The costs of the journey back to Warsaw were high. As Bertha told *The Kingston Standard* in 1921, in the process of leaving she "lost everything in Russia, her money, baggage and private belongings." Presumably, Zofia suffered much the same fate. This was not an unusual story, as it was an extremely insecure time for travellers, women in particular, and robbery was very common. But that was not the end of their troubles. *The Kingston Standard* also reported that Bertha "could not even draw her money from the bank, as the law was then that only 500 roubles a month could be drawn out of the bank."

Bertha made no effort later to expand upon the trauma of her last months in Petrograd or her flight to Warsaw. Ultimately, in 1921, *The Daily British Whig* would pronounce that "Miss Crawford does not like to talk of the terrible sights or sounds of war."

Entr'acte –
The Great Train Robbery

*N*ear *dawn, July, 1918. The Ukrainian Steppes.* The train carriage, which has been rocking slowly as it creeps along the poorly maintained tracks, suddenly comes to an abrupt halt, noisily slamming against the coupling of the carriage in front. Zofia, whose head has been resting heavily on Bertha's shoulder as she slept, slides off the wooden bench. The dogs wake up as she falls on top of them. Bertha was dozing fitfully, but she is not even slightly rested.

Bertha hadn't quite understood when they boarded this train why they had been able to get seats. On most of the other parts of this long journey, the train has been so crowded that one, if not both, of them have had to stand for endless hours. Their only thought has been to keep moving north and west across the country, towards refuge across the border in Poland. But once they started the journey, their fellow passengers began to mumble about the bands of anarchists and thieves—the distinction between the two seems very vague—who have been targeting the trains on this line. So, as she helps Zofia up from the filthy floor, Bertha guesses that that is the cause of the commotion, and also why the train has been so empty on this part of the line. Bandits.

The carriage is dark. The candle was put out hours ago, and only the faintest light is breaking outside the carriage. Bertha jumps back as a bandit on horseback knocks the glass out of a window with his rifle butt. Cold air rushes in.

"Get out. Now!" shouts the bandit, his barely intelligible Ukrainian only adding to Bertha's sense of dislocation.

The passengers fumble down the carriage steps, clutching at bags and bundles they don't trust out of their sight. A peasant in a dirty sheepskin coat relieves them of whatever they are holding as they reach the ground. Bertha resists, clinging to her club bag briefly, and then tumbles backwards to the ground as she lets go. The little dogs bark in her defence and then yelp as they are tossed aside by a tall leather boot.

Looking up from the gravel rail bed, Bertha sees that the man has hand grenades hanging from his belt. And also that he is really only an overgrown boy. Zofia grabs at the dogs to silence them.

As Bertha gets up, another bandit pushing his way along the slanting edge of the rail bed puts his grimy hand on her chest to shove her out of his way. As she falls further down the embankment, she gasps as the brooch pinned inside her chemise stabs her chest.

But she keeps quiet. Like all the women around her, she is acutely aware of the danger of drawing any attention. All of them silently pray that it is only the baggage these men want this morning. The bandits seem relaxed, taking their time to go through each carriage before moving on to the baggage car, loading up their horse-drawn carts with loot. But, from time to time, disputes break out about who will get what, and a ruthless tension rises and falls.

Bertha and Zofia insinuate themselves into a huddle of women of indeterminate age and station. Bertha is wearing her oldest, plainest clothes, which are none the better for being worn for many days straight now. She is not the only one whose faded linen skirt hem swings like a richer fabric once did, nearly giving away the coins sewn into it. Her cropped, wavy hair is hidden beneath a faded floral peasant kerchief. She is fairly sure she doesn't look particularly foreign or middle class, but she keeps her mouth shut, exchanging only a glance with Zofia. It wouldn't take more than a few words for Bertha's accent to give her away.

Not for the first time, Bertha wonders if she should have just thrown away the brooch from the Grand Duchess. But she can't quite bring herself to let go of that last reminder of her dream—although, by now, a dream is all it seems to be. In a conscious attempt to escape from reality, Bertha puts her mind back to that evening more than three years before, recalling her excitement at the invitation to the Winter Palace.

That night, Bertha had felt like she was on top of the world. She had chatted with Zofia in nervous animation as the carriage clattered its way across the great snowy square between the palace and the Admiralty. But she had quieted herself by the time they'd made their way across the interior courtyard to the entrance.

Zofia had whispered advice as they'd walked up the grand marble staircase, knowing very well that Bertha had no experience with court etiquette. "You must make your lowest and slowest curtsey for the Grand Duchess," she had advised, "and then don't say anything unless she says something first."

Inside the great hall, there had been nothing but a quiet murmur of voices, everyone constrained by the grandeur of the building. A soft light had gleamed from crystal chandeliers dangling from the ornately painted ceiling, and the gilded plaster mouldings had seemed to glow. The whole effect was overtly splendid and clearly designed to impress—and keep lesser mortals in their place. And yet the Grand Duchess, only eighteen years old and dressed in a simple (although clearly expensive) white gown, was a slight and reserved girl. Not at all the imposing presence that Bertha had expected a royal princess to be.

The whole ceremony had gone quickly. One by one, the painters, singers, and dancers who had participated in the fundraising evening a week earlier had stepped forward to receive their awards.

At the time, Bertha had been quite taken with her little silver brooch. But now, her feelings are decidedly mixed. The brooch might establish her credibility with any White forces she meets in the future, but, at present, it risks creating a fatal impression that she is a counter-revolutionary.

Bertha watches as the bandits, lit by the pink flush of a slowly rising sun, unload the trunks from the baggage car. She sees one pause as he pulls out her trunk, studying the Roman letters of her painted name and the remnants of foreign labels peeling off the end. She has a moment of acute fear, but, like most peasants, this bandit is illiterate. He shoves the trunk on top of his cart and then whips his run-down horse into a trot behind the departing trail of bandit wagons.

Bertha shrinks back among the women, mentally disowning those possessions—and, with them, all the events and experiences of the past four years. The important thing is to forget these things as soon as possible. And to get far away from this place, fast.

It turns out that the bandits are making off with the train, too, and the engine engages with a hiss of steam. Trains are a prime military asset in this mobile war, and the engine and carriages are the ultimate booty. The cars pull away into the early morning, leaving the passengers in stunned groups along the tracks. There is little debate about which way to go. Given that the bandits are travelling forward, the passengers will follow the tracks back the ten kilometres to the previous station.

Bertha follows Zofia and the other women and does what many people in Russia have been doing since the revolution—she puts her head down and puts one foot in front of the other. The dogs follow close at her heels.

CHAPTER ELEVEN –
A Return to Stability,
1919–1921

*As she re-established her career in newly independent post-war Poland,
Bertha updated her image with platinum blonde hair styled in the latest marcel wave.
However, her musical taste remained firmly classical.*

Zofia and Bertha arrived back in Warsaw in July 1918, to find that the Germans were no longer a threat. In fact, Bertha must have found it more than a little ironic that the German occupiers from whom she and Zofia had fled in fear three years before now offered a kind of protection for the Polish people against their previous overlords, the Russians. It must have been even more surprising to find that the Germans in Poland did not represent any real danger to Bertha, either, despite the fact that the Canadian Expeditionary Force was in hot battle with the German army on the Western Front in the summer of 1918. In the relative safety of Warsaw, Bertha felt comfortable enough in August to place newspaper advertisements, in bold type, telling the city that she had just returned from singing in opera and concerts in Russia and would now be offering lessons in the old style of bel canto singing from 2:00–3:00 pm at Zofia's new address. However, Bertha was not so at ease that she let her family know where she was. For how could she have explained that, in contrast with her compatriots fighting in France, she was no longer really at war with the Germans? In fact, Bertha never told the Canadian public that she spent five months, from July to November 1918, living under the protection of her country's sworn enemy.

So it must have been with mixed emotions that thirty-two-year-old Bertha returned to Warsaw. She was coming back to a city that had been Zofia's lifetime home, and Bertha must have wanted to share in her friend's great relief at returning from three years' exile. But for Bertha, Warsaw had been more like a temporary stopover when she had first stayed there a full four years before—just one of many transitory places she had hung her hat in the eight years since she'd left Canada. How long did it take Bertha to realize that Zofia's Warsaw home had the potential to become a more permanent base for herself, too?

While Bertha had managed to hang on to her two "constant companions"—her Griffon Belge dogs—she had almost no material possessions to show for her four years in Russia. Zofia, on the other hand, came home to a vastly improved scenario: the promise of an independent homeland, where her wealth and status remained intact and where she could rapidly reconnect with her family and a network of influential friends. And Bertha, as her companion and protégé, would soon be making use of those assets, too.

As Zofia—who was now taking on her Polish title, the Baroness Kosińska—regained access to her property and inheritance, she was returned to the comfort, stability, and status she had left behind in 1915. It was probably the inheritance from her father that enabled her, within a few weeks of her return, to buy a large house. Seven aleja Szucha was a fashionable address in one of the elegant Warsaw neighbourhoods where the intellectual and cultural life of the city was concentrated. The upscale address was only one block from the Royal Lazenki Park and the Belvedere Palace, which would soon be the home of Marshal Pilsudski, the most famous military leader and behind-the-scenes political force in post-war Poland. Zofia's big house on aleja Szucha did not survive the Second World War, but the footprint of the address, and the other buildings on the street, suggest that it was a substantial building with plenty of space for long-standing guests. After almost twenty years of on-and-off journeying through England, Italy, and the farthest limits of the Russian Empire, the purchase of this grand house suggests that forty-eight-year-old Zofia had decided that her travelling days were over. Perhaps she hoped that, with a stable home to offer, she might lure her son John back to Warsaw. She probably had no idea that John, now a naturalized British subject, had just become an officer in the British army and had no plans to ever live in Poland again.

In the meantime, Zofia welcomed not only Bertha into this new house, but also the dogs they both loved. Bertha must have quickly felt at home, for she rapidly expanded her pack from the original two Griffon Belge up to six, acquiring two more Griffon Belge, adding a toy terrier, and finally rescuing a stray Spitz from the streets of Warsaw. Together, they all settled down to await the much-anticipated end of the war.

Initially, it could not have been obvious that Warsaw was the best place for thirty-two-year-old Bertha to rebuild a viable musical career, given the political and economic turmoil that characterized the new Poland. When the Germans finally agreed to a general armistice on November 11, 1918, they withdrew westwards from Warsaw to their pre-war borders, while the Soviet army moved forwards into the positions that the Germans had evacuated along the Eastern Front. Between these indistinct borders were the 150,000 square miles where the country of Poland would be re-created. In the eastern provinces of the collapsing German Empire, Polish populations rose up and took control of the area around Poznan. But it would be months before the Treaty of Versailles endorsed the formal process to recognize a newly independent Poland.

Nevertheless, it was a heady time for Polish patriots—and for foreigners like Bertha who had developed an affection for the Polish people—as their dream of Polish independence became a de facto reality. But the challenges were huge. The war had wrought massive damage to the infrastructure of the country. It had destroyed 1.8 million buildings, including homes, schools, and churches, and had damaged the majority of water systems and railway bridges. What is more, a third of all draught horses—the engines of reconstruction—had been killed off. Inflation was rampant, and earnings eroded rapidly. Even more challenging, the new state of Poland brought together lands that had previously been part of three different empires—German, Russian, and Austro-Hungarian—each of which had had different official languages, laws, and currencies. They even had different railway gauges, not to mention different traditions of managing musical enterprises. Consolidating, harmonizing, and rebuilding the three zones into one coherent country was a difficult task, and, in the short run, the Polish government met the demands with only limited success.

Did Bertha pause to consider whether it would be better at this point to go back to her family and the relative tranquility of Canada, even if that meant she would not be returning as the celebrated prima donna she had been in the early years of the war? Or did she know that any chance of reasserting stardom on the opera stage was best if she remained in Europe? And was it indecision on this front that still kept her from cabling her family? Indeed, as late as January 24, 1919, *The Toronto Daily Star* reported that Bertha's anxious parents were "in complete ignorance as to the whereabouts of their daughter, or even whether she is still alive." In London, Minister Kemp reacted to this newspaper report by writing again to the British Foreign Office in February, asking for more help with locating Bertha. On March 14, 1919, the only answer that the British Consul in Helsinki could supply was that Bertha and Zofia had left Finland more than a year before, in November 1917, on their way to Warsaw, but he had no more recent news.

What would her parents have thought if they had known that, in fact, on January 24, Bertha was not only safe and well, but was making her first return appearance in Warsaw in a concert helping to cement the creation of a new country? More than just harmonizing laws and administrative structures, the Polish state needed to reintegrate the divided Polish national identity. To this end, opera and music were more than just entertainment—they became highly symbolic art forms that were used to promote and consolidate Polish culture and national unity. In the new Poland, important historical and political events would regularly be commemorated by concerts and special opera productions, with the top leaders from the government, army, and church all symbolically in attendance.

The concert that Bertha appeared in on January 24, 1919 was "In Honour of the Allies," whose support had been so critical in winning Polish independence. So, once again, Bertha's nationality was as important as her voice in this performance. Bertha sang as a soloist with the Warsaw Philharmonic Orchestra, returning to the hall where she had first appeared back in 1914. There, she reconnected with the resident accompanist, Dr. Urstein, with whom she would build a productive working relationship that would last many years.

Did Bertha already know Emil Mlynarski (1870–1935), the dynamic and well-travelled Director of the Warsaw Philharmonic Orchestra, when she was invited to sing at this special concert in celebration of the Allies? Their paths may well have crossed when he was with the orchestra of the Bolshoi Theatre in Moscow between 1916 and 1918. And, as he had worked for five years before that with the Glasgow Orchestra, he spoke good English, which might have made it easier for Bertha—who spent so much of her time in Europe speaking French—to build up a rapport with him. This may explain how Bertha came to be chosen as a soloist for the first big concert conducted by Mlynarski in the newly independent Poland on his return to Warsaw in January 1919. Like the Petrograd charity concerts that Bertha had sung in a few years earlier, the program included pieces and artists chosen to represent different countries in the coalition. There was English, French, Italian, and American music. Bertha, who was still described in some newspapers as an 'American,' sang an Italian aria, some English and American songs, and even a Polish song.

Warsaw Philharmonic Orchestra conductor Emil Mlynarski chose Bertha as a soloist for his patriotic concert, "In Honour of the Allies," putting her at the centre of one of Poland's most important stages in her first post-war appearance, in January 1919.

For an artist trying to re-launch a career after a long hiatus, Bertha had a very auspicious start. Mlynarski's endorsement of her potential as a concert soloist so soon after her return to Poland must have been incredibly valuable in her subsequently getting high-profile concert engagements. Mlynarski, who was a particularly well-respected member of the Polish musical establishment, had been the first Artistic Director at the Warsaw Philharmonic Orchestra from 1901 to 1905, and he was again heavily involved with both the Philharmonic and the Warsaw Opera in the 1920s. Trained at the prestigious St. Petersburg Conservatory, he arrived home in Warsaw at the end of the 1890s with the ambition to promote Polish music in opera and develop a symphonic orchestra. He fulfilled his first ambition during his four years' directing the opera at the Warsaw Great Theatre from 1899 to 1903, and then he moved on to spend four years building the newly formed Warsaw Philharmonic Orchestra. By the 1920s, Mlynarski was almost bald, and his moustache and flaring eyebrows were completely white, but his energy was undiminished. By all accounts, he was a dominant force in the Warsaw music scene.

In contrast with the limited professional possibilities that had been available to Bertha during the years of revolution and civil war in Russia in 1917 and 1918, singing under Mlynarski with the Warsaw Philharmonic put Bertha back in the top tier of concert performers from the first month of 1919. The Warsaw Philharmonic had been established in 1901 under the patronage of a group of Polish aristocrats, financiers, and musicians. One of the leading instigators was Aleksander Rajchman, who later led the Warsaw Opera when

Bertha was there in the summer of 1915. The Philharmonic Hall was an impressive and elegant three-storey building that rose to a fourth storey over the central hall. The auditorium was superior to the Warsaw Great Theatre and had seats for 2,000 people, all of which had a good view. The building was reputed to have been modelled on the Paris Opera, and the façade had distinctive round corners and a central row of columns in front of a third-storey balcony above the entrance stairs. Two sets of allegorical bronze figures graced the parapet of the roof, and the interior was decorated with panels painted by Polish artists.

Bertha made many repeat appearances as a soloist with the Warsaw Philharmonic Orchestra during the 1920s.

As the premier Polish musical institution outside the ambit of the Russian-dominated Warsaw Theatre Directorate, the Warsaw Philharmonic had been the most important cultural centre in Poland before the war, and so it was well placed to build on that reputation in the newly independent Poland. In the 1920s, the weekly Friday concerts at the Philharmonic were the favourite meeting places of music lovers, musicians, and critics—all the top figures in the intellectual and cultural life of the city. Despite the fact that it was not the opera, the Warsaw Philharmonic was a promising place for Bertha to begin to put her career back on track after her war experiences in Russia, and she appeared at least twice more with Mlynarski's orchestra in the next few months.

During this period of rapid change in her life, when exactly did Bertha finally decide to tell her family where she was? Kemp's answer from the British Consul in Helsinki suggests that the Helsinki pension owner already had a forwarding address for Bertha at Zofia's house on aleja Szucha in Warsaw. Had Bertha informed the Helsinki pension of her new address in Warsaw but not told her own family in Toronto? Did some of her letters home get lost in the mail? Or had she simply been waiting until her feet were back on the ground—and, more importantly, on the stage—before contacting them? In any event, the Crawford family probably knew by the middle of March 1919 at the latest that Bertha was safe in Warsaw, at which point it seems likely that some long letters crossed the Atlantic. The Crawfords certainly must have been surprised to find out that, despite a narrow escape from the turmoil of the Russian revolution, Bertha still had no immediate plans to leave Eastern Europe. In fact, she would make no real plan to return to Canada until she was once again definitively a prima donna.

Meanwhile, despite the setbacks to her career resulting from the war and revolution, Bertha was actively making up for lost time. In addition to her rapid return to the stage in Zofia's hometown, Bertha was getting good work in other parts of Poland, too. Almost immediately after her comeback appearance in Warsaw, Bertha found another receptive audience in Lodz, an industrial city that was located about a hundred kilometres southwest of Warsaw and had a population of about half a million people in 1919. Alfred Strauch (1877–1934), a Lodz bookseller turned impresario, had established the new Lodz Symphonic Orchestra less than a year before, and, driven by his personal passion for music, he set about bringing in high-quality conductors and soloists to work with his orchestra. Strauch took it as a matter of honour to organize prestigious concerts in Lodz, whether they were profitable or not. He hired the respected Bronislaw Szulc (1881–1955) as orchestra director, and he also regularly brought in the top conductors who were working with the Warsaw Philharmonic as guests. As early as February 1919, with her reputation riding high in the Warsaw papers, Bertha was invited to make the short hundred-kilometre train journey from Warsaw to be one of Strauch's guest stars in her first concert with the Lodz Orchestra.

Felix Halpern (1866–1942), the learned music teacher, writer, and music critic at the Lodz newspaper *Glos Polski* (Voice of Poland), was immediately taken with Bertha's singing, identifying her upon her first appearance in the city as "a star of the first order of the coloratura repertoire, able to combine total artistic achievement with sophisticated technical ability." He admired both her "technical bravado" and "sweet lyricism," and commended how she executed even clichéd opera arias with expression and spontaneity. While Bertha had to be pleased with such strong praise, if she sent the glowing review home to her family (as she had done in the early years of the war), she didn't ask them to show it to the press. For the time being at least, Bertha appears to have been waiting for a very particular kind of review before she would share any more successes with the Toronto papers. In any event, Bertha sang with the Lodz Philharmonic Orchestra in February and March, 1919, and was regularly invited back for various Strauch productions in Lodz.

It is unlikely that Zofia accompanied Bertha on short journeys like these, now that she was settled in her new home in Warsaw. After all, with Bertha now in her early thirties, and with post-war Warsaw society rapidly becoming more modern and liberal, the necessity of a chaperone was fading. However, it is quite possible that Bertha travelled with a maid to help her with things like her hair and her wardrobe. But henceforth, Zofia's role in Bertha's life would subtly shift as she evolved into the doyenne of a home base where Bertha could be confident she would be welcomed to stay after yet another tour of guest appearances.

Meanwhile, Bertha's relationship with both the Warsaw and the Lodz orchestras flourished in the years following the war. The fact that she began to appear repeatedly alongside the most prominent conductors in Poland says a lot about the respect she earned as a performer. The programs for these symphonic concerts followed a standard pattern. The orchestra would be scheduled to perform two or three major pieces, generally concertos or symphonies. Bertha would come on in the interval between these longer pieces to provide a change of pace by singing two or three of the showier arias from her Italian opera repertoire. In addition to regularly singing arias from the operas that she also performed in full at other times, like *Rigoletto*, *The Barber of Seville*, and

La Traviata, in these concerts she might also further demonstrate her coloratura form by singing arias from operas that she did not have the opportunity to perform with a full cast, such as "The Shadow Song" from Meyerbeyer's *Dinorah*, or an aria from Donizetti's *Lucia de Lammermoor*, or sometimes "Qui la Voce" from Bellini's *I Puritani*. Now in her prime, Bertha's vocal technique was mature and consistent, and the Polish critics were often very positive. In April 1919, when she worked with the conductor Mateus Glinski (1892–1976) in Warsaw, reviewers wrote about her coloratura vocal technique that "arpeggios, trills, staccato, stamina, range, for Miss Crawford all these things are like her 'daily bread.'" Despite not getting any roles in full opera at this time, Bertha's concert appearances were building her a solid reputation.

Along with this professional success (and the income that came with it), Bertha was probably also encouraged to stay on in Warsaw by an expanding social circle. In addition to her longstanding friendship with Zofia, Bertha struck up an acquaintance with the eccentric American doctor, Violet Berger (1878–19??), around this time. Perhaps the two North American women met in the popular café of the Bristol Hotel when Berger was staying there. Berger, who was about ten years older than Bertha, had been born in Austin, Texas. Her parents were immigrants to the United States from the Rhineland area of Germany, and she probably spoke both German and French fluently. Widowed while still young, she studied medicine in Europe and then in New York before the war. In 1915, just before leaving for Switzerland to finish her medical studies, she married a first cousin, Carl Berger, in New York. However, she never spent much time with him, as, for the next decade, she lived mostly in Europe while he stayed on in New York, and eventually she divorced him.

Bertha would have found an affinity with Berger's taste for adventure and her determination to make her own way in the world. After qualifying as a doctor at the age of nearly forty, Berger joined the medical service of the French army and then worked for the American Red Cross in France until the end of the war. Then, in 1919, she was recruited in Paris by the Polish pianist and patriot, Ignace Paderewski, who, together with his wife, convinced Berger to come to Poland to work for the newly formed Polish White Cross. Berger travelled to Warsaw with the Paderewskis in July 1919 and lived for several years in the Paderewskis' Bristol Hotel in the very centre of the city.

Berger was a strong, independent professional who lived as a single woman and led an active public life. She seems to have been inspired by the new feminist values, which had begun circulating at the turn of the new century in Poland just as they had in Canada and the United States. Like Bertha, Berger had moved beyond the old-fashioned ideas of how a woman should live. She had, perhaps, a 'devil may care' attitude and showed little concern for the opinions of staid society matrons. Like Bertha and Zofia, Berger had travelled extensively and had worked as an equal to men all her life. Hence, it is unlikely that friends like Berger would have suggested to Bertha that this was the time to go running home to her parents, celebrity or not.

Nevertheless, as she entered the 1920s, Bertha was still working towards regaining her place at the centre of an opera stage. Perhaps, in her mind, this was the only way she could justify a return to Canada—as a triumphant, bona fide prima donna—and restart her Canadian singing career. But as she settled into a comfortable life in the Polish capital, niggling doubts about realizing a long-term return to Canada must have started to infiltrate her subconscious. She would have learned that her sister Lucia now had a second child—a son, Ernest, born at the end of 1918—and that her soldier brother Lorne had returned from France to Toronto in May 1919. Howard, with his wife and daughter, were running a small grocery store near her parents' house. All her siblings had grown up and were settling down in Toronto. But could Bertha really see herself abandoning the career opportunities of Europe to settle down amongst them? Probably not, especially if she thought she would be perceived not as an established opera singer, but as a middling performer whose success had plateaued.

Therefore, the success of her recent concert appearances in Warsaw and Lodz must have encouraged Bertha that Poland had the better potential for re-establishing a major singing career—if not yet in opera, then (at least for the time being) through prominent concert performances. Indeed, while the historical sources about Bertha are very thin for this period, it seems likely that she continued to get engagements in the fall of 1919 and through the winter of 1920, both in Warsaw and in the Polish provinces. Her friends and colleagues must also have encouraged her to keep working. But life in Poland still lacked the stability of life in Canada. While the First World War had officially come to an end in many parts of Europe, this was not the case in Poland

and Russia. In the background, the war over the Polish territories on the Eastern Front had only taken a brief pause at the end of 1918 before fighting resumed in early 1919, this time between the newly constituted Polish army and Russian Bolshevik forces.

As the Polish–Soviet War heated up in early 1920, Bertha was acutely aware of how the fighting was going, as her friend, Dr. Berger, was conscripted out of the Polish White Cross and into the Polish Army Medical Corps. Berger was given the highest-ranked medical commission in the Polish army as a Lieutenant-Colonel, and she took charge of medical services for wounded soldiers—a highly unusual appointment for both a foreigner and a woman. Indefatigable and unshakeable, Berger was often at the front, following the Polish army. In the summer of 1920, following a daring advance by the Polish army deep into Ukraine, the Soviet army drove the Polish forces back towards Warsaw in what appeared to be an unstoppable rout. Berger stayed at her post back in Warsaw as the Soviet army approached, perhaps the only American woman to remain in the city. Very uncertain of the outcome, Bertha hovered on the edge of leaving, reluctant to give up her foothold in a city she was coming to love. As she waited, she showed her respect for Berger's efforts by volunteering to sing for the wounded in her friend's hospital, but this can only have heightened her sense of the mounting threat.

The eccentric American doctor Violet Berger was a good friend of Bertha. Bertha sang for the wounded soldiers in Berger's Warsaw hospital during the Polish–Soviet War in 1921.

In August 1920, less than eighteen months after leaving behind all her money and belongings in Russia, Bertha came very close to losing everything again. She got caught up in the kind of panic that she hoped she had left behind when she escaped from Russia in 1918. As she later told *The Toronto Star Weekly*, she became so alarmed with the possibility that Warsaw would fall to the Soviet army and be looted that she packed her belongings and sent her trunks to the port city of Danzig, presumably in preparation for boarding a ship out of the country. Did Zofia warn her not to risk staying to face the Bolsheviks? Was Zofia herself thinking about leaving? Bertha later claimed that she was convinced not to flee by the English and French Consuls, although surely Zofia's advice was more important overall. As it was, the Polish army finally stood its ground outside Warsaw, and the Soviet army took its turn to retreat in disorder back to the east. In the end, Bertha must have been very relieved when an armistice was eventually signed between the Polish and Soviet governments in the fall of 1920 and peace finally settled over Poland. In retrospect, although she could have taken the opportunity to return to Canada at this point, it is clear that she wanted to stay where she was and continue building her career in Poland. Indeed, the idea of a proud return to Canada would have to wait a while yet—at least until she reclaimed a starring opera role. In the meantime, Warsaw had become her true home.

What are we to make of the fact that Bertha now found herself living in Zofia's home and slipping into a more permanent relationship with her sometime patron and longtime friend? Bertha was probably earning enough money to support herself now (although whether she ever earned enough to support a lifestyle befitting an aspiring prima donna is questionable). Consequently, the modern reader may inevitably wonder just what kind of bond existed between these two women, who had travelled and shared a home together for so many years. Certainly, in Bertha's era, the concept of the 'Boston marriage'—where two women lived together without the financial support (or control!) of a man—was current. And there were examples of contemporary Canadian women artists who lived as lifelong companions, such as the prolific novelist, Mazo de la Roche (1879–1961), and her cousin, Caroline Clement, or the Toronto-based sculptors, Florence Wyle (1881–1968) and Frances Loring (1887–1968). But to automatically assume that such associations resembled a modern same-sex relationship would be inappropriately anachronistic. In Bertha's day, strong—even devoted—friendships between women were frequently platonic. Indeed, it was an era when many people assumed that most women were non-sexual, particularly if they weren't married. Did Zofia and Bertha see themselves like a mother and daughter? As close friends?

Or as something else? A century later, such questions are extremely difficult to answer.

In the meantime, Bertha seems to have been strongly focused on her work both in and around Warsaw. In October 1920, she returned to the stage twice at the Warsaw Philharmonic, where she sang to sold-out audiences with Emil Mlynarski and with the conductor Zdzislaw Birnbaum (1878–1921). The papers said "she roused admiration for her vocal training, her breathing and foremost her truly impressive efficiency in all the combinations of the coloratura technique." She even travelled as far afield as the southern city of Lwow (Lviv), which also had been under siege during the fighting in August, and received a strong review for a concert in Krakow on the way back.

As 1920 drew to a close, Bertha's steady work over the previous two years to build her reputation with Polish audiences through concert work finally paid off in the form of ample opportunities to sing in full opera again. The re-creation of the Polish state inspired a flowering of artistic activity in the 1920s, and, by the peak year of 1922, there were five opera companies operating in different Polish cities, all aspiring to work on an ambitious scale. Many major theatres remained the property of municipal governments, but, unlike before the First World War, not one of the opera companies or orchestras was under state control. Some companies were sponsored by municipal governments, while others were private ventures funded by entrepreneurs or groups of artists and directors who would lease a municipal theatre for the season and run their own show. Most companies presenting a season of opera hoped to offer about forty different titles in Polish, Italian, French, and German. At the top of the list were the Italian classics of Verdi and Puccini, with Rossini's *The Barber of Seville*—including the soprano role of Rosina that Bertha specialized in—being the most popular. Despite the growing fashion for cabarets and variety shows in Warsaw, live opera and operetta performances remained very popular across Poland throughout the 1920s. During a typical opera season, the Warsaw Great Theatre presented a different opera every night, seven nights a week, with two performances on at least one day of the week. All this activity meant that even an artist with a limited opera repertoire like Bertha could aspire to find work on the opera stage. Finally, her work on the best concert stages across Poland was about to pay off.

One of the companies that Bertha had her eye on was the new opera company launched at the municipally owned Poznan Great Theatre in August 1919. Poznan, a city in the far west of Poland, was an overnight train journey from Warsaw. Of its pre-war population of 150,000, about half had been German, as it was part of the German Empire. However, after political control was taken over by Poland, most of the German population left. Polish artists were brought into administrative positions alongside the new Polish politicians, and the Polish musician Adam Dolzycki was hired as the first Director of the new Poznan Opera Company. In contrast with the Warsaw Great Theatre, the Poznan Great Theatre was a very new building, constructed only a decade earlier, in 1909, by the Prussian authorities. The building had a rather severe neo-classical façade dominated by six imposing ionic columns and a large bronze winged Pegasus on the peak of the roof.

The Poznan opera building may have been new, but the tradition of opera was very well established in the city. Indeed, over the next twenty years, the Poznan Opera Company proved to be the most stable of all the opera companies in Poland. From its inception, with Dolzycki directing the opera company and a new ballet company installed, the Poznan Great Theatre quickly became one of the most important music venues in the new Poland. Fortunately for Bertha, she already knew Dolzycki from their time together at the Warsaw Opera Company in 1914, and she would have reconnected with him when he was in Warsaw in 1919.

Adam Dolzycki, Director of the new Poznan Opera Company, hired Bertha in 1921 for eighteen guest appearances in prima donna roles, which she would leverage for her return to Canada.

Dolzycki was the same age as Bertha, still only thirty-four years old in his second season in Poznan in 1921. He wore his hair in a thick, unruly mop and posed with an almost melodramatic seriousness for his portraits, perhaps hoping to look older than he was. Like Bertha, he had spent the war in Russia, building his talents in the larger Russian music scene as he composed and conducted. In Poznan, he was known for his impulsive and exuberant interpretations of music, as well as for finding unconventional solutions and making creative use of theatrical opportunities. The potential to work with a dynamic young director—particularly one who had innovative ideas about modern staging for the old opera standards—may have seemed particularly attractive to Bertha.

Probably on the advice of Dolzycki, in January 1921, the directors of the Poznan Opera Company invited Bertha to be a guest artist for two performances of *Rigoletto*. At Bertha's Poznan debut on January 27, the people of Poznan liked what they heard. The review of her debut performance in the *Goniec Wielkopolski* (Wielkopolska Messenger) boded well for more appearances: "Ms. Crawford guest starred [as Gilda] . . . and proved to be an outstanding performer of the part . . . The artist's voice sounds like a flowing instrument and although small, it is extremely graceful. Impeccable technique and skill." The directors of the opera company liked how Bertha was received, and what initially looked like a short contract gradually grew into an extended series of eighteen appearances over six months, from January through June 1921, in performances of *Rigoletto, The Barber of Seville,* and *La Traviata,* as well as in Gounod's French version of *Faust*.

The role of Marguerite in *Faust* was a new role for Bertha. The story follows the classic tale of Faust, who sells his soul to the devil, Mephistopheles, exchanging renewed youth and sensual pleasures during his lifetime in return for helping the devil in the underworld after death. Faust's prize is the seduction of the innocent Marguerite. She has his child, but he abandons her. Another fallen woman of the opera canon, Marguerite finishes the opera dying in prison, alone but repentant, after killing her child. The role is demanding in that it requires vocal versatility to move from portraying childish innocence in the opening scenes, through love and rejection in the act four, and finally madness and death in the opera's final act. In the opening scene, the singing demands a lyric soprano; by the last act, however, the role moves towards a dramatic soprano voice.

Bertha's ability to carry off the extended range of emotions and singing in this role suggests that, by the early 1920s, she had developed a mature operatic technique. Indeed, the length of her run with the Poznan Opera Company confirms the fact that, in the Polish market at least, she had become a true prima donna. How must Zofia have felt as she watched the young, unsophisticated girl she had taken under her wing nearly ten years before become incontrovertibly recognized as a mature, cultured star? Surely it was the achievement of this longtime goal that made Bertha feel that the time was finally ripe for a return to Canada. In retrospect, it seems unlikely that Bertha had any intention of severing her relationship with her new audiences in Poland, but she intended to at least seriously test the Canadian waters before she decided where her future really lay. Thus, leaving most of her dogs in the care of Zofia in Warsaw, Bertha set sail for North America in the summer of 1921.

The fact that Bertha chose to go back to Canada in 1921, immediately following her long run singing opera at the Poznan Great Theatre, suggests that she had always dreamed of arriving back in Canada riding on a wave of success as a genuine opera star. She had had many opportunities to go home since her first debut in Italy seven years before, but up to this point, she had always delayed. Clearly, she was waiting for the right moment—and that moment arrived when she had indisputable proof that she was a bona fide prima donna with a significant number of operatic appearances to her credit and a collection of consistently positive reviews to prove it. Finally, by the middle of 1921, she could confidently go home as a star.

Entr'acte —
The Myth in the Making

*O*ctober 27, 1921. *The Daily British Whig office, 306 King Street, Kingston, Ontario, Canada.* Bertha sips the hot coffee and settles into the armchair, absorbing the comforting heat of the nearby coal fire. She has come to this interview directly from the train station. She hasn't had a bite to eat since she left Toronto early that morning, so she is savouring this small refreshment. Over the rim of her cup, she sizes up the young journalist as he sizes her up in return. What should she tell him? she ponders. And what will he write? Unlikely to be the same thing, she expects.

She is not completely comfortable speaking to the press. She has had many reviews in European papers, but interviews there are not so common. But now she has her instructions from Isaac Suckling, her new Canadian manager, and she has to trust his judgement about what the Canadian press and its readers want to hear.

This is the first of two interviews Suckling has booked for Bertha today with the Kingston papers. They hope to get coverage in the evening editions in advance of tonight's concert. It will be her first concert in Canada in ten years, and she is tense. She is anxious to create a particular impression—to show off the European sophistication she has gleaned from her relationship with Zofia—while subtly implying that she hasn't lost touch with her roots in small-town Ontario.

"Can you tell us how you came to be in Europe before the war, Miss Crawford?"

The journalist has a copy of Suckling's advance publicity materials, but he wants to hear the story in Bertha's own words. Bertha takes another sip and begins to recount her training in England and Italy. It is tedious to have to retell this story so often, but she agrees with Isaac that it is necessary.

"You're going to have to establish your credentials as a highly trained musician," Isaac had suggested when they'd first met in September. "Don't expect that the public will know where you have been. People like me may have followed your progress in the musical journals, but most people will only remember your church work in Toronto back before the war. They have no idea what you have done since then."

Bertha's family has shared some of her European press clippings with Canadian journals like *Musical Canada* and *Saturday Night* over the years, so she has had some press coverage in Canada while she was away. But that had all dropped off after 1916, as Russia began its slide into chaos. Now Isaac has decided they need to tell her story, and tell it to as many newspapers as possible, if they are to generate good box office returns from her Canadian appearances.

Isaac thinks it should be a proper prima donna's story. In his view, the people want to hear about her being 'chosen' for training by the 'best in the business' and then becoming an 'overnight sensation' on a major opera stage. Basically, he wants her to recount how a little Canadian girl made good on the stages of Eastern Europe. And to be honest, it is the story she has always dreamed of coming home to tell. But now, however many times she tells it, she can't forget how far that tale seems to be from her reality.

But reality or not, *The Whig* journalist is ready for this story. Already he has jotted down in his little notebook some observations about her 'golden hair' and her 'long dark lashes,' her 'slender girlish figure' and her 'bright vivacious face.' He sees all the classic features of a heroine from a fairy tale.

"And where were you, exactly, when the war broke out?" he asks.

Bertha puts her mind back seven years and tries to recapture where she was and what she felt. She doesn't really want to talk about those experiences, but Isaac says they should play up the dramatic parts of her story, like how she 'escaped' from Warsaw with the Germans 'snapping at her heels.' Which isn't exactly how she remembers it. But she gives the journalist what he wants to hear.

"Well, there were guns, guns all day, and all night bombs dropping in the street. Oh, it was terrible." She waves her hand vaguely and assumes he will fill in the details.

"I understand you came to know the Russian Imperial family before the Revolution," the journalist says, leaning forward in his seat now.

This is the kind of juicy detail his readers will really want to hear about. The good burghers of Kingston who read *The Whig* have not lined up with Canadian labour in support of the Bolshevik cause. Indeed, many feel a romantic sympathy for the assassinated Imperial family and are fascinated with the details of their lives and tragic deaths.

"Make the most of your contact with the royals," Isaac had recommended back in Toronto. "The Canadian public can't get enough stories about royalty, and it all adds to your mystique."

"Mystique?" Bertha had asked, raising her eyebrows. Well, she would have to cloak her encounters with the Imperial family in quite a bit of mystique, because really, she only saw them at a few official functions, and mostly from a distance. It would be quite a stretch to say she 'knew' them.

However, she knows there are very few Canadians who got even that close to the Imperial family, so if that gives her some distinction, she will take it. She will do what is necessary to get the public to buy tickets. She hopes that these romantic stories will become less relevant after people have bought their tickets, and heard her sing. But until then, she and Isaac will use these tales to draw in the audience.

"Well," she addresses the attentive journalist, "I recall a charming evening at the Winter Palace, where I met the Grand Duchess . . ."

The journalist's pencil snaps to attention and marches rapidly across his notepad.

CHAPTER TWELVE –
Transatlantic Times,
1921–1923

Arriving in New York in 1921, Bertha must have been apprehensive about how she would be received after ten years abroad.

*C*oming home to Canada after ten tumultuous years in Europe could not have been a simple transition for Bertha. She must have envisaged her homecoming countless times in the decade since she'd left, but now that it was at hand, the anticipation must have been tinged with a considerable degree of apprehension. After leaving Poland at the end of July 1921, she drew out the journey over August with a visit to her old London friends the Weatherlys in Kensington before getting on a North American–bound ship in Liverpool. She arrived in New York on September 4, 1921.

In these days of air travel, it is easy to forget how slow the journey across the Atlantic would have been in 1921, and how much time a woman travelling alone by sea would have to think (and to work up her anxiety). Bertha was now set on an irreversible track towards her return to the Canadian stage, and one cannot help but suspect that she cared deeply about how she would be received there. Indeed, there are signs that as soon as she arrived, she was concerned about how she appeared to the public. When she filled out her immigration forms in New York—in the neat, rounded copperplate handwriting that she had learned at the Elmvale School—she slipped the 'h' back into Bertha, reverting to the Canadian spelling of her name. She also shaved five years off her true age of thirty-five—a common bit of vanity—and listed her occupation as a 'domestic,' an almost humorous subterfuge given that she was travelling first class. Probably she wanted to forestall any unscheduled meetings with the New York journalists who trolled the docks looking for celebrity 'stories' coming down the first-class gangplank. In any case, she intended to keep some control over her story and how it was told. For instance, she must have written home to her family from Poland many times in the last couple of years, but she didn't ask them to publicize her Polish successes; the stakes were too high for her to risk being portrayed in the Canadian papers as anything but the prima donna she strove to be.

Bertha began the formal process of crafting her image as a significant opera star with a visit to the Fifth Avenue studio of Herman Mishkin (1871–1948). An immigrant from the Russian Empire, Mishkin was the premier American photographer of opera stars of the day, and he had been specializing in studio portraits of top-of-the-line opera singers since he won the contract to be the official photographer for New York's Metropolitan Opera in 1908. Bertha would have hoped to benefit from his reputation for helping performers, who were generally more accustomed to conveying dramatic action across a large stage, to appear more refined before the camera lens. Newspaper copies of Mishkin's publicity photos of Bertha dressed for the role of Gilda in *Rigoletto* remain the only extant photos of Bertha in the costumes she wore on stage as a prima donna.

In New York in 1921, Bertha had her portrait taken by the top opera photographer of the day, Herman Mishkin. Here she is in costume as a boy for the final act of Rigoletto.

Mishkin captured a Bertha who looked quite different from the young woman who had left from Montréal before the war. She had been dying her hair blonde since she arrived back in Poland in 1919. She wore it short, in the shingled fashion so popular in the 1920s; this style also suited her hair, as it naturally curled around her face and fell into 'marcelled' waves without tedious time spent with the curling tongs. And she sounded different, too; one Canadian journalist would comment that she now spoke English with a very slight French accent.

What was the reunion like when Bertha arrived home to see her family after ten years? The big house on Parkside Drive, which John Crawford had bought around the time Bertha left for England, was a quieter home now. Her two youngest brothers were grown up and at work all day. Lucia and her husband had recently moved into their own Toronto home, as had her eldest brother, Howard, and his wife a couple of years before that. Although her parents had been in the prime of their lives when Bertha had left them, John and Maud—now sixty-three and fifty-eight, respectively—were moving towards old age by the time she returned.

John Crawford must have been happy (and relieved) to see Bertha again after so long—and certainly he would have felt more than just a little proud. Despite the turmoil of the war years, his daughter seemed to have found the success they had dreamed of together. While he probably wasn't a man given to bragging in the normal run of things, we can imagine John, after a Sunday service, letting slip to his friends in the church lobby about Bertha's appearances on the big stages of Warsaw and Poznan, or about her upcoming concerts in Canada. And what did Howard's and Lucia's children think when their legendary travelling aunt finally turned up in the flesh? Lucia's one-year-old daughter, Evelyn, certainly came to treasure a porcelain doll that her Aunt Bertha had brought her, as she passed it on to her own daughter a generation later.

Did the Crawford family think Bertha was home for good? Bertha was certainly thinking about spending more time in Canada; she had been working to make this possible for years. But the fact that she had left all but two of her beloved dogs in Poland suggests she had always had plans to return to Warsaw. Still, one reporter went so far as to suggest that she had "had enough of Eastern Europe" and would be singing in Canada and the United States for the next few seasons. To be sure, Bertha would have been well aware of the kind of attention that Canadian artists returning from overseas could draw, and she must have hoped to turn that interest into more than just a short-term advantage. We may never know how long she really planned to stay—but it seems highly unlikely that she expected this homecoming to Canada to be a permanent return.

It must have been gratifying for Bertha to discover how many old friends still remembered her. Soon after she returned, Edward Schuch, her old voice teacher, arranged a special tea for her to meet—and sing with—his new generation of students. And Marietta Ladell, the artist she had gone on her first tour with in 1907, held a luncheon in honour of Bertha and two other singers. Even Flora Eaton, who by then was Lady Eaton, invited Bertha to a social event at her home. Friends and colleagues were pleased to welcome her back—and, more than that, they seemed pleased to welcome her back as a bona fide prima donna.

Was Bertha concerned about whether she could still please Canadian audiences, which were so unlike the Polish audiences she was now used to? Did she feel some culture shock as she took stock of how different Toronto was from Warsaw? The Toronto that Bertha returned to in 1921 had grown by a third, to a population of more than half a million, but it was still not much more than half the size of Warsaw. Ninety percent of Torontonians were Canadian- or British-born, and they were predominantly Protestant. What is more, after years of lobbying by the Protestant temperance movement, Ontario now had prohibition. Did Toronto society seem bland and narrow compared with the cosmopolitan population of Warsaw, where Bertha had socialized with expatriates from many countries, had lived and worked alongside Catholics, and had performed with many of the greatest Jewish musicians of her day?

On the other hand, Toronto was much less class-bound than Warsaw, where Bertha's Polish friends held fast to their titles and positions. And, as a woman, Bertha probably appreciated that the gender divide in Canada had narrowed since the pre-war years. For instance, in 1920, Toronto had elected its first woman councillor, Constance Hamilton. What is more, during Bertha's trip home, she may well have taken the opportunity to vote, joining all other Canadian women who voted for the first time in a federal election on December 6, 1921. However, she would not have met as many professional women in Toronto as she knew in Warsaw, where, in addition to women musicians, she had female friends who were doctors, lawyers, journalists, and artists.

From a musical perspective, 1920s Toronto offered a serious musician like Bertha only one real option for performing, and it wasn't in grand opera. While some aspects of the Toronto entertainment scene had changed radically since she left, others had remained much the same. Supported by the Protestant hierarchy, choral groups and chamber music ensembles were still the mainstay of the Toronto musical establishment, and the recently defunct Toronto Symphony Orchestra was about to be revived. But while there was an amateur Toronto Operatic Chorus that gave occasional concert presentations of full operas, there was still no permanent opera company—and nothing close to the financial interests necessary to subsidize one. Groups like the Toronto Conservatory and Hart House Theatre were struggling to build a tradition of local opera performance in Toronto, but the already limited market for grand opera was shrinking, being squeezed from several directions.

The biggest musical competition came from the growing popularity of jazz music. In the previous few years, American jazz records began to be sold in Canada, and foreign and local performers were experimenting with the new sound. The Toronto music critics who covered classical music in the 1920s were very uneasy about the influence of jazz and were not sure whether it had a place in venues for so-called serious music like Massey Hall. But the general public knew what it liked, and the growth of jazz was unstoppable. At the same time, on the theatrical front, everyone had learned to love an outing to see the moving pictures on the 'silver screen.' Where the 1912 Toronto City Directory had listed about twenty theatres, the 1921 edition named almost a hundred—and virtually all of those new theatres were primarily venues for silent movies. What's more, the actors who had triumphed in these silent films were now international stars whose fame far exceeded that of the previous generation of prima donnas. The silent movies that Toronto's own Mary Pickford made in the early 1920s were shown around the world, and some grossed more than one million dollars. Inevitably, the gains of these new entertainment businesses were the losses of opera.

There did, however, remain a significant audience for recitals by opera singers, and a steady flow of international stars stopped in Toronto during their tours. Bertha knew that a recital—or a recital tour—would be the best way to capitalize on her operatic skills in Canada. The fact that, up to this point, Bertha had resisted publicizing her considerable post-war European success suggests that she knew this return tour needed to be carefully staged. She also knew that, if she was to be taken seriously on the Canadian stage as an internationally successful prima donna, she should be represented by a manager of some repute who would 'reintroduce' her to North American audiences and arrange her recitals. When she had lived in Toronto as a young woman, she had not had the kind of career that merited an ongoing relationship with a professional manager—so it would be a sign of how far she had come that she no longer dealt with the details herself. Moreover, after ten years of being out of touch with the Canadian public, she needed the support of a manager who had his finger on the pulse of current audiences.

For the winter of 1921–1922, Bertha put herself under the management of the preeminent impresario of classical music in Toronto, Isaac Edward Suckling (1862–1938). Suckling's feet were planted firmly in the heart of the

Toronto music business. His father had founded a music publishing and sales business and piano store, which had flourished on Yonge Street for about twenty years beginning in the mid-1870s. Starting out by selling concert tickets through the family music store, and then underwriting and promoting concerts, Isaac Suckling became the first manager at Massey Hall in the 1890s. He then worked as an independent music manager for several years, managing the Canadian appearances of some of the biggest international opera stars of the era, including sopranos like Adelina Patti, Lillian Nordica, and Nellie Melba. After a fifteen-year break, during which he worked as an agent for the Canadian Pacific Railway, he returned to the concert management business in 1919. By the 1920s, he was one of the top concert managers in Toronto, if not the country. If Bertha wanted to return to Toronto stages as a prima donna, then Suckling was the obvious choice to act as her manager.

Suckling was planning a series of fifteen recitals in Massey Hall over the winter of 1921–1922 featuring artists with prestigious international reputations, and Bertha was the only artist he booked to appear in two of these recitals. Bertha's name was given equal billing in Suckling's advertising for the series with international stars like the expatriate Canadian tenor who sang with the Metropolitan Opera in New York, Edward Johnson; the Italian soprano Amelita Galli-Curci; the New York Symphony Orchestra under the direction of Walter Damrosch; the Polish-American pianist Josef Hofmann; the Polish violinist Paul Kochanski; the English contralto Clara Butt; the French soprano Emma Calve; and the Lithuanian-Jewish violinist Jascha Heifetz. Clearly, Bertha's Canadian career was being re-launched within the premier recital series of the season.

Suckling thought strategically about how to make the most of Bertha's return to Toronto as a long-absent daughter of the city. He knew all too well that Canadian audiences suffered from an inferiority complex that could leave them sceptical about their own musical artists. Indeed, Suckling had experienced some difficulty getting local audiences to turn up to see the internationally renowned—but Ontario-born and raised—tenor Edward Johnson when he had made his first return appearances in Canada the year before. So, initially, Suckling appealed to Torontonians' subtle snobbery by reintroducing Bertha as a member of 'society.' In the first weeks after she arrived, he accompanied Bertha to a recital by Edward Johnson, to a performance by Polish violinist

Paul Kochanski, and to a production of the opera *Tosca* by Antonio Scotti's touring opera company, thereby ensuring that she was seen about town and was mentioned in Toronto's society columns in the company of prominent socialites from the latest Blue Book.

Then Suckling set out to establish, in the public's mind, that Bertha's dramatic story was an authentic example of the established legend of the prima donna. He circulated publicity materials widely and sent Bertha to do personal interviews, so that at least seven newspapers in Toronto, Kingston, Guelph, and Peterborough published articles detailing Bertha's adventures in Eastern Europe over the previous decade. Suckling and the Canadian journalists worked together, almost subconsciously, to fit Bertha's story into the standard mould. Using quotations from Bertha to supplement the narrative provided in the publicity brochure, the stories followed a similar pattern and corresponded with the expected trajectory of the North American opera singer as she rises to fame in Europe.

In the best example of this, Hector Charlesworth of *Saturday Night* wrote fulsomely that Bertha was "probably the most distinguished coloratura soprano produced by Canada within the present century;" he then worked his way through her early church success in Toronto, her specialized training in Europe, her debut in Italy, and her sudden rise to fame in Russia, where she "at once obtained an engagement at the immense . . . People's Opera House" and then had a multinational career based on "successes . . . in cities which are musical by instinct and ruthless in rejecting the incapable singer." The Canadian public was not expected to be interested in a complex story that included ups and downs and compromises. While Bertha's real life had different ingredients from the simple myth, the journalists—if not Bertha herself—glossed over these details and emphasized instead the predicted triumphs on the stage and the meetings with royalty. To Suckling's credit, the result appears to have been considerable interest in Bertha's long-overdue return to Canada.

Having carefully prepared an audience by melding Bertha's story with the legend of the successful prima donna, Suckling sent her off to test out her repertoire on a receptive and sophisticated small-town audience. Her first recital in Canada after her ten-year absence was in Grant Hall on the campus of Queen's University in Kingston. Her maturity as a musician was set off by the participation of two up-and-coming young men: a twenty-two-year-old baritone, Douglas Stanbury, who had also studied with Bertha's teacher Otto Morando; and a twenty-year-old violinist, Harry Adaskin. A glowing review in *The Kingston Standard* declared that Bertha had "appeared at ease on the stage and her singing was nothing short of wonderful, her clear rich voice sounding . . . with bell-like clarity," and that "she had entirely captivated the audience." But the appreciation and good reviews in Kingston did not completely calm her nerves about appearing before her hometown audience in Toronto after so long.

In her first concert in Canada in ten years, Bertha appeared alongside the young violinist Harry Adaskin at Queen's University in Kingston.

If being recognized as a prima donna by her hometown audience really mattered to Bertha, then her performance on November 9, 1921 may have been the most important event of her career. For while Suckling saw the prima donna legend primarily as a marketing ploy, on some level Bertha must have still believed in the dream. Deliberately creating suspense, Suckling arranged that, for this first re-appearance in Toronto, Bertha would sing just one opera aria in Massey Hall in the middle of a concert by the extremely popular New York Symphony Orchestra and its celebrity German-American conductor, Walter Damrosch (1862–1950). Her nervousness—not apparent in Kingston, but noted in Massey Hall—suggests that she cared much more about recognition during this brief hometown appearance than at her full-length recital in Kingston two weeks before. Was it not a huge gamble for Bertha, to invest so much of her hope in this one short appearance? Would her hometown audience once and for all crown her as a star? In this ephemeral moment of return, so much could go wrong. But this moment was integral to completing her dream of becoming a prima donna. It was the culmination of the triumphant return home that she had been working towards for ten years.

It is not surprising that Bertha felt nervous as she took the stage at Massey Hall. She was certainly facing a sceptical audience of discerning tastes. All of Toronto's top society names were represented, from the Lieutenant Governor on down. Even more importantly, the most significant music critics were there. E.R. Parkhurst from *The Globe* was in his seventies and approaching the end of his career, but he was still bullishly optimistic about Canadian talent. Sitting nearby was the next generation of more sophisticated writers already at the peak of their careers: Hector Charlesworth of *Saturday Night* and Augustus Bridle of *The Toronto Daily Star* and *Musical Canada*. Augustus Bridle (1868–1952), a friend and colleague of both Parkhurst and Charlesworth, had been a music critic since Bertha's early days in Toronto. Like Charlesworth, Bridle was an advocate of cultural nationalism who believed in promoting Canadian performing arts and artists as a bulwark against the pressure of American commercial interests in music and theatre. While Bridle was inclined to support Canadian artists, he and his colleagues hadn't seen Bertha perform since she was singing in church ten years before. They were well prepared for the possibility that, despite the glowing advanced publicity they had all participated in, she might turn out to have overreached herself. Charlesworth spoke for them all when he suggested in his review that he had braced himself for disillusionment that evening.

Bertha was determined to surprise these critics. She had to wait while the orchestra played through its opening number, Rachmaninov's Second Symphony in E Minor, which ran forty-eight minutes long. *The Evening Telegram* reported that, by the time she came on, she was "manifestly nervous, but if she let her nervousness have any effect on her singing no one noticed it." She came on stage looking splendid, wearing "a charming frock of silver cloth, the bodice, front and back panels were green and silver sequin with flounces at the side of green tulle, caught with a jewelled girdle." She had a green jewelled bandeau around her blonde hair, a matching bracelet and pendant of emeralds, and silver shoes. Without a doubt, she captured the full glamour of all those prima donnas of old. Her voice was confident as she launched into "Caro Nome" from *Rigoletto*, an aria she had been singing for years. This time, she drew on all the lessons she had accumulated through ten years on the European stage.

The critics agreed in advance that "Caro Nome" was an admirable test of coloratura technique, and they were immediately impressed as Bertha began singing. This was not the performance of a minor church soloist. As he sat through the aria, Parkhurst was delighted with how she "excelled in vocal flights and in the exact adjustment of the intervals of the trill." Bridle marvelled at her "almost perfect intonation . . . wonderful breath control and versatility of technique" and was charmed by her "very engaging personality on stage." And Charlesworth noted with satisfaction that her voice "has a subtle vibrancy and carrying power that fills every corner of the vast auditorium without the slightest sense of strain." A reporter for *The Mail and Empire* thought her voice possessed the "sparkle of a diamond." Their praise went far beyond the pat encouragement offered to a Canadian who had made a good effort. Bertha had earned the accolades in her own right, and the reaction of the audience reinforced it.

Parkhurst described how, after she finished singing, the audience sat "thoroughly astonished" before erupting into a "perfect furore of applause." In Bridle's words, "the crowd were captivated" and gave "a sincere ovation for a highly gifted Canadian." Bertha was delighted and turned immediately to thank Damrosch. She left the stage, but had to return to acknowledge the applause several times and receive six large bouquets from the audience. Finally, the audience quieted as she sang her prepared encore, "The Shadow Song" from the opera *Dinorah*, which includes a duet with a flute. Again she was recalled three times by the sustained applause, but she claimed she had no music for a further encore and withdrew with apologies. Had Suckling told her that the key was to leave the audience wanting more? While the critics all managed to come up with their own adjectives, they could only agree that the brief appearance had been a triumph. For Charlesworth it was a "decisive triumph," while Parkhurst felt it was an "incontestable and brilliant triumph." For Bridle, it was "as sincere and as well-deserved a triumph as ever could have been accorded to a musical artist anywhere." Bertha would not have disputed Charlesworth's conclusion that she had had "a most triumphant home coming!" No prima donna could have asked for more.

Bertha's challenge now was to make the most out of this initial success. In December, she received further recognition of her new status in Canada as a serious musician when she got an invitation from Toronto's Women's Musical

Club to give a recital as part of their annual series. The Club, whose members were mainly musicians married to well-off bankers and industrialists, had been organizing exclusive chamber music concerts since the turn of the century. The Club's musical tastes were completely classical, and, before the war, when Bertha was singing mainly church music and sentimental ballads, she had not had the repertoire to be invited to sing for its members. However, her appearance singing Italian arias with the New York Symphony Orchestra in Massey Hall now put her in the category of classical musicians with an international reputation who could be enjoyed by even the most discriminating society matrons. For her recital for the large audience of society women, which took place in a hall at Jenkins Antique and Art Galleries on Grenville Street, Bertha dressed the part of an international star. *The Globe*'s social column noted that Bertha wore a slinky black satin dress with a wired Spanish lace overskirt and a black hat trimmed with feathers, although it neglected to mention her program.

Confident from her reception in Toronto, in January 1922, Bertha decided to test the waters in Montréal and sing for Canada's most famous opera patron, Brigadier General Frank Stephen Meighen. After Meighen had folded his sponsorship of the Montréal Opera Company in 1913, he had moved his resources to support a new musical project: a band formed under the auspices of the Canadian Grenadier Guards, the Montréal regiment that he had led during the First World War. After the war, the Guards built up a strong reputation as a concert band with a repertoire of classical music unusual for a military band. In the early 1920s, the band gave an annual series of winter concerts at His Majesty's Theatre in Montréal, where Meighen underwrote the appearance of Canadian and foreign solo artists. For the 1922 season, the band committed to invite only Canadian soloists, and Bertha was one of these artists.

She made her Montréal debut with the Canadian Grenadier Guards Band on January 29, 1922. With the exception of opening with "Caro Nome" in Italian, her other program numbers were all songs in French by Saint-Saens, Paradies, Meyerbeer, and Cesak. In her first ever performance before an audience predominantly made up of native French speakers, there were mixed reviews of her abilities in that language. *Le Canada Musical* said her voice was very agreeable, but her French pronunciation so bad that one could not understand her words. *Le Patrie*, on the other hand, commended her excellent diction in French. Overall, her performance was well received, but the Montréal press could not match the rapture generated in her hometown papers. This remained the only appearance she ever made in Québec.

Could Bertha have looked up Zofia's son John while she was in the province? John had returned to Canada in 1920, when he began a five-year stint with the Québec-based pulp and paper industrialists, The Laurentide Company, as a teacher in their private school in Grand-Mère. It is impossible to know if he met up with Bertha in Canada, but there is no evidence to suggest that their paths ever crossed. In any event, John was to spend most of the rest of his life in Canada, far from the reach of his mother or any of her friends.

During February and March 1922, Bertha spent six weeks in New York. Was she hoping that she might cash in on her successful appearance with Damrosch and the New York Symphony Orchestra in Toronto to get a similar engagement with them in New York? In December 1921, a brief mention in *The New York Times* alluded to this possibility. Unfortunately for Bertha, whatever her hopes for this trip were, there is no evidence that any major opportunities materialized for her in New York, which was probably a disappointment. Perhaps she chose to put off a minor New York debut in the hope of making a more major appearance after her reputation was fully re-established in Canada.

Undeterred, Bertha returned to Ontario in time for a five-city tour organized by Suckling for the spring of 1922, to take advantage of the strong reviews and excitement they had generated in the province the previous fall. The tour was anchored on her appearing, once again, in one of Suckling's Massey Hall recitals, but he bracketed that appearance with recitals in Peterborough and Hamilton before, and Owen Sound and Guelph afterwards. For this mini-tour, Bertha worked with two Canadian accompanists—flautist Daniel F. Dineen (1876–1926) and piano accompanist Ralph Angell—in a program designed to show the full breadth of her well-developed talents. Bertha used Dineen's flute accompaniment to great effect to accentuate her vocal performance in songs like "The Shadow Song," "The Nightingale" by Alyabyev, and "Moon Dear" by Manuel Klein, as well as Bellini's aria "Qui la Voce." Two flute solos by Dineen—"Les Diamants de la Couronne" by Daniel Auber and

"Cracovienne" by Tulsee [sic]—added breadth to a program otherwise dominated by vocal numbers. Ralph Angell also interjected a solo piano piece by Liszt among the songs.

Bertha made sure that all of her programs in Canada showed the full range of her singing styles. Defining herself first and foremost as a specialist in Italian opera, she opened (and often closed) her performances with one or more popular Italian opera arias, which allowed her to show off her finesse in coloratura technique. After the opening group of Italian arias, her second group of songs was often in French, with favourites being "Le Petite Rose" by Cesak, "Le Papillion" by Foudrain, and "The Polonaise" from Thomas's opera *Mignon*. Reminding the audience of the breadth of her travels, she might include a group of songs in Russian, usually her favourites by Rimsky-Korsakov, Gretchaninov, and Alyabyev. Often the final group of songs for the evening would be art songs in English.

By performing American art songs, Bertha was making a point of presenting a parallel identity to her guise as a European opera singer, essentially reclaiming her roots on the Canadian side of the Atlantic. She had used songs like these during the war to represent herself as a North American to European audiences. When she was home in Canada, however, Bertha's repertoire of art songs served the distinct purpose of putting her in the avant-garde camp of Canadian cultural nationalists, represented most famously in the visual arts by painters like the Group of Seven and Emily Carr, who looked for indigenous inspiration in the Canadian natural environment. However, given the very limited number of art songs written by Canadians about Canada, Bertha had to resort to American songwriters to express her feelings for her native land. She continued to use songs by members of the Indianist Movement, such as Charles Wakefield Cadman and Thurlow Lieurance. She often performed songs like Cavanass and Lieurance's "By the Waters of Minnetonka" and Cadman's "The Moon Drops Low" and "From the Land of the Sky Blue Water." She also frequently included songs written by American composers on the subject of nature, like Richard Hageman's "Nature's Holiday," Roland Farley's "The Night Wind," and Louis Campbell-Tipton's "The Crying of the Water." It was, however, very difficult for her to use her repertoire to make a firm statement about being Canadian, mainly because there were almost no Canadian composers in her era writing art songs for soprano soloists.

In fact, during the Hamilton recital of the short five-city tour, Bertha sang the only song by a Canadian composer included in any of her Canadian recitals in the 1920s—and that was a generous condescension, as "That Heart of Gold" by Bertie Aikin-Green was a parlour song written for amateurs to sing at home. Alberta 'Bertie' Aikin-Green (1873–1924) was a Hamilton composer who published at least eight songs between 1916 and 1922. Publishing sheet music was big business in Canada in the era when the parlour piano was the primary source of family entertainment, and a popular song could sell tens of thousands of copies. Stylistically, however, virtually all Canadian songwriters drew on the same techniques found in popular songs of the day from Britain and the United States, so while the lyrics often had a strong Canadian theme, songs like Aikin-Green's did not represent a distinctly Canadian sound. Most of Aikin-Green's songs fell into the popular category of patriotic songs, but her most recently published song, "That Heart of Gold," was a simple sentimental song. In recognition of Aikin-Green's help in arranging the Hamilton date on the 1922 tour, Bertha included Aikin-Green's latest composition in her Hamilton program. Aikin-Green was obviously thrilled to have her song performed by an artist of Bertha's stature, for she subsequently published the song with the tagline "Sung with Great Success by Miss Bertha Crawford!" It was the last song in Aikin-Green's song publishing career, as she died two years later, in 1924, at the age of fifty.

When Bertha appeared in Massey Hall in the middle of this spring 1922 tour, Toronto audiences were finally given a chance to hear her sing a wide range of songs. Sharing the stage with Alberto Salvi, an Italian harpist based in New York, she presented herself in the height of fashion as befitted an established star. Her dress was an elegant pale pink crepe de chine affair, with the lace-edged hem cut in deep points; its bodice was accented with artificial flowers and flashed with crystals, silver, and net. And while the reviews were all excellent, her talent was now expected—even taken for granted—by Toronto's music critics. Indeed, their write-ups no longer suffused with the delighted surprise that had met her earlier Toronto appearance in the fall of 1921, though they were glowing nonetheless. E.R. Parkhurst from *The Globe*, who had attended all the big recitals that season, described Bertha's recital as one of Suckling's "most brilliant successes." Bertha, he wrote, "showed herself a mistress of the coloratura, the brilliant passages of her music being delivered with rare, clear-cut definition and purity of voice. She astonished her hearers by the perfection of a long sustained trill, proceeding from pianissimo to forte, and then dying away almost to the vanishing point, and then renewed with fresh brilliancy." The reviewer from *The Toronto Daily Star* remarked on "her conservation of vocal energy and wonderful voice control" and on "the same versatility of her technique which has resulted in the perfect blending of voice and music." *The Toronto Evening Telegram* compared her favourably with the Italian soprano Amelia Galli-Curci, who had appeared the previous fall, saying that Bertha sang faultlessly and with greater intellectual appeal than Galli-Curci. *Saturday Night* said her voice "possesses remarkable resonance and fills a great auditorium with the utmost ease."

By the time she reached Guelph at the end of this mini-tour in mid-April 1922, Bertha had already heard from the directors of the Poznan Opera Company in Poland, inviting her for another round of guest appearances. Did the possibility of returning to Poland after only eight months in Canada come as a surprise to Bertha? Or had she already realized that the best way to maintain momentum in her career now was to repeatedly play on the novelty and mystique of being 'just returned from North America' in Poland and 'recently back from Europe' in Canada? Certainly, it was clear that there were no opportunities to appear in full opera performances in Canada, although the market for recitals was promising.

So, after completing the mini-tour in Owen Sound and Guelph, and after having committed to another recital with Suckling in the fall, Bertha left Canada via New York and London to return to Poland. Invigorated by the potential for success on both sides of the Atlantic, she was embarking on a new strategy to build a transatlantic profile by keeping a foothold on the stages of the two countries. It was a plan that risked leaving her disoriented in both places as she repeatedly moved between two very different worlds, but it would maximize her earnings, her career success, and—perhaps most importantly—her artistic mystique. In addition, it must have pleased both her family and Zofia to know that they would all be seeing her regularly as she split her time between Toronto and Warsaw.

POZNAN — Teatr Wielki

On her return to Poland in 1922, Bertha was again invited to be a guest soloist at the Poznan Opera.

What did it feel like to be arriving back in Warsaw after three-quarters of a year in Canada? Stepping down from the cab in front of 7 aleja Szucha, did Bertha sense that this arrival—rather than her return to Toronto—was the more genuine homecoming? Did she have a quiet moment to reflect about whether she was more comfortable in Zofia's house than she was with her own family—before she was overwhelmed by the excited barking of all those dogs, that is? Was it something of a shock to realize how familiar it felt to step back into the upper-class world of the Baroness after so many months with her middle-class parents? Did she feel shy when she greeted her long-time patron after their lengthiest separation in ten years? Or did they just pick up where they had left off the summer before?

Bertha's new transatlantic strategy was already working when she arrived in Poznan in time for a May 17, 1922 production of *Rigoletto*. The semi-anonymous Dr. W.P., writing for the *Kurjer Poznanski* (Poznan Courier), described Bertha as "the well-known coloratura soprano" who was an excellent example for Poznan audiences of what "the better foreign theatres have," for "her example is a demonstration of what the cultivation of the rational school can do with the voice." Bertha sang at least five times in May and June 1922 with the Poznan Opera, and at least once with the Warsaw Philharmonic Orchestra.

After a summer based with Zofia in Warsaw and travelling to Poznan for opera engagements, Bertha returned to her parents in Toronto in the fall of 1922. On October 17, she made her third appearance in Massey Hall under Suckling's management. This time, she shared the Massey Hall stage with a Welsh pianist, Marie Novello. By this point, Bertha was a confirmed transatlantic star, so if that had been her goal in returning to Poland for the summer, then her gamble had paid off. *Saturday Night* introduced Bertha as "freshly returned from a sea [sic] after several months of operatic triumphs in Warsaw and other cities." Augustus Bridle at *The Toronto Star Weekly* was again effusive about Bertha's "perfectly astonishing vocal capabilities for coloratura work." He pointed out how the fact "[t]hat she can charm her own friends in public in the city of her birth is a high tribute to her remarkable achievement in vocal art." Edward Wodeson wrote in *The Evening Telegram* that "The warmth of her reception left no doubt as to the place Miss Bertha Crawford holds in the hearts of musical Toronto."

Back in Canada in the fall of 1922, Bertha's manager, Isaac Suckling, paired her with another international star, Welsh pianist Marie Novello.

There is no question that Bertha had found a warm place in the hearts of her Canadian audience. However, as so often before, she seems to have been driven to look for something more—preferably a starring role on the opera stage. Indeed, she would not be able to completely fulfill the prima donna dream until she had sung in a full opera in North America. And so, in January 1923, for the first and only time in her career, she gambled on a contract to sing in opera in the United States. A rather disorganized but enthusiastic opera company existed in the American capital under the direction of a Canadian expatriate, Edouard Albion (1887–1972).

Albion came from Port Stanley, Ontario, but had spent most of his life in the United States. After a short and not very exalted career singing opera, he married and settled in Washington, DC, where he taught singing. In 1919, he established the fledgling Washington Opera Company. Most of his musicians and singers were amateurs, and he himself never took a salary. But Washington could summon keen audiences, salted with national politicians and foreign diplomats, which gave his company a certain cachet beyond its modest abilities.

Albion was a dedicated visionary and a problem solver who was undeterred by minor setbacks, and Bertha offered a solution to a casting challenge he faced in 1923. The company performed intermittently, hiring guest soloists when it could, sometimes from Europe but often Americans. It had been idle for more than a year when Albion decided to take on a couple of performances of *Rigoletto*. He secured a German baritone, Joseph Schwartz, for the role of Rigoletto, but his first choice for Gilda, Luella Melius, fell through, and they scrambled to find a replacement. Albion's connections in Canada must have suggested Bertha, for she came in at the last moment. But if Bertha was a lifesaver for Albion's production, then Albion was also throwing Bertha a line at a time when her North American opera options were drifting away.

It must have felt strange to Bertha to be arriving as a relative unknown in Washington when she was already recognized as a celebrity in Poland. Be that as it may, Bertha knew how to look the part of the glamourous international guest star. Mishkin's photos of Bertha in costume, dressed for her role as Gilda, were used by several of the Washington papers. For the first acts of the opera, she wore a stylized Renaissance costume that matched the sixteenth-century setting of the plot. The dress had simple straight lines with a full-length pale satin overdress in two panels, each bordered with decorative braid. The long back panel trailed along the floor and was joined to the shorter front panel at the sides by criss-crossed strings of beads, revealing a dark satin underskirt beneath. The neckline was modestly scooped, and beaded cap sleeves left her arms and the edge of her shoulders bare, suggesting an innocent young girl. On her head she wore the long blonde wig that was de rigueur for the part, and she topped it off with a little beaded cap that matched the beads on her dress. In the last act, where Gilda appears *en travesti* (in disguise as a man), Bertha's dark tunic had long sleeves ending in pointed, lace-trimmed cuffs that only reached to her knees, which were hidden (or were they revealed?) by dark tights. Over the tunic she wore a cape, and most of her hair was hidden by a boyish cap trimmed with a dangling white plume. It was a costume that was no more revealing than a flapper's dress in the 1920s, but it would have been scandalous only a decade before, in the pre-war era of floor-length gowns.

Bertha must have been optimistic when she agreed to this contract to play Gilda, even though she probably knew that the quality of the company's productions varied greatly and was unlikely to compare favourably with professional companies in Europe. Still, she must have hoped that a successful debut in North American opera might lead to better engagements. Bertha sang well, and, although her second performance was less impressive than her first due to a cold, the press was kind. Furthermore, she made the most of the opportunity to sing for a Washington audience by scheduling a recital on the following Friday evening. The wife of the Polish Consul even invited 125 guests to a tea in her honour. Overall, however, the experience must have been depressing, as it would have reminded her that what she had achieved in Europe could not be recreated in North America. Indeed, after finally getting an opportunity to sing in a full opera production in North America, the standard must have fallen disappointingly short of what she had experienced in Petrograd and Poznan. An amateur company like Albion's could never afford the investment in costumes, sets, and musicians that the government-subsidized companies in Europe could. Furthermore, in comparison with the avant-garde staging put on by Dolzycki in Poznan, Albion's traditional production would have seemed pedestrian. If this was the best that North America could offer her, then she might do better to stay in the sophisticated music market in Poland. Bertha hadn't yet abandoned her plan to play both sides of the Atlantic, but her experience in Washington emphasized the limitations of this strategy.

After returning to Ontario briefly to sing in Ottawa and Hamilton, she headed to New York in May to catch a steamer back to Poland. In the week before the ship sailed, however, Bertha stopped in Ridgewood, Brooklyn to meet up with her friend, Dr. Violet Berger, who was booked on the same ship. Violet took Bertha down to WHN, the Ridgewood Radiophone station, where, on a Friday evening, Bertha stood before a microphone for the first time and sang some songs for an unseen radio audience of New Yorkers. It was her first taste of this new technology, which would play an important role in her career over the next few years. Certainly, it must have been an eye-opening experience to realize how many more Americans she reached from the small studio as compared to the big stage in Washington.

Back in Poland and staying again with Zofia, Bertha glowed with her North American aura, as the *Kurjer Warszawski* (Warsaw Courier) presented her as "recently returned from America, where she had real shining artistic triumphs in New York, Washington, Toronto, and other cities in the United States and Canada." As her transatlantic strategy fed her star persona in the press, did she also begin to receive star treatment around the theatre and on the street? Were there always flowers in her dressing room? Were there fans lining up for autographs, or photographers catching her out walking her dogs? And could she leverage this transatlantic star quality into more work?

Keeping up her profile, she took a booking to appear with the Warsaw Philharmonic under a newly appointed conductor, Grzegorz Fitelberg (1879–1953). Fitelberg himself was just back from Russia, and he was probably familiar with Bertha's work there from his time in Petrograd in 1915. Reviews of the recital suggest that in Poland, like in Toronto, Bertha was increasingly appreciated for her ability to combine technically superlative singing with a warm connection with her audience. *Gazeta Warszawsaka* (Warsaw Gazette) said, "The admirers of masterly vocal techniques ... enjoyed great delights while listening . . .", and the learned composer and editor of *The Musical Quarterly*, Felicjan Szopski (1865–1939), wrote in the *Kurjer Warszawski* (Warsaw Courier) that, "Miss Crawford touches with her song the chords of deeper feeling in the bosom of the audience."

In one particularly high-profile engagement, in July 1923, Bertha was hired by Mlynarski to sing with the Warsaw Opera Company opposite the fifty-year-old Polish bass Adam Didur (1874–1946). Didur, who had sung with Mlynarski at the Warsaw Opera from 1899 to 1903, was, by the 1920s, mainly singing with the Metropolitan Opera in New York. However, using a similar strategy to Bertha, he often crossed the Atlantic in the summer off-season to travel to Poland, where he was adored as one of Poland's most successful international stars. The popular press credited him with being able to breathe life, and even exuberance, into the most hackneyed roles of the classic Italian repertoire. In July 1923, Bertha sang Rosina in *The Barber of Seville* with Didur as Don Basilo. If she had not been at the peak of Polish fame before, then appearing opposite this celebrated national son was confirmation that she was at the top in Poland now.

Nevertheless, while Bertha came back to continued artistic success and celebrity in Poland, she also came back to an extremely unstable Polish economy. The Polish tax collection system was underdeveloped, and tax avoidance was a national tradition. As the government printed more money to cover the resulting deficit, hyperinflation took over the economy. However much Bertha earned, the value of any local savings she had was eaten away. The crisis was reaching a peak by the fall of 1923, when, for example, the newsstand price of *Bluszcz,* a Polish women's magazine that Bertha would have read from time to time, was in the process of rising from 1,500 marks a copy in February to the 500,000 marks it would reach by the end of December. The only recourse for most people was to turn whatever cash they earned into a useable product or foreign currency as fast as possible, although this rapid spending only increased the pressure on the currency.

As Bertha was still fortunate to be living as a guest of Zofia, she was in a better position than most. But everyone in Poland was feeling the pinch of inflation, and it cannot have been easy to keep up the appearance of an international star, dressed in the most fashionable gowns and being seen in the most fashionable places. Bertha, however, had options. She probably could have simply relied on Zofia's backing, but, having worked so hard to have at least some independence as a musician, that would have been an embarrassing step backwards. And so the uncontrolled inflation must have been an additional incentive for Bertha to perform again in North America, where she could continue to accumulate stable dollars while keeping afloat her transatlantic reputation.

In what now looks like a last attempt to scale the peak of success on the New York stage, Bertha contracted with an experienced New York concert manager, Antonia Sawyer (1856–1941), to arrange a New York debut in the fall of 1923. Sawyer had been a singer herself, working mostly as a church soloist and in recitals, but she retired from singing and became a manager to musicians in 1911. It was an unusual role for a woman to take on in her time, but she felt it was the best way to use her experience in music to support herself and her invalid husband. She was both well organized and matronly, and it turned out she had a talent for taming the egos of sensitive artists while helping them to earn good money for themselves (and for her agency). She came to specialize in managing the North American tours of musicians who were based in Europe. After ten years in the business, Sawyer had earned a national reputation and was a member of the Board of Directors of the National Musical Managers' Association. If anyone could help Bertha to achieve this last mark of prima donna success—that is, to gain artistic acclaim and fame on the New York stage—it was Sawyer.

Bertha probably took advantage of a standard management arrangement with Sawyer. Sawyer is known to have charged between fifteen and twenty percent of her clients' gross concert earnings for her services, which was probably typical for the industry. In return, she arranged engagements with venue managers, negotiating a set fee or a percentage of the gross taking (with or without a minimum guarantee); she also arranged publicity, made the travel arrangements, collected the earnings from the concerts, and forwarded the artists their portion of these earnings. Sawyer also offered a personal touch; for instance, she would meet her international clients as they came down the gangplank at the New York docks, and she often accompanied them on tour. She could provide counsel on how to structure a successful recital career, and she even gave fashion advice on appropriate dress to meet the expectations of the American public. For an artist like Bertha, based for so long in Europe and with few professional contacts in the United States, services like these were well worth the agent's fees.

Being met at the docks by Sawyer must have made Bertha feel like 'a somebody' and helped to soothe her inevitable qualms about this all-important appearance. She could hardly have been expecting anything to top the affectionate reception she had received during her first return appearance at Massey Hall in Toronto two years before, but she must have been at least hoping for a strong response from the New York audience, which would be the ultimate definition of the successful return of a prima donna. Bertha's New York debut recital was booked in the Aeolian Hall, a popular venue for debut recitals and the building where Sawyer had offices on the fourteenth floor. Bertha appeared there on the evening of November 27, 1923, probably wearing the dress she used at the only other concert she gave that month: "a gown of cerise chiffon velvet with draping of gold lace." She was supported by a flautist, Edward Meyer, and the piano accompaniment of Richard Hageman, the Dutch-American composer whose art songs she had often sung in recital. Hageman was also a conductor for the Metropolitan Opera. Perhaps Bertha hoped that he would provide an entré for her at that most prestigious New York opera, but there is no evidence that anything more came of their one appearance together. Her recital began with three Italian arias followed by a group of six French art songs. The third set was a group of five American art songs, and then, for the finale, she sang her favourite—"The Shadow Song" from *Dinorah* with the voice-flute duet.

Sawyer ensured that Bertha's appearance got the range of press coverage that a prima donna would hope for, and positive reviews appeared in seven New York papers. Apparently, Bertha drew a large audience that gave her a long ovation. The reviews, on the other hand, were short, and they were good but not stellar. *The New York Times* hedged about a "too silvery fineness" and "the gritted teeth of a throaty crescendo," while *The New York Herald* found that her coloratura work was "for the most part well done." *The Musical Courier* was more generous, concluding that she was "an artist of high rank," and *The New York Tribune* said her "voice is easily that of prima donna proportions." *Musical America* remarked on the "unbelievably rapid tempo" of her encore, Valverde's "Clavelitos," which—unusual for Bertha's repertoire—was a Spanish song. Despite this modest praise, the reviews found nothing to single Bertha out as a performer of exceptional note. New York was a very big city in 1923, and there were performances by aspiring sopranos every week. Indeed, another soprano had appeared at the Aeolian the very afternoon that Bertha had debuted. So, although Bertha did well to get so many notices, there was nothing about her appearance that was remarkable.

While the art songs she featured were a lot more up to date than the Italian arias, papers like *The New York Tribune* felt that Bertha's program "contained nothing radically different from those being sung throughout this season and many past." Compared with the Canadian soprano Eva Gauthier (1885–1958), who had dared to combine classical songs with jazz in a recital at the Aeolian three weeks before, Bertha did not court musical controversy. And unlike in Toronto, her Russian and Polish experience did little to catch the imagination of New Yorkers. As a Canadian she was foreign, but not foreign enough to be exotic. Her singing may have been good, but good singers appeared in the city all the time. So, like her forgettable American opera debut in Washington earlier in the year, and like her minor radio appearance, the recital at the Aeolian was the kind of modest, finite success which demonstrated that there was little prospect of Bertha's career taking off in the United States.

Did the mediocre response to her recital in New York leave Bertha with doubts about her future in the American market? Did she begin to re-evaluate the transatlantic element of her career strategy? There is no evidence that she had any more engagements in the United States or Canada after the Aeolian recital, but when she went back to Poland for the summer of 1924, she had not rejected the possibility of more work in Canada. By this time, she had built up a significant nest-egg from her North American earnings—almost undoubtedly kept, for the meantime, in an American or Canadian bank—which she would have been happy to increase. But by the end of 1923, in the aftermath of her anti-climactic New York debut, it may have looked like her North American success had plateaued, while her reputation in Poland was bigger than ever and still climbing. And so, after three years of struggling to make a sustainable impression in the North American market, Bertha returned to Warsaw in early 1924 with a renewed incentive to make the most of the Polish market, where she was already well on her way to becoming a major star.

Entr'acte —
Wrapping Up the Album

*B*oxing Day, 1923. 369 Parkside Drive, Toronto, Ontario, Canada. The dining room table has disappeared under the mess. Bertha's collection of newspaper clippings covers most of the surface. Directly in front of her is the black scrapbook she bought in New York City, opened to the first blank page. On her right, a brush sticks out of the glue pot. It is a bit daunting, trying to organize three seasons of a career into one tidy album. After the letdown in New York, the temptation is just to sit and reread all of the encouraging reviews and put off deciding how to sort them. But she wants to tidy up at least one aspect of her life, and she is determined to do it before they have to set the table for the family dinner.

She reaches out and stirs the clippings around, then tosses in the latest clippings from New York amongst last year's notices from Washington and all her other Canadian recital reviews. "If I glue them in randomly," she reasons, "it will look like there are more events." Only someone reading very carefully will notice that there is more than one review for most recitals. She reaches out for the first couple of clippings and starts pasting.

Lucia comes in. Her little girls pound noisily past the doorway behind her. Evelyn is clutching the new doll that her aunt had brought her all the way from Warsaw a few months before.

Jane Cooper

Edith sticks her head in the door. "Don't forget, you said you'll take us to the pictures tomorrow, Mom!" And then she disappears towards her grandmother in the kitchen.

Lucia looks over her shoulder. "My goodness, she loves those Mary Pickford movies. She's such a modern little girl." Then she looks down at the clippings. "Are you taking all these back to Poland this time?"

Bertha sighs. "No. They're not much good to me over there. Not enough people read English. Anyway, I left a file full of Polish notices at Madame Kosińska's."

"So you're going to leave them here for your next trip home?" Lucia makes it sound like an idle question.

"Hmm." Bertha concentrates on her brush work. She hates to let on to Lucia how unsure she is about another season. Despite the satisfactory reviews from her New York debut, Mrs. Sawyer has not been able to book any follow-up engagements. The dream that a New York debut could lead to guest performances on American opera stages has come to nought. Suckling may have some ideas for more Canadian engagements, but they are unlikely to be opportunities of the quality she can get in Poland.

Lucia sits down and starts reading clippings. Spread out like that, the clippings form an impressive portfolio of the work of a well-respected artist. "You've had such good recitals here these last couple of winters," she observes. "So many good reviews. Surely you could do another Massey Hall recital?" The question hangs as Bertha pastes another page.

Maud walks past the dining room door. "You're taking up the whole table—right before dinner?" She comes in for a closer look. "Oh. I've got some clippings you mailed from Russia somewhere."

"You have?"

"They're in the desk." Maud pulls down the front of the drop-leaf desk and rummages. She pulls out an envelope and passes it over. Bertha shakes out three clippings. One is in Russian, two in Polish.

Bertha is surprised to see that they are from 1915. "This is from my Petrograd debut." She turns the narrow strip of Cyrillic text slowly in her fingers. It seems out of place among the Toronto reviews—a glimpse of a world so far removed from here. Her mind flashes back to how it felt, standing on the stage in that big Russian auditorium, listening to the applause, the cries of *bravissima* echoing around the room, and the thud of flowers dropping onto the stage from the balcony. She'd like to hold on to that lost feeling of wonder, but she knows it is as ephemeral as the blooms were. She will put these foreign-language clippings at the end of the book.

She pulls out the four Polish reviews from last spring, which Antonia Sawyer gave back to her before Christmas. Bertha had mailed them to New York to help Mrs. Sawyer with her publicity for the Aeolian Hall recital. Evidently, Mrs. Sawyer didn't think she could do anything more with them. The agent probably thought it was a kindness to return them, but, to Bertha, it felt like confirmation of the end of their business relationship. Bertha could have been insulted, but honestly, she can't blame Mrs. Sawyer for being realistic. Not when Bertha prides herself on always coming around to a realistic assessment of her options.

And Bertha knows that, realistically, her best options now are for work in Poland. If she wants to keep singing in operas, and not just recitals, then she'll need to go back to Europe. Singing opera in North America just isn't going to happen. It never was more than a pipedream. She can see that now.

Bertha can't deny how disappointed she is by how the Americans seem so wrapped up in grabbing the new and throwing out the old, and Canada is being dragged along in their wake. In with the movies, out with the opera. Europe has plenty of cutting-edge arts—racy cabarets and saucy operettas—but they are finding ways to keep their opera fresh at the same time. That's what she loves about Europe: it's not an either-or world that pits the new against the old. There is more give and take in how they adjust to change.

So, she'll put together the album and leave it with her parents to lend to Suckling, just in case anything comes of his ideas. But she is beginning to think there aren't many serious opportunities for her here. Not artistic opportunities, anyway. She will check the New York-to-Danzig schedule and book a Baltic-American Line steamer in the new year.

Bertha picks up the last clipping on the table and pastes it down. She has filled all the pages in the album. She closes the cover on her Canadian recital career and gets up to help her mother set the table.

CHAPTER THIRTEEN –
Choosing Poland,
1924–1926

The marriage proposal from Zofia's cousin Count Karol de Hauke presented Bertha with one of the most difficult decisions in her life.

When Bertha arrived back in Poland in the spring of 1924, at the age of thirty-seven, she found herself at a crossroads, both professionally and personally. On the professional front, there can be no question that, in contrast to her reception in North America, where—to use a modern term—she remained a 'B list' artist, in Poland, Bertha was already on the 'A list' of opera stars. She had not abandoned the idea of further touring in Canada, but the previous three seasons had shown that it was an uphill battle to build a reputation as a real star in both Canada and Poland. More to the point, it was becoming clear that she could be a bigger star in Poland than she would ever be in Canada. Within a few months of her return to Warsaw, she was boasting to Suckling in a letter, "I have renewed my successes in Poland, both in opera and concert, singing again in *Il Barbiere de Seviglia*, *La Traviata* and *Rigoletto* and such enthusiasm I have seldom heard, being forced to repeat my arias. I gave two concerts in Warsaw and others in Posuan [Poznan], Lemberg [Lviv] and Cracow [Krakow] . . ."

While the universal language of music had allowed Bertha to integrate so well into the Polish musical world, her foreignness continued to give her a special cachet. In Poland, Bertha found something that North America was never going to offer her—a warm affection that is reserved for the outsider who commits to the cause of a resurrected nation. While the critics continued to laud her technical abilities in performances before the musical elite, they also alluded to her wider popularity, as she was increasingly taken to heart by a broader Polish audience. "My Warsaw following is delightful," she told Suckling. "They crowd around the stage door and hundreds of them escort me to my car. They are wonderful in their sincerity for an artist." In a period of continuing economic uncertainty and constant political crisis, it seems the Polish people appreciated those foreigners who showed commitment by returning to Poland and by speaking out in support of the new Polish Republic. Bertha found a receptive national audience that loved her in part because she was a Canadian who had made a commitment to live in Poland—and it made no difference to her wider Polish fan base whether she was successful in Canada or not.

By 1924, Bertha had begun to appear in concerts and venues that appealed to a wider Polish audience than the more select crowd that patronized the

Warsaw Great Theatre and the Warsaw Philharmonic. For example, on the evening of May 24, Bertha appeared in an ensemble concert headed by a Polish tenor, Stanisław Gruszczyński (1891–1959), a singer who had no formal opera training, but who had succeeded in building a very popular following, not only in operatic roles, but also in film and theatre. In the spring of 1924, the Warsaw Opera and the Warsaw Philharmonic were in the throes of another financial crisis and were not paying their artists. Gruszczyński, along with a number of other big-name singers, including dramatic soprano Helena Zboińska-Ruszkowska (1877–1948), Dmitri Smirnov (the Russian tenor whom Bertha had sung opposite in 1914), and a German concert pianist, Wilhelm Backhaus (1884–1969), put on a popular concert to prove their star power and earn some income. The venue they chose for the concert was the Warsaw Circus Hall.

Unlike North America, where circuses usually appeared under a 'big top' tent, many Eastern European cities had a permanent building for their circuses with a purpose-built circular auditorium. When the circus was not performing, the round hall offered an excellent place for concerts. The Warsaw Circus Hall was an elegant domed auditorium, with a star-patterned circular parquet floor surrounded by ornately decorated banks of seating and topped off with chandelier lighting and a built-in pipe organ. As a theatre-in-the-round, it offered the full audience an unobstructed view, with acoustics that suited individuals and small groups of singers.

In the ensemble concert in the Circus Hall, Bertha could see a payback for having risen to the ranks of a famous opera star in Poland—a return that she knew she would never find in Canada. Under the leadership of Gruszczyński, the artists had cut out the middle man to organize this concert themselves. Balancing the shared risk of renting the hall against the advertising advantage of sharing their reputations, there was little chance that these prominent opera stars would lose. Promoting the show in the popular press to reach a wide audience, they were probably expected to sing only the best known opera arias accompanied by a piano. As no rehearsal, costumes, or sets were needed, a joint concert in the Circus Hall was probably easy money. As time went on, Bertha began to regularly earn money in events like this in the company of the top performers in Poland. The fact that she was invited to join in these popular concerts, in addition to the more elite engagements with the Warsaw Opera and the Warsaw Philharmonic, suggests that Bertha had cemented her reputation as a guaranteed crowd pleaser who could bridge the distance between highbrow tastes and mass audiences. Indeed, by the middle of the decade, Bertha's name consistently topped the list of performers in popular ensemble concerts like this one.

Recommitted to the Polish stage, Bertha's relationships with former colleagues continued to benefit her as she gained even more success in Warsaw. For instance, after the opera director from Poznan, Dolzycki, took up a new appointment with the Opera Company at the Warsaw Great Theatre, he continued to give Bertha work as an occasional guest star in opera. In June 1924, Adam Didur and Bertha repeated their performance of the year before in *The Barber of Seville* at the Warsaw Great Theatre, with Bertha earning "unreserved admiration" by singing, in Polish, Frederic Chopin's variation on a theme from Bellini's *The Puritans* during the singing lesson scene. She appeared with Didur again at the Warsaw Great Theatre the following night in *Faust*. The enthusiastic reviewer from *The Illustrated Weekly's Theatre and Film Review* lauded how "the well-known Canadian Nightingale" sang the coloratura parts with "phenomenal efficiency, refined taste and high culture." Her "delicious and exquisite craftsmanship" made her a singing a "North Star."

Bertha's Warsaw appearances opposite Adam Didur, a Polish star from the Metropolitan Opera in New York, were another mark of her success in Poland.

The week following their appearances at the Warsaw Great Theatre, Bertha, Didur, and their co-star, the Italian baritone Benvenuto Franci, milked the buzz about their opera appearances by joining with Gruszczyński and other local Polish opera stars for a 'Grand International Concert' in the Warsaw Circus Hall. Bertha sang in at least two more of these Circus concerts that summer, and, as the rate of inflation dropped considerably, her take-home earnings improved.

Nevertheless, there was much more on Bertha's mind in the summer of 1924 than her successes on the stage and how much money she was earning. For, at the age of thirty-eight, Bertha came face to face with what must have been one of the most difficult personal decisions of her life. Finally, after living the life of a single career musician for twenty years, Bertha found herself with an offer of marriage—and from a Count, no less.

Karol January Stanisław de Hauke (1889–1940) probably met Bertha at some kind of de Hauke family event. Karol was a first cousin of Zofia, although he was almost a generation younger. Zofia's mother was a sister of Karol's father, and the two Warsaw families were closely intertwined with each other and with their Stackelberg cousins in Petrograd. Zofia's mother was godmother to one of Karol's sisters, and Karol's godmother was Konstantin Stackelberg's mother. Karol's elder brother lived at 21 aleja Szucha, less than two hundred metres from Zofia's house, and Karol must have visited his relatives on the street often. And, as Bertha was a de facto member of Zofia's family, it is very likely that she was included in numerous family events. Of course, Karol may have first become acquainted with Bertha on the stage, possibly even ten years earlier when his cousin Zofia had first returned from her European travels with a young Canadian protégé in her care. Indeed, he may have visited family in Warsaw after he completed university in 1914, at the time when Bertha was singing with the Warsaw Opera Company. Had he first fallen in love with her then? It is impossible to know. De Hauke family legend maintains that he and Bertha bonded over her favourite dog, which he would look after for her, perhaps when she travelled outside of Warsaw after the war. At any rate, it is clear that, by the early 1920s, they had met enough times for Karol to fall in love and propose marriage, and for Bertha to have accepted—at least tentatively.

What kind of man could tempt Bertha to trade in her independence in favour of matrimony at this point in her life? Unlike the fiancés of so many of the storied opera singers, Karol had no connections with the world of music or the entertainment business; he was neither a musician nor a manager, although he must have had a taste for Bertha's style of singing. Of all the possible professions, Karol was a career soldier in the artillery of the Polish army.

In addition, he was a Count by birth, born into a titled Warsaw family with generations of service in the Tsar's army, which could hardly have been further removed from Bertha's rural Ontario roots. However, while Karol appears to have taken more pride in the military ranks he earned than in his inherited noble title, Bertha was keenly aware of how marriage to an officer with a title might dovetail with the image of the truly successful prima donna.

Although he was three years younger than Bertha, Karol had seen more of the serious side of life than she had, and he had more formal education. He was already a volunteer in the Russian army in 1908, when Bertha was still living at home with her parents. After that, he completed a four-year degree in engineering at the Technical University of Riga. His lifelong membership in Arkonia, a Polish academic fraternity founded at his university, was emblematic of his early identification as a Polish patriot. And, like most educated Poles of his class, he was multilingual; in addition to his Polish mother tongue, he was fluent in German (he had attended a German-speaking university), Russian (he had served in the Russian army), and French (the language he most probably spoke with Bertha).

Ironically, despite his years of soldiering, Karol was not a fierce or aggressive-looking man. In his photos, he looks to be something of a mild character, clean shaven with rather gentle eyes. With his slight, narrow-shouldered frame, he was probably no taller than Bertha. In fact, Karol is remembered by his daughter as being a cheerful and compassionate, and, above all, a humble man. Despite his title, he never had any personal wealth, and he always lived in military apartments. He was a caring officer towards his men and was a deeply religious Catholic. Even at war, he always ended the day by reciting the rosary with fellow soldiers.

While Bertha was singing on the stages of Petrograd in the early years of the First World War, Karol had been fighting for the Russian Tsarist Army in the trenches of the Eastern Front. However, in the first year of the revolution, he transferred to the newly formed First Polish Corps, and, by early 1918, he was fighting *against* Russia's Bolshevik Red Army. Karol was arrested and interned by the Bolsheviks, but then released. By the middle of January 1919, he was back in Warsaw, where he joined the army of the new Polish Republic, the institution he would serve for the rest of his life. He won the highest decoration for bravery during the Polish–Soviet War, and then, between 1922 and 1924, he was assigned to study at the recently created Higher Military Academy in Warsaw in preparation for a more senior command. Already thirty-five years old when he became engaged to Bertha, Karol had spent much of the previous decade at war, often in appalling conditions. One can only wonder how the stress of his experiences had affected his outlook on life. In any event, as the emerging Polish Republic stuttered towards a semblance of stability in 1924, Karol must have been hoping to find a more steady personal life by starting a family.

How would Bertha's life change if she accepted Karol's offer of marriage? Marriage did not have to be a barrier to her continuing to sing professionally; on the contrary, it might even enhance her career. But could she really settle down to simultaneously run a household? And what if there were children? Thirty-eight may be towards the upper edge of the age range for becoming a new mother, but it is still very possible. However, children would highlight the question of Karol's Catholicism. The idea of a Crawford raising Catholic children would be an anathema to the rest of her Presbyterian family, but it was the expectation with marriages to Catholics in that era. Inter-denominational marriages may have been common in the de Hauke family, and not a big concern for Warsaw society. But in 1920s Ontario, where the Protestant triumphalism of the Orange Lodge still held great political sway, it was almost unheard of; certainly, no one in Bertha's family had ever married a Catholic.

On the other hand, for all her prima donna fame and success, there could be no doubt that Bertha would be 'marrying up' if she wed Count de Hauke. Indeed, marrying into the de Hauke family, with its extended reach across Europe and cousins situated in several royal households, would officially bring Bertha into the upper classes. And, having lived like a member of Zofia's family for more than ten years, marriage would cement her place as a legitimate relative. But the price of a marriage to a patriotic army officer like Karol would be the commitment to stay in Poland for the rest of her life. While Bertha would have wanted to keep open the option of more transatlantic tours in the future, a Polish patriot like Karol would never be interested in more than a temporary visit to Canada. Such factors could hardly have been passing concerns for Bertha, and she must have spent long hours weighing all the considerations.

While Bertha thought through her options in Warsaw, the news of her engagement was leaked to the Canadian press. A personal letter she wrote to

Isaac Suckling around August 1924 was directly quoted in *The Collingwood Bulletin*, a local newspaper published near Elmvale. While it seems that she had accepted the engagement, Bertha was obviously ambivalent about the idea of marrying: "should I cede to the arduous [sic—ardent?] appeals of Count Charles [Karol] de Hawke [Hauke], a colonel in the Polish army, and settle down?" Bertha wrote, implying that the question was very much open in her mind. And then, revealingly, her preeminent concern turns out to be the impact on her career (although, granted, she was writing to her Canadian manager). Would she draw a better audience if she was married? "I believe it might mean more artistically, as single blessedness does not seem to attract in America . . ." Furthermore, as she noted, there might be an added attraction if the marriage was to a man with connections—albeit distant ones—to royalty: "it would appeal to many from the historic relations of his family, as his great aunt married the Prince of Hesse, whose sister was the wife of Czar Alexander II of Russia." Ultimately, only after she had addressed these career implications did Bertha raise the question of affection, and even then it was with considerable caution: "I still feel that I prefer a long engagement," she confessed. "Then one can thoroughly decide, and if one finds after that that one is still in love, then marry." Hardly the words of a woman swept off her feet.

Strangely, while this story was copied a week later in *The Barrie Examiner*, no mention of this piece of news was made in *The Elmvale Lance* or in major newspapers like *The Globe* or *The Toronto Daily Star*, although surely it would have been of considerable interest to Toronto readers. Did somebody spike the story? Was it Suckling perhaps, aghast to find a piece of his personal correspondence being quoted in the press? Or did someone from Bertha's family appeal to the Toronto journalists for privacy, perhaps because of the unfavourable implications of Bertha's potential marriage to a Catholic? And what did Bertha herself think when news filtered back to her in Warsaw that her private soul searching was now the stuff of public gossip? The personal tone of the letter suggests that she had had no intention of these musings being fed to the press. The article in *The Collingwood Bulletin* also suggested that there were plans in place for Bertha to come to Toronto in the fall of 1924 for a concert with the Canadian tenor Edward Johnson at Massey Hall and that she was in negotiations with Suckling for a cross-Canada concert tour. In the end, neither of these bookings came to pass. Had the leaked correspondence created a rift in Bertha's relationship with Suckling? Certainly, she never worked with him again. Or did news of the engagement cause tension between Bertha and her strict Protestant family? We will never know. What is clear, however, is that Bertha did not return to Canada for another ten years.

Private details such as how long the engagement with Karol actually lasted, or who ultimately chose to end it, are lost to history. In any event, there are strong indications that, by the middle of the decade, Bertha was certain she would not be setting up a household with Count de Hauke. Did the thought of sacrificing some of her independence scare Bertha away from marriage? Did she want to preserve maximum flexibility to pursue her career? Did the difference in religion turn out to be more of a barrier than she initially thought? Or was it just that Karol, the devoted staff officer, turned out to be a bit dull? Of course, it is just as likely that it was Karol who called the whole thing off. Karol had never forgotten his first teenaged love, a married woman from Riga. It was around this time that he finally confirmed that she had survived the revolution as a widow, and he went to great lengths to help her escape from Bolshevik Russia. Did Karol realize then that his heart lay elsewhere? One has to wonder how she felt about the demise of what was probably the best offer of marriage she'd ever had in her life. Was she heartbroken? Disappointed? Or was she simply relieved? Moreover, what was Zofia's reaction? Was she happy to find that she was not going to lose her companion of so many years? Or was she slightly offended that Bertha had opted out of an opportunity to marry into her family? So many questions are impossible to answer at this far remove.

In the meantime, through the mid-1920s, Bertha pushed ahead with her career in Poland. Her professional reputation continued to grow, crossing not only the class divide, but also reaching out into the provinces. From her home base in Warsaw, she was welcomed for concert engagements in places like Lublin to the southeast, Krakow and Lwow (Lviv) to the south, and Wilno (Vilnius) to the northeast. But her most extensive exposure on provincial stages in the second half of the decade was with the Opera Pomorska, which was established in the province of Pomerania, west of Warsaw, at the beginning of 1926. The company was based in the municipal theatre in the city of Torun, but it also performed in municipal theatres in the two nearby cities of Bydgoszcz and Grudziądz. The Director and chief conductor was Jerzy Bojanowski (1893–1983), whom Bertha knew from her appearances in

Poznan with Dolzycki. Unlike the older Polish artists who escaped to Russia to perform during the war, Bojanowski had served in the military, first with the Russian army and then with the new Polish army, until 1920. In 1921, he was back in Poznan, teaching and conducting at the opera, where he probably conducted Bertha on occasion. This might explain why, when he came to work with the Opera Pomorska in 1926, he hired thirty-nine-year-old Bertha for a series of guest soloist appearances.

It was in the middle of a run of nine opera performances of *The Barber of Seville* and *Rigoletto* under Bojanowski's direction, in the first half of 1926, that Bertha was invited to experiment with an entirely new form of concert that would once again change the trajectory of her career.

Entr'acte —
A Stage in the Air

20:15, July 4, 1926. Radio Poland studio, second floor, Land Credit Society Building, Kredytowej Street, Warsaw, Poland. The studio door closes softly behind Bertha, and a dense quiet descends on the room. She nods silently to some familiar musicians, who are sitting quietly before their music stands. She sees Władysława Ordon-Sosnowska and Aleksander Zelwerowicz from the National Theatre leaning close to a microphone. They are reading from one script, sharing it between themselves. They have nearly finished their dramatic reading of one of Mark Twain's humorous stories.

This evening's program is all in honour of American Independence Day, and Bertha will be up next, in the guise of an American singer. She has no qualms about impersonating an American in her first appearance on the Polish airwaves. Her cousins in Massachusetts would probably laugh if they knew, but Bertha is not going to turn down such a novel opportunity over a minor detail like nationality.

The studio is only a couple of hundred feet square and is thickly carpeted from wall to wall. There are no windows or natural light, and the effect is slightly claustrophobic. Deeply folded draperies cover all the walls and are tacked in ruffled layers across the ceiling. Bertha thinks this might be what it feels like to be inside a large, expensively lined coffin. The hush in the room certainly reminds her of a funeral parlour. Fortunately, the smiles from the musicians belie the sombre décor. She slips into a heavily upholstered chair against the wall and waits for her cue.

At the signal of the director, Bertha steps up to the microphone. It is a strange contraption—a shiny metal cylinder suspended on a carpeted sling inside an open wooden box frame. It sits about five feet off the ground atop a four-legged wheeled frame. An electric cable disappears under the curtain and through the wall.

Bertha is far more uneasy in this quiet little room than she would be on a public stage. Will this bizarre instrument really capture her voice and send it out across the city? And who is listening? The newspapers say there are many thousands of radio receivers already in homes across the city and even out in the provinces. If that is true, then there are many more listeners out in there than would fit in the largest concert hall in the country. But she can't see their expressions or hear their applause. Reacting to the mood of the audience is automatic for a seasoned performer like Bertha. But how will she find inspiration in this dead space? She breathes in and tries to conjure up her friends listening across the city.

* * * * *

20:30, July 4, 1926. The drawing room, 7 aleja Szucha, Warsaw, Poland. Zofia Kosińska adjusts the left-hand dial on the small wooden box and settles back into the sofa. Her guests take their seats as the maid passes around a tray of cocktails. Several of the household's many dogs lie scattered around the room. Everyone waits expectantly for some music to emerge from the curved metal horn that sits on top of the box and projects the sound of the radio.

The Baroness is feeling uncommonly modern this evening, hosting a party to listen to Bertha's first radio broadcast. Zofia can't imagine what her own parents would have thought of this new technology. She is not completely sure what she thinks of it herself. Her father, at least, would have liked it. He'd spent his life developing new techniques for surgery, so he probably would have seen some value in this new communications technology. But there is some lively disagreement among her friends about how to make the most of this new potential for Poland.

"Surely freedom for the Polish people must mean freedom to listen to whatever is most popular. I thought we got rid of censorship with the Russians!" One of the women defends the notion of letting the market determine radio programming.

Zofia's old friend Zdzislaw Debicki, the editor of *The Weekly Illustrated*, is adamantly opposed to that idea. "I can't agree. It is the responsibility of the intelligentsia to lead the nation, and radio will be an amazing tool to reach the ordinary people. We must take this opportunity to teach the Polish people about their history, the fundamentals of their national culture, the great music that is their heritage. We can use this tool to bind together our people all across the country!"

Zofia is not surprised by Debicki's excited response. Debicki has been a hot-headed Polish patriot since his university days, which was why he missed so many of her father's lectures and eventually ended his youth in exile in Russia.

"Shhh," another member of the party calls for quiet.

The speaker crackles and the sound of a piano emerges out of the depths of the horn. It is a little faint, and the sound certainly isn't like what could be heard in a concert hall, but everyone in the group leans forward, entranced anyway. The opening bars come to an end, and there is a momentary pause during which they automatically visualize—although they cannot hear it—Bertha sucking in a breath.

Zofia is surprised when she finally hears the sound of Bertha's voice. It is what they have been waiting for. But how improbable, to find Bertha somehow inside that small wooden box.

Much more surprised than Zofia are Bertha's dogs, which perk up their ears. One of them jumps up and stares at the radio in astonishment, then runs around the room and out the door. It can't understand where Bertha is. The listeners hush the other dogs, but one of them will have none of it. He puts back his head and yips, matching Bertha's top notes just like he does when she practices. The group breaks into laughter.

"So you are not so sure about these radio broadcasts either, then?" Zofia comforts the confused animal.

"We will just have to wait and see where it takes us all," pronounces Debicki.

CHAPTER FOURTEEN –
Public Lives and Private Dramas,
1926–1934

Prof. Ludwik Urstein was the accompanist with whom Bertha had the longest relationship. After first meeting in 1913, they picked up again in 1919 and frequently worked together at the Warsaw Philharmonic and on Radio Poland.

𝒫erforming in concerts and operas in the provinces in the 1920s had certainly built Bertha's reputation with audiences in concert halls all over Poland. However, it was the new medium of radio that cemented her reputation as a definitive star, as she was able to reach a truly national audience of all kinds of people sitting in their living rooms. In July 1926, forty-year-old Bertha had her first engagement with the recently established Radio Poland. Bertha had sung on American radio over three years before, but Poland was a late entry into radio broadcasting as compared to North America. By 1926, there were more than five hundred stations broadcasting in the United States and perhaps sixty in Canada. It was not until April 1926 that Poland caught up with the rapidly developing world of radio and began daily broadcasts from its first station in Warsaw.

Singing in a radio concert allowed Bertha to reach a live audience of a size unimaginable earlier in her career. When Radio Poland was launched in 1926, there were already somewhere between 7,500 and 20,000 radio sets in the country, with sales increasing rapidly after that. During its first year, Radio Poland scheduled forty-four hours a week of live broadcasts, with about sixty percent being concerts and twenty percent lectures. The balance was made up of advertisements and public service announcements. Early broadcasts were at the mercy of new and unstable technology, and while the quality of the sound was lamented by the critics, they all saw the huge potential for this new technology that could reach a mass audience. From Radio Poland's earliest years, the Polish critics argued that the radio broadcasts were an opportunity to bring high culture—meaning lectures by professors and performances of classical music and opera—to people who might never make it into a concert hall. The mass audience might want to hear more popular music, but—according to the critics at least—a technology this revolutionary was a cultural asset that should be used in a structured way to raise the musical understanding of the masses.

In this environment, as a classically trained musician with a reputation for pleasing all kinds of audiences, Bertha was well placed to become a radio star. From the earliest months of Radio Poland's broadcasts, Bertha was regularly hired for the 20:30 prime-time concert, during which she was called upon to raise the cultural awareness of the audience. She quickly developed a very good relationship with the microphone, and the journal *Muzyka* (Music) was soon reporting that Bertha's radio performances in particular were "supremely successful." And she was already very comfortable working with the main accompanist at Radio Poland, Dr. Ludwik Urstein. By now, Urstein was one of her oldest colleagues in Warsaw, and she had sung with him at the Warsaw Philharmonic and in numerous other venues on many occasions since they'd first met before the war in December 1913.

Bertha also had the advantage of being able to play the chameleon with her international identity. She turned up in broadcasts at different times to present the best of American, English, and French music—and, of course, Italian opera. On July 4, 1926, she helped celebrate the one hundred and fiftieth anniversary of American independence. Typical of early Radio Poland broadcasts, the program combined educational lectures with music. The broadcast began at 16:15 with the American national anthem, and it included lectures by Polish professors on American history, contemporary America, Polish–American relations, and travel in America. There were also readings from works by the most famous American writers of the previous century, Edgar Allen Poe and Mark Twain (presumably in translation). And then, starting at 20:50, Bertha rolled out her modern American repertoire in three musical interludes of nine songs in total. She included Charles Cadman's art songs inspired by American Indian music, "From the Land of the Sky Blue Water," "Far Off I Hear a Lover's Flute," and "The Moon Drops Low," as well as songs inspired by American nature, like Richard Hageman's "Nature's Holiday" and Campbell-Tipton's "The Crying of Water." Unusual for Bertha, she was also persuaded to sing an old sentimental American parlour song, "Silver Threads Among the Gold."

While Bertha dabbled with this new medium of radio throughout 1926, at the age of forty, she must have been thinking about the future of her career in a world where the musical scene was quickly changing—and where she was not becoming any younger. Perhaps she already sensed a need to look for new directions as she completed the 1926 opera season with Opera Pomorska in July and joined in another ensemble concert at the Circus Hall in August. Well aware that the natural way for a prima donna to leverage her fame on the opera stage after retirement was to move into teaching, in September 1926, Bertha added her name to a newspaper notice for the Moniuszko Music School in

Warsaw, offering voice lessons. However, the notice was not repeated, and it seems likely that the experiment was short and that Bertha did not take to teaching. Instead, she returned to the opera stage to sing Rosina's part in *The Barber of Seville* with Opera Pomorska twice more in January 1927, in what would be her final appearances in opera. Did she realize at the time that she would never sing in a full opera production again?

As she entered her fourth decade, there is nothing to suggest that Bertha's voice had diminished in quality with age, but it was inevitable that the competition to portray youthful characters like Gilda and Rosina was now coming from women twenty years her junior. At the same time, the opera companies of Poland were slipping into another period of financial crisis. For instance, the Opera Pomorska folded a few months into 1927, and the Warsaw Great Theatre Opera Company fell into financial difficulty. By the late 1920s, only Poznan and Lwow (Lviv) had reasonably stable companies. At this point, after fifteen years of chasing the dream of the prima donna, did Bertha make a choice to retire from opera in the face of shrinking opportunities? Or did she continue to hope that more invitations to sing as a guest soloist in opera would come her way? Perhaps she just segued naturally into a routine where almost monthly appearances on national radio—a medium where beauty and youth had little advantage—came to define her as a star of the new airwaves as much as of the old stage.

It may have been a sign of her growing confidence in her place in the hearts of Polish listeners that, around 1927, Bertha slipped into a more settled existence in her own Warsaw apartment. It certainly reflected her confidence in her personal financial situation, for, in the mid-1920s, she lent the majority of the money she had saved from her North American concerts—perhaps as much as $10,000 USD—to Zofia to fund some major renovations at 7 aleja Szucha.[3] In return, Bertha got her own apartment in the building, which she occupied rent-free in lieu of interest on the loan. By this time, it seems clear that the engagement with Karol was officially off—indeed, it may have ended

---

3   While a Polish newspaper later suggested that she had accumulated as much as $10,000 USD—roughly equivalent to $100,000 USD in today's currency—that was probably an exaggeration, as it is unlikely she could have saved that much from her eighteen North American performances over the three years, less her travel expenses.

months or even years earlier—and that Bertha had committed to a life as a single career woman. However, at least for the time being, Zofia and Bertha's close friendship seems to have remained intact, despite any drama that might have accompanied the broken engagement with Zofia's cousin. Nevertheless, Bertha's relationship with Zofia was bound to evolve.

"All my life it seems," she later confessed to *The Toronto Daily Star*, "I had been living in hotels and trunks." Presumably, up to this point, Bertha had felt something like a guest in Zofia's home, even though she had felt confident to cite 7 aleja Szucha as her address in Poland for many years. Through lending Zofia the money to renovate the house, Bertha definitively moved onto an equal footing with the Baroness, as she was able to balance out the early years of debt to her patron and make a public show of living independently. In fact, although it would later come back to haunt her, Bertha had such faith in her equal relationship with Zofia by this point that she lent her former patron the bulk of her savings without any formal agreement for repayment. Beyond a doubt, after fifteen years together, their relationship was steeped in trust and defined by comfortable common interests.

In addition to music, one of these common interests was animals. In 1927, building on their shared passion for animal welfare, Bertha helped Zofia to found the Polish League of the Friends of Animals. Lending her name to a worthy charity like the League was just the kind of thing that an established prima donna like Bertha was expected to do. But we can assume that a dog lover like Bertha also genuinely shared the League's interests, which ranged from medical care for strays and support for circus animals to anti-vivisection campaigns and opposition to the ritual slaughter methods used by kosher butchers. Indeed, this genuine belief in the cause was probably why Bertha offered a room in her new apartment for the League's office. She also hosted a fundraising event and took her dogs along on the annual 'Day of Kindness to Animals,' joining the large procession of animal lovers and their pets on a march through the streets of Warsaw to raise awareness and money.

As a founding member of the Polish League of the Friends of Animals, Bertha—along with her dogs— enjoyed the annual parade for the 'Day of Kindness to Animals' in Warsaw.

Bertha must also have enjoyed the opportunity to socialize with a wider group of people than she met through music. For instance, through the League, she met people like Zdzislaw Debicki (1871–1931), a nationalist poet, essayist, and editor of a major Warsaw publication, *Tygodnik Ilustrowany* (Weekly Illustrated); Oskar Saenger (1873–1930), an industrialist with big interests in forestry, pulp and paper, and banking; Maurycy Trybulski (1883–1944), a domestic livestock specialist who was particularly interested in poultry breeding, but also a friend of dogs and cats; Romuald Mandelski, a veterinarian experienced with government animal care inspections; and the Prince Janusz Franciszek Radziwill (1880–1967), who was a member of the Polish parliament and a horse enthusiast. The League also brought Bertha into contact with the most powerful people in Poland, as its honorary board included Marshal Pilsudski and his wife. Pilsudski, a storied national war hero, was the military leader who had engineered a coup to take over the government a year before, in 1926, and was very much the power behind the government. Also on the honorary board were the Polish President Moscicki and his wife, as well as the Minister of Internal Affairs and the Minister of Agriculture. These men may not have been the crowned royalty that the old-fashioned opera singer seemed destined to associate with, but, in the new Polish Republic, they were the next best thing.

As political and economic stability settled temporarily over Poland in the second half of the 1920s, Bertha enjoyed a busy concert schedule for a while. Through 1927, she sang almost every month on the radio, appeared in a couple of ensemble concerts at the Circus Hall with other top performers, and travelled as far west as Poznan and as far east as Wilno (Vilnius) to sing in solo recitals. And, "famous for her great and wonderful vocal technique," she was still in demand at the Warsaw Philharmonic and appeared with guest conductor Bronislaw Szulc. While she was no longer getting opera engagements, her popularity with the Polish public continued to ensure that she had plenty of work.

Irrefutable confirmation of Bertha's established standing as a prima donna in Poland turned up in 1928, when a Polish music poll was published. In recognition of the anniversary of ten years of Polish independence, Mateus Glinski's *Muzyka* (Music) magazine offered its readers the opportunity to vote for the top Polish musicians and musical organizations. The individuals whom readers selected as the top three Polish conductors—Emil Mlynarski, Grzegorz Fitelberg, and Jerzy Bojanowski—were all men with whom Bertha had worked repeatedly during the previous decade. Likewise, the top three orchestras selected—the Warsaw Philharmonic, the Poznan Opera, and the Lodz Symphony Orchestra—were organizations with which Bertha had been a frequent guest artist. Most significantly for Bertha, however, one commentator from the Lodz *Pravda* (Truth) predicted that many *Muzyka* (Music) readers would have a difficult time identifying truly 'Polish' stars to vote for. After all, he said, if they voted on the basis of pure popularity, then many would want to vote for Bertha Crawford in the category of top Polish singers.

Bertha must have been proud to see that she was considered one of the most recognizable singing stars in Poland. But was she unsettled by the implication that, however genuine her commitment to her Polish audience, she could never truly be considered a 'one of theirs'? Had the legends of all those well-travelled prima donnas of old prepared Bertha for the possibility that a successful international singer who is accepted as a star in many countries may eventually belong to none?

Unfortunately for Bertha, acceptance as a favourite Polish singing star in 1928 did not translate into continuing financial security. In October 1929, along with the rest of the world, the Polish economy began the long slide into the Great Depression. Beginning with the collapse of the New York stock market, the Depression spread around the world, lasting in some measure until the Second World War. All parts of the Polish economy were hit hard, and many artists had trouble making enough money to get by. As the Depression took hold, Bertha's ability to earn a good living would have gradually evaporated as her paid engagements became increasingly rare. Did she begin to regret passing up the financial stability that marriage to Karol would have brought? Was she even a little jealous when she heard, in 1929, that he had married the widow he had rescued from the Soviet Union and was starting a family?

Like her fellow musicians across the country, Bertha was caught in a progressively tight financial squeeze. The opera companies of Poland collapsed completely, and not one opera troupe remained active by 1931. Alfred Strauch, the music impresario from Lodz who had often hired Bertha to perform in the 1920s, became so depressed over the financial crisis that he hanged himself in the lobby of the Lodz Philharmonic Hall. Indeed, as the Depression set in, even popular artists like Bertha were falling on hard times, and it is difficult to imagine that, at forty-three years of age, she could have got by without the support of friends.

Therefore, it is doubly tragic that, at some point around 1930, Bertha and Zofia's friendship of some eighteen years dissolved in a bitter quarrel which, despite the efforts of friends to bring about a reconciliation, descended into a series of convoluted court cases. It is frustrating that we do not know how the dispute began or the subject of the initial disagreement; reports in some Warsaw newspapers about the legal saga were replete with ironic commentary as the case wended its way through the ninth, tenth, and eleventh district courts. The outcome of these cases in the short term is not clear, but there seems little doubt that any residual support that Bertha might have had from Zofia ceased after this point. So, from this point onwards, Bertha likely would have needed to work to cover even her most basic expenses.

Be that as it may, as the Depression progressed and Bertha moved into her mid-forties, she was invited to sing in concerts less often—although how much of this was a result of the economic situation and how much due to her increasing age is difficult to gauge. However, she was still hired to sing on radio quite often. Sales of radio sets had increased rapidly since the establishment of Radio Poland in 1926, and the government encouraged the production of cheap radio sets. Furthermore, it upgraded the broadcast equipment so that the signal from Warsaw soon reached the whole country. As a result, by the early 1930s, Bertha was regularly reaching families listening beside 200,000 licensed sets across the country. With her repeated radio appearances, Bertha kept up her strong reputation across Poland even as her earning power eroded.

Indeed, following one radio concert she gave in August 1931, a vignette was published in the Torun paper *Slowo Pomorskie* (Word of Pomerania) showing that forty-five-year-old Bertha had become a household name among ordinary readers in Poland and was on par with Ada Sari (1886–1968), the most famous contemporary Polish coloratura soprano. In the vignette, the writer recounted his Sunday dinner around the family dining table.

"Images and pictures – a wonderful invention

... Indeed—the atmosphere at the table was shaping up to be tense. It looked like a heated 'family chat' was developing. What to do? Where to get oil to calm the turbulent waters of a red-hot passionate discussion? Suddenly, my eye fell on the shiny bronze surface of the Philips radio. Ah! How very easy! I rushed to the receiver. I snapped on the contact and shook the screws of the capacitor. What is it? There it is! The trills of a nightingale . . . Ah! Today in the Warsaw studio, Bertha Crawford, the 'Canadian nightingale' is singing. Although she is a 'Berta,' her voice is very light. Like a clerk in front of his boss.

Out of the Philips flowed the miraculous coloratura singing of Gilda's aria from *Rigoletto*.

- Wait! Quiet! Hush! Crawford is singing.

- Who? Crawford? I thought it was Ada Sari . . .

- Ada Sari's voice is even lighter.

- Not so good! Crawford has the most beautiful coloratura voice. Shh.

- No! Ada Sari!

- Hush! Be quiet... such wonderful singing...

At the table there was silence. You could hear a pin drop. All that could be heard was the discreet clink of cutlery. And the sweet sounds of the aria floating out of the Philips... Well, is the radio not a wonderful invention? This sower of peace and reconciliation should be recommended for a Nobel Peace Prize."

Further confirmation of Bertha's continuing star power came in a 1932 article in *Ewa: Pismo Tygodniowe* (Eve: Weekly Letter). In its comparison of the programing on Polish radio with the larger German radio service, Bertha was included on the list of "glittering stars of the first magnitude" whose appearances on the Polish airways in 1932 proved that Radio Poland's programing was second to none.

Did comforting press like this help Bertha to avoid thinking about how her position as a working musician was becoming tenuous? She had not sung in opera in five years. If the economic conditions by 1932 no longer allowed her to fill a concert hall, and if she didn't want to teach, then what did she think her options were as a middle-aged opera singer? We can never know. Did she see change coming? Did she realize that her days in Poland were numbered? Or did she think that, as they had for so many years, things would all work out?

It must have been a welcome distraction when, in both 1932 and 1933, Bertha was invited to be a summer house guest of Prince Janusz Radziwill, the wealthy politician and nobleman whom she had met through the Polish League of the Friends of Animals. As was the fashion among wealthy and powerful European aristocrats in the 1930s, the Radziwills hosted large house parties at their castle at Nieswiez, and Bertha was among the well-connected guests invited to enjoy hunting and other seasonal pursuits. The estate at Nieswiez, less than twenty kilometres from Poland's far eastern border with the Soviet Union, was just one of many properties owned by Prince Radziwill's rich family. Restored in the 1880s, Nieswiez Castle is really a set of buildings built on a mound around a courtyard. Like a castle in a fairy tale, it is surrounded by a moat and overlooks a small lake. Among its many rooms is a theatre hall with seating for about 120 people.

Bertha's summer visits to Nieswiez should have been the culmination of a career that, through her hard work, had brought her to such social peaks. They should also have been a reminder of how she had achieved—and was maintaining, however tenuously—the status of a classic prima donna. But while Bertha later implied that she was at Nieswiez as a guest, it seems that there was also an informal understanding that she would accept requests to perform from time to time, to help the Prince create a privileged atmosphere for his guests. Consequently, while she made it sound like an honour to spend her summers in a charming country setting with rich and influential people, she may effectively have been reduced to 'singing for her supper.' This can only have reminded her that, while the successful prima donna might rise to circulate among the highest ranks of society, she was foremost a performer who would never be quite an equal member of that society.

Indeed, in retrospect, it looks like Bertha's footing in Polish high society was always a bit shaky. Certainly, it could only withstand so much undercutting by snide court reporters. By the time Bertha and Zofia's final dispute made it to court in 1933, the demise of their friendship had taken on all the hallmarks of a messy divorce. Their relationship reached such a low point that Zofia insisted that Bertha leave her apartment at 7 aleja Szucha. Bertha reacted by demanding the return of the $10,000 USD of savings that she had invested in Zofia's house several years earlier. In her court defence, Zofia claimed that she had already repaid, and she produced receipts that won her the case. Bertha retaliated, alleging that the receipts were forgeries, and continued her complaint with the prosecutor.

Whatever the outcome of this legal battle, which we may never know, the resulting publicity could only have been devastating. One Warsaw newspaper picked up the story of the celebrity breakup and salted its report with delicate innuendo. Leading its story by describing Bertha and Zofia as 'estranged friends,' the paper went on to relate how the two women had a long-established 'warm friendship,' but recently that friendship had 'been torn apart' and Bertha was now demanding money from her 'ex-girlfriend.' The subtle article could be read in many ways, none of which was flattering to Bertha or Zofia—particularly the implication that the two middle-aged women were spatting ex-lovers. Had Bertha realized, when she began pursuing her personal battle in the public courts that she was setting herself up to be outed by the press?

Ultimately, whether or not she got any money back from Zofia (and that seems unlikely), Bertha must have been mortified that she emerged from the court drama not only with her reputation tarnished, but also with no place to live and a greatly reduced fortune. The fact that Bertha had accumulated a decent nest-egg in the first place demonstrates that she had been—up to this point, at least—a responsible manager of her money. Of course, financial ruin was not an uncommon debacle for the flighty prima donna who is seduced by the extravagant lifestyle of the famous. Nonetheless, being bilked of her savings was most definitely not one of the career turns that John Crawford's careful daughter would have expected. Surely, her thrifty Scottish roots railed against this turn of fate.

Could she have risen above the scandal and gone back to work to recoup her lost funds? Could she have made a fresh start at the age of forty-seven? Apparently, Bertha thought she could not—at least not in 1930s Warsaw. Consequently, after twenty years of living in Eastern Europe, where she had built an extended career and become a household name in Poland, Bertha found herself homeless, short of money, and with relatively few options. Finally, stinging from the betrayal of her oldest friend, she made the decision to return to Toronto.

Entr'acte —
The Final Return

May 10, 1934, 3:00 pm. Earlscourt Park, St. Clair Avenue, Toronto, Ontario, Canada. The children around Evelyn Pearson are getting restless. Some of the boys have moved back from the sidewalk and are playing catch with a baseball on the edge of the park. They have already been waiting for half an hour, and not all the young people in Evelyn's class are excited about this homecoming parade. However, for a lot of adults who remember this daughter of Toronto from back before the Great War, this is by far the most exciting of all the events so far celebrating Toronto's centennial year. And although she would never say so, Evelyn is also very curious to see how Toronto will welcome home this great star who has been away for so long.

Evelyn enjoys a parade. At fourteen, she is a thoughtful girl, happy to quietly observe the people around her and wonder about them. And watching people watching other people can be particularly interesting. While she keeps her eyes on the street, she listens to the teenaged girls in her class gossiping and giggling around her.

"Do you think she is really still beautiful?"

"My mother says she's over forty! I don't think you can really count as beautiful at that age, can you?"

"My mom says she hasn't lived in this country for more than twenty-five years. Do you think she really thinks this is 'home'?"

"Hey! You hear that?" The boys drop their game and crowd up behind the girls.

The sidewalk is lined with people as far as Evelyn can see in every direction. A distant roar starts to build north up McRoberts Avenue as the first car in the long cavalcade comes into sight. The sound of the cheering crowds rolls towards the schoolchildren as the car glides closer.

Standing on tiptoes and peering between the front row of students, Evelyn finally gets a glimpse of the world-famous star, who is sitting up on the back of an open car with her ankles primly crossed. She is not a tall woman, but she is instantly recognizable.

Evelyn is a little disappointed. She can't see anything like a ball gown or jewels. The woman in the car is dressed in a neat blue belted coat with a little blue suede hat perched on top of her short blonde curls. But she is waving her arm to the crowd and smiling that million dollar smile, so there is no mistaking who she is.

"Hi, Mary!" yells one of the boys behind Evelyn as the car finally turns the corner onto St. Clair Avenue.

Evelyn can just hear as Mary Pickford calls back a cheery "Hi!" in return.

An hour later, Evelyn is running down St. John's Road. She turns onto the front path at Number 107 and bounds athletically up the front porch steps. She pauses to catch her breath, then scrubs her shoes on the doormat and calmly opens the front door.

She hurries along the hall and into the kitchen to find her mother. "I saw her, Mother! I saw Mary Pickford!"

Lucia looks up at her youngest daughter from the sink where she is peeling potatoes for dinner. "So, what did she look like?"

Evelyn considers her words. "Well, she is quite small, actually. But she has a big smile. And she looked like she was really happy to be in Toronto. Can you imagine that? A Hollywood star happy to be in Toronto?"

In fact, Lucia finds that a bit hard to believe. But then again, Hollywood probably isn't all that the papers make it out to be. Nowhere is. And Lucia is happy to be in Toronto. But then again, she has rarely been outside of Ontario. So she is not really in a position to judge other places.

Evelyn relaxes her back against the door jamb as she continues, "There were crowds and crowds of people. You wouldn't have believed it. I never saw so many people! Well, maybe when we went to see the Prince of Wales." Evelyn was only seven when the Prince visited Toronto, but seeing royalty certainly left an impression on her. "So, why do you think Mary Pickford is called 'America's Sweetheart' when she is really a Canadian?"

Lucia pours the dirty water down the sink. "Well, I guess Canada doesn't look like a very important place when you are away from it."

"What do you think, Mother?" Evelyn is suddenly wistful. "Will the city have a parade when Aunt Bertha comes home?" Evelyn is old enough to know the answer to that question but still young enough to get lost in school-girl dreams.

"No." Lucia dries her hands and hangs the towel on its hook. "I don't imagine they will."

CHAPTER FIFTEEN –
An Uneasy Return,
1934–1937

In her late forties, when she returned to Toronto,
Bertha was still a stylish—and apparently fit—woman.

The fact that Bertha travelled home from Poland in May 1934 in second class (rather than in first class, as she had travelled in the 1920s) suggests that she was now conscious that she must be careful with her money. Indeed, this return to North America was a stark contrast to her 1921 arrival, when her triumphant homecoming was so carefully timed to coincide with her rising star in Europe. Her low-key arrival in New York on May 26, 1934 was not completely unnoticed, but the interview published in *The Washington Post* the following week did not make any hay out of Bertha's career as an opera star. Rather, the journalist was more interested in Bertha's perspective on the situation of Polish women.

Bertha was happy to talk about the wide opportunities for professional women in the country she had left behind and about how there were more women sitting in the parliament in Poland than in any other country in the world. She was proud of the advances made by her Polish friends and perhaps already nostalgic for the Polish society in which she had spent many happy years. But her most telling comment came when she described how few Polish women would "sacrifice a family life for a career, as they do in America." Was she comparing them with herself, as she faced the reality that she had no husband or children to fall back on in this difficult period of her life? Was she questioning if she had made the right decision not to marry Karol de Hauke?

Fitting back into a life in Toronto with her middle-class family, after twenty-five years of living the life of a celebrity in Europe, cannot have been an easy process for Bertha. She dallied for a couple of weeks in New York, perhaps testing the waters for potential work and visiting friends, but the social column of *The Toronto Daily Star* reported that she was back in Toronto and at home with her parents by June 20. Unlike her 1921 homecoming, there were no reports of teas held in her honour, or meetings with old voice teachers and adoring students, or luncheons hosted by the who's who of Toronto society. In fact, except for *The Toronto Daily Star*'s brief mention in the social column, nobody in Toronto society—apart from her family, of course—seems to have paid much attention to Bertha's return at all.

A month after her arrival in Toronto, *The Toronto Daily Star* did send out a reporter from their Women's Department to find out how Bertha was reacting to being back at the Crawford family home in Toronto. Like *The Washington*

Post, *The Toronto Daily Star* showed limited curiosity about Bertha's history as a singer and was more interested in her experiences as a Canadian woman who had made a life in Eastern Europe. They also honed in on her fashionable dress, a "rose blouse of dotted Swiss, a pale blue crepe skirt and a white and rose novelty necklace. Very long ear-rings of antique silver set with turquoise..." They were charmed by the antics of her beloved Griffon Belge dog, Sylvestre, who had come with her from Poland. However, reading between the lines, there were also clues about how removed Bertha had become from Canadian life. For instance, the article discussed her love for the rich dishes and many courses of a Polish dinner prepared by her Polish cook; her friendship with Prince Radziwill and the summers at his castle; and her fluency in the Polish language and how, when she spoke English now, there was an "attractive hesitancy." There was also a final suggestion that Bertha planned to give some concerts in North America and then return to Poland. Was this actually her real plan? Or was it wishful thinking that made her current situation in Toronto more bearable?

We can only imagine what it was like for Bertha to come 'home' for good to the house on Parkside Drive, which had never really been her home. Bertha's parents were getting on: John Crawford was seventy-eight, and he had been retired for some years; and Maud was seventy-one. Was Bertha prepared for the fact that her parents, although still strong, were moving distinctly slower than when she had last been home ten years before? And what was Bertha's relationship with her mother like? After all, Maud had built her entire life around marriage and children—things that Bertha had effectively rejected many years before. And how would Bertha explain the downturn in her career to her father, who had always been so proud of her success?

We might also wonder about Bertha's relationship with her younger brothers. All three of them were married now, but only Howard had a child, and none had gone far from home. Howard, who ran a confectionary store, lived with his wife and daughter about four blocks from his parents. During these Depression years, Lorne and Clarence and their wives had moved back into the family home on Parkside Avenue. Lorne was an accountant, while Clarence did clerical work for the Gas Company. While they probably were relatively interested in meeting their sister again after so many years, it is hard to imagine that Bertha's conventional brothers and their wives could find much in common with this unmarried older sister. And what did Bertha have to share with them after living so long in a big European city and moving in social circles peopled with titled nobility, influential politicians, and cultured artists?

Perhaps the most important question is whether Bertha found some solace and support from her sister. Lucia is remembered from her later years as a quiet woman who was sometimes stern but always practical and self-disciplined. While they may have had notably different personalities, especially in their later years, there is nothing to suggest that Bertha was ever estranged from her sister. One of the few dates that Lucia recorded in her datebook in the 1930s was the day that Bertha returned in 1934, so Bertha's homecoming was obviously very important to Lucia. However, according to the memories of Lucia's son and Bertha's only nephew, Ernest Junior, Bertha came to visit Lucia's home only one time in the 1930s. While Lucia, her husband, and her three children did live a little farther from the family home than Bertha's brothers, it was only a distance of about four kilometres that separated them. Perhaps something else was responsible for the sisters' limited contact after Bertha's return—and that something may have been Lucia's husband, Ernest Pearson.

Family memories suggest that Ernest Pearson was a taciturn man, and that the Pearson family put a high value on propriety and restraint. Ernest had lost his father early, and he had been forced to make his own way in life from his teenaged years. He is remembered as a proficient handyman, a conscientious saver, and a man who favoured the non-fiction writing of the newspaper over the imaginary worlds of novels. He was a member of the Masons and the Orange Lodge, both highly conservative organizations. By the 1930s, he was working as an electrical inspector for Ontario Hydro—a job that had, at its core, the enforcement of rules. Toronto in the 1930s was still a very straight-laced place, and the Pearsons were comfortable with conformity.

We can only surmise how much the Pearsons really knew about Bertha's lifestyle in Europe and the nature of her career as a professional musician. Nevertheless, it cannot have escaped their notice that, for more than twenty years, she had accepted—even when the prospect of marriage was offered—the companionship and patronage of a widowed older woman. That on its own would have made Bertha's life unconventional by Toronto standards, and, like much in a prima donna's life, it would have left room for speculation, whether warranted or not. It may be that Ernest Pearson had come to his own conclusion that there was something not entirely proper about how Bertha had led her life or how opera singers in general carried on. Perhaps he was uneasy about exposing his children to alternative lifestyles at their impressionable ages. Or maybe he could not reconcile himself to the idea that she had considered marriage to a Catholic. Of course, Bertha herself might have been responsible for the tension. Was she uncomfortable with Ernest and his conservative outlook? Whatever the reasons, it seems that Bertha had a more distant relationship with her sister's family in the last years of her life than one might expect for a woman who had spent the first half of her life in such close contact with her sister. This situation is all the more puzzling given that the Pearsons maintained strong family ties with the rest of the Crawford family and often visited Lucia's parents both at their home and at their cottage.

Bertha stayed in her parents' home for a few months after she arrived back in Toronto in June 1934, but by 1935 she was listed in the Toronto city directory as living at 205 Shaw Street, a narrow brick Victorian row house where she was a tenant. It was a far cry from aleja Szucha, and it epitomized just how far behind Bertha had left her comfortable Warsaw life.

It would not have taken Bertha long to realize that nothing in Toronto would compare to the life she had led as a prima donna in Poland. It would also have been immediately clear that the impact of the Depression was just as profound in Canada as it was in Eastern Europe. During the previous winter of 1933, one-third of all workers across Canada were out of work, and one-fifth of the Canadian population—more than a million and a half people—depended on government relief to survive. Things were slightly better in industrial Ontario as compared to the rest of the country, but even so, when Bertha came home in 1934, 120,000 people in Toronto were on relief. However, upon her arrival, Bertha found her fellow Torontonians doing their best to put on an optimistic show by celebrating the hundredth anniversary of the incorporation of the city. These centennial celebrations had kicked off in March 1934, a few months before her return, with a service of thanksgiving and prayer. Multiple committees of prominent citizens decorated the streets and arranged parades, public addresses, musical pageants, religious activities, sporting events, flower shows, and commemorative books. Everything about the centennial celebrations was designed to raise the spirits of a city that, like the rest of the country, was reeling from the impact of the worldwide economic collapse.

One of the many public events planned for the city's centennial was a full day of public appearances for Hollywood's most famous star, the ex-Torontonian Mary Pickford. In stark contrast with the world of entertainment twenty-five years before, when both Mary and Bertha had left Canada to build their respective careers, the opera stage no longer represented the peak of fame and fortune. Mary Pickford's 1934 welcome, which included a reception and parade, encapsulated the city's pride for its most famous daughter and highlighted how the dream of the prima donna had been replaced by a new fantasy: the dream of the Hollywood film star and her fairy tale rise to fame. Since Pickford had left Toronto in 1910, she had become one of the most recognizable women—and one of the highest earners—in the world through her work as an actress and movie producer in Hollywood. Without a doubt, by the 1930s, the biggest international celebrities were movie stars, not opera singers.

It was not only the general public that now identified opportunities and fame with Hollywood and the movies. Bertha's old singing teacher, Otto Morando, had left Canada for Los Angeles in the late 1920s. Despite years of teaching voice to performers destined for the opera stage, by the time he died in the 1950s, he would be best remembered as a singing coach of movie stars like Pola Negri, Norma Shearer, and Joan Crawford, rather than of opera singers like Bertha Crawford.

Indeed, the professional environment that Bertha returned to in North America in 1934 offered few opportunities to make a living for the singers that Morando had trained for the classical stage. Audiences were now gravitating to vaudeville, radio, and film. Letters to Otto Morando written by some of his ex-students in the early 1930s give a glimpse of how dire the situation had become for more traditional professional singers in big North American cities. One male student wrote bluntly to Morando from New York, saying, "It has been the worst year I have experienced ever since I have been here, and things don't look very bright for the near future . . . you have just got to take what they will offer, or go hungry, because there are hundreds willing to jump in and take these engagements . . . don't let any-one tell you that things are good in New York, they are not . . ." From Vancouver, one of Morando's female students described a similar situation for singers trying to find work in Canadian cities: "There is no money in music and hasn't been for the past year. The musicians who rely solidly on their art have been very badly hit . . . I am trying to keep my voice in good condition and am trying to go ahead rather than slip back. You once told me that it is impossible to stand still. However, I have great difficulty in trying to keep up to speed. It is so simple to slow down, isn't it?" Of course, slowing down was something that Bertha had been doing for several years already.

Touring to small towns to sing no longer offered a viable alternative for Bertha, either, as concert party tours were no longer able to make a profit. After years as the Managing Director of the Community Chautauqua of Canada, Bertha's old friend, the impresario Wallace Graham, was overseeing the tail end of the era of long concert party tours in western Canada. In 1935, the touring circuit he managed through Manitoba, Saskatchewan, Alberta, and British Columbia—the western Canadian circuit where Bertha had made a name for herself in 1909 and 1910—came to an end.

Bertha was in fine form for her performance in Varsity Arena at the University of Toronto during the 1935 Promenade Symphony Concert series.

It is not surprising, then, that when Bertha finally got a chance to sing in a concert, it was through a charity arrangement designed to give work to underemployed musicians while providing subsidized access to culture and entertainment for low-income Torontonians. The concert, staged in August 1935, was part of a summer series of Promenade Symphony Concerts arranged by the conductor Reginald Stewart (1900–1984) under the auspices of the Toronto Musical Protective Association. The weekly concerts were held in the University of Toronto's Varsity Arena on a midweek evening from May to October, with ticket prices kept low and most seats going for just twenty-five cents. The profits were shared across a large orchestra in addition to any soloists, so there was not much money to be made from just one appearance. But Bertha was in no position to turn up her nose at any earnings she could get. The fact that she would now consider an appearance in a hockey rink was a stark indicator of how far down the musical ladder she had slipped in just a few years.

Despite being a charitable venture, Stewart's concert series did provide a serious musical environment where Bertha could legitimately demonstrate the continuing strength of her singing. Bertha knew Stewart from the 1920s, when he had been a young guest pianist at Bertha's 1923 concert at the Royal Connaught Hotel in Hamilton. Like Bertha's father, Stewart was a Scottish immigrant, and he kept his distinctive accent all his life. He advanced his career by becoming both a teacher and a radio music director, but he became best known as a conductor and was remembered for being the person who founded the Promenade Symphony Concerts in 1934, the year before Bertha sang in them. Comparing Stewart with the conductor of the Toronto Symphony Orchestra, a violinist who performed with them both later wrote that Stewart "looked like a more exciting conductor. Perhaps to some he also sounded like one." Invariably, Stewart was a highly professional conductor, and, despite the pedestrian nature of his hockey rink concert venue, he set high standards for his performances. He would not tolerate applause from the audience between movements or noisy tuning from his musicians, so Bertha, at least in this respect, could have expected a professionally satisfying background for her singing.

There is no question that Bertha could still sing at a high professional standard. She was forty-nine years old in 1935, but her vocal cords were still strong and supple. However, she might have been worried about the acoustics of the arena venue. It is one thing to project one's voice to a couple of thousand people in a modern concert hall specifically designed for musical performances. It is quite another to make oneself heard by more than 5,200 people crowded along the benches of an oblong hockey arena. In fact, even the promoters must have had some concerns about the sound quality, as they installed a special 'sound-screen' to improve the acoustics inside the rink for the 1935 season. So, when Bertha finally appeared on the Promenade stage in August 1935, more than a year after her return to Toronto, she had good reason to be nervous. Similar to her homecoming appearance on the Massey Hall stage in the early 1920s, Bertha may have felt that she once again had something to prove—that she could still please a Toronto audience after another ten-year absence from the stages of the city.

Bertha was only scheduled to sing one opera aria, "The Bell Song" from the opera *Lakme*, to lighten the mood between the orchestra's performances of operatic pieces such as Wagner's *Ride of the Valkyries* and the ballet music from Gounod's *Faust*, and Rossini's *William Tell Overture*. The audience members, most of whom were unfamiliar with her earlier career, were not expecting much. However, at least one journalist was listening with an open mind. For perhaps one of the first times in Bertha's career, her appearance was being covered by a woman journalist, Pearl McCarthy (1895–1964), who was writing for *The Mail and Empire*. McCarthy, who had come of age during the First World War and had degrees from both Toronto and Oxford universities, was part of a new generation of Canadian cultural nationalists. While committed to the idea of building nationalism through culture, like Parkhurst and Charlesworth a generation before her, McCarthy was generally sceptical about what others had written and liked to get the facts for herself. And so she admitted to being pleasantly surprised by how, "after [Bertha] had sung a few bars, everybody began to sit up and lean forward. The listening became more and more tense. When she had finished her first aria the crowd applauded; after her second encore [a Latin American tango-foxtrot, 'Serenata Criolla'] they cheered, and even after her third [a classic English folk song, 'Long, Long Ago'] they were loath to let her go."

The writer from *The Evening Telegram* concurred that there was no doubt about Bertha's welcome, noting how "[t]he ovation accorded her was warmingly spontaneous" and that her "long experience abroad has set its distinguishing mark upon her singing." And *The Toronto Daily Star* reported that "It was like a sudden, unexpected homecoming of a member of a family last night when the Canadian-born coloratura, Bertha Crawford, gripped the hearts and imaginations of more than 5,000 people." For that evening, at least, Bertha must have been pleased.

However, while Bertha must have found it gratifying to be received again so warmly by her hometown audience after such a long absence, she must have been doubly frustrated that the successful appearance did not result in any follow-up engagements. In fact, the charity concert of 1935 was the last public singing performance of Bertha's life. On her death, *The New York Times* suggested that she had 'retired' after this concert, but it is hard to imagine that she was in any position to give up working at this point in her life, or that she wanted to. There is also no evidence that Bertha ever taught singing in Canada (or tried to). Perhaps her brief experiments in in Warsaw had confirmed for her that she would never enjoy teaching. As it was, during the Depression, there was a greatly reduced pool of students who could afford lessons, and it would have been a very challenging time to set up a new practice.

There is no way of knowing what Bertha's long-term plans were at this point in her life. She does not appear to have been working as a musician. And, unlike during difficult periods earlier in her career, there is no evidence to suggest that she had a musical patron. However, it does seem that she was trying to recapture at least some semblance of her life as it had been when she was a working musician, if only through her choice of housing.

At some point in 1936, Bertha left the rental house on Shaw Street and moved into a suite in Toronto's Carleton Park Hotel. The hotel, which overlooked the Allen Gardens on the south side of Carleton Street, advertised one-, two-, and three-room furnished apartments with private 'shower baths' available at daily, weekly, and monthly rates, with optional maid service (but no 'beverage room'). It is easy to imagine that Bertha, a woman who had rarely kept house for herself, liked the idea of moving into a furnished, serviced hotel and found it a more convenient option than renting a house. But more than that, as she had spent so much of her life living in hotels when she travelled for work, she may have found that the hotel environment gave her a comforting illusion of being 'at work'—or, at the very least, prepared to leave for work at any time, despite her lack of actual employment. What is more, for a single woman living alone, the hotel would have offered a home that pulsed with life and activity. However, while it was neither a luxury hotel nor a seedy one, it still seemed to be a suspect place for her to live in the eyes of some members of her family. Indeed, Bertha's nephew remembered that the Pearson family thought there was something not entirely seemly about the fact that Bertha was living in a hotel—perhaps even dangerous.

In fact, it may have been because she was living in this hotel that, initially, nobody recognized that Bertha had become suddenly and unexpectedly ill in the spring of 1937. Lucia recorded in her diary that on Tuesday, May 25, 1937, Bertha was rushed to the Toronto General Hospital with pneumonia and placed in an oxygen tent. Presumably, Bertha had been ill for several days by that point, but had delayed asking for anyone's help. Was she waiting, in her delirium, for Zofia to appear and take care of her, as she had done over so many years? What is clear is that, by the time Bertha was taken to hospital, she was already seriously ill, and her condition deteriorated quickly. In the days before antibiotics, severe pneumonia was difficult to treat, especially if treatment started late, and it was the most common infectious cause of death in Canada.

The pneumonia may have been brought on by influenza. A particularly virulent strain was circulating that winter. As an insurance company report noted, "influenza and pneumonia caused more deaths during the winter months of 1937 than they have at this season for several years past . . . and the death rate from pneumonia is the highest since 1931." Perhaps Bertha was already run down, and maybe even depressed about the state of her career. She was always a slim woman, and she ate lightly—she had told *The Toronto Daily Star* in 1934 that she only took coffee for breakfast and ate sparingly at her two meals a day. Consequently, she probably did not have strong reserves for fighting a serious illness.

Bertha died after only a day in hospital, at 5:30 pm on Wednesday, May 26, 1937, three years to the day after she had arrived back in North America. She was fifty years old. It was particularly tragic that Bertha, a singer who had been complimented so many times in her life for her breath control, succumbed to a disease of the lungs.

Ironically, after such limited recognition as a professional singer in the last years of her life, Bertha was again treated as an international prima donna in death. The 'Canadian prima donna's' death was marked in all the Toronto papers, and death notices ran in community papers across Canada, including Regina, Winnipeg, Barrie, and, of course, Elmvale. A short obituary even appeared in *The New York Times*. All reiterated the tales of her distinguished talent and legendary successes in Russia and Poland and noted how she had achieved great success as a prima donna. Perhaps the longest obituary, which ran in *The Globe and Mail*, came closest to capturing the reality of Bertha's life. In truth, sometime arts reporter Blanche Robbins was clearly disappointed that, in the end, reality had failed so badly to match up to the dream. Despite being "idolized" during a "dramatic and glamourous career", outside of the musical community, "[e]ven in Toronto, where her career had its beginning, the passing of Bertha May Crawford, went unnoticed by thousands." As far as Robbins was concerned, the real tragedy was that "the most distinguished coloratura soprano produced within the present century in Canada" had died a forgotten 'has been.'

And Bertha might well have agreed. After all, considering that she had not been able to attract a crowd to fill a concert hall in several years, Bertha would probably have been galled to know that at least 200 people turned up for her funeral. Included were "many representatives of Toronto musical circles," some of whom harked back to her earliest work in Toronto. The recently retired music critic Hector Charlesworth, who had written about Bertha's career since she was a teenager, was there. So was Charles Aylett, who had taken Bertha's publicity photos in 1909. Even the ageing Scottish-Canadian soprano Flora McIvor Craig, who once sang with Bertha at a Robbie Burns night in 1906, paid her respects. Where had all these people been in her final years?

Bertha had no will—an indicator of the suddenness of her death—and the family delegated Lucia to settle Bertha's estate. When Lucia finished taking stock of her sister's assets, it became clear that, for all her years of performing on stages across Europe and North America, Bertha had accumulated almost nothing of tangible value. Of course, had she been able to retrieve her savings from the investment in 7 aleja Szucha, she might have had more to show for it, but as it was, there remained only $25 worth of clothing and jewellery, a mere $25 worth of household goods, and savings of just over $800 in cash and stocks—roughly the equivalent of ten months' average earnings in Canada in 1937. Bertha did not die broke, but she certainly had no long-term financial cushion in the bank.

Would Bertha have preferred to leave a different legacy? Did she ever aspire to follow in the footsteps of all those prima donnas of her childhood and write her own version of the prima donna's memoir? And how would she have told that story herself? Would she have tailored her memories to fit the established legend of the prima donna, where the hard work of the talented singer is rewarded by a steady rise to spectacular fame and a 'happily ever after' conclusion? Or would she have told it like it really happened, with its ups and downs, its compromises and adventures, finding friendship and love in unexpected places—a jangled medley combining new and old tunes running through major and minor keys, with plenty of sharps and flats and codas?

Had she written her own memoir, so many things about Bertha's life might be clearer. We might understand better the nature of Bertha's friendship with Zofia and why it came to such a dramatic end. We might appreciate more about Bertha's relationship with Karol de Hauke and comprehend why she wavered between Poland and Toronto during the height of her career. As it is, we may never know. If there were telling personal papers in her rooms when she died, no one knows what happened to them.

Bertha was the first of her family to be buried in the family plot in Toronto's Park Lawn Cemetery, three weeks short of her fifty-first birthday. By the time her name was chiselled onto the family memorial some years later, this Canadian musician, who had seen remarkable success singing opera in Italy and Russia and who, for fifteen years, had been a well-loved singing star in Poland, had become little more than a footnote in her family's history.

Requiem — Packing Up the Pieces

Monday, May 30, 1937. No. 354, Carleton Park Hotel, Carleton Street, Toronto, Ontario, Canada. The manager lets Lucia into the room. "She was only paying one month at a time, so you'll have to get her things out by the end of tomorrow, Ma'am."

"Oh, I don't suppose it will take that long." Lucia is still numb with the shock of last week, but she isn't going to show her grief to this tactless administrator. "You can just leave me to it." As she hopes, he goes away.

The family has delegated Lucia to collect Bertha's things and settle her estate. Her parents are elderly now, and they tire easily. It takes all of Maud's energy to keep up with running the large household on Parkside Drive. And John Crawford, well, he is an old man with a broken heart. So it has fallen to Lucia, who has always been the practical one, not to mention the sibling who was closest to Bertha. Their younger brothers were always wrapped up in their boys' world, and then, by the time they were old enough to really appreciate their singing sister, she was gone.

Lucia surveys the room. She was right—it isn't going to take long. She is amazed when she realizes how few possessions Bertha has. Bertha had such a big life, with such far-flung travels, but it hasn't resulted in a lot of possessions.

There are enough clothes to fill two suitcases. On a shelf there is a Polish–French dictionary and a stack of sheet music. In a drawer she finds a bankbook. She opens the cover; $385. There are also some bank stock certificates. Worth a bit more than $400 maybe. There is a jewel case, but nothing in it looks valuable. Lucia picks out a little enamelled silver Easter egg hanging on a chain. "That looks Russian," she thinks. "Is that the only thing Bertha has left from Russia?" She thinks she might give it to her eldest daughter, Edith, to remember her aunt by.

She looks around. Is this really all that an opera singer has to show for more than thirty years of singing?

"Well, perhaps it makes sense," thinks Lucia. "Bertha never was interested in things. She wanted people, glamour, adventures, and music—always the best of music. Things were never important to her." Lucia thinks of how much stuff there is in her own home after more than fifteen years. None of it is expensive or luxurious, but there are plenty of things—and she is comfortable with the stability that implies.

She retrieves a few letters from the desk, mostly written in French or Polish. And some kind of journal, also written in French. Lucia can't read these. "Perhaps someone can translate them some day," she thinks.

Lucia packs Bertha's bags quickly and efficiently. She feels sad, but also embarrassed. It all feels too intimate, like an invasion of Bertha's privacy. Lucia doesn't want to dwell on this.

She picks up the phone and asks the manager to call a taxi and to fetch Bertha's last remaining dog, Sylvestre, from the chain in the back alley. She doesn't start to cry until she and the dejected old dog are in the back seat, safely on their way home.

EPILOGUE

The dream of the prima donna always concludes with two final promises—that the singer will live happily ever after and that her life will be remembered and celebrated. It turns out that those parts of the fairy tale often don't come any closer to reality than the other parts of the fable.

We have no way to gauge the condition of Bertha's mind in her last few years. However, it seems unlikely that it would have fit into a 'happily ever after' mould. As an expatriate returned from a dynamic European capital, she must have often felt like a fish out of water in the provincial milieu of 1930s Toronto. At the same time, like all opera singers of her day, she faced the challenge that her art form was declining in the face of competition, most particularly from the movies. To top it off, she had woken up from her prima donna dream to find that her approaching middle age had coincided with an unprecedented worldwide Depression, which meant little work and perilously little money. The economic downturn had caused two out of three of Bertha's brothers to move back home. Perhaps she also would have had to join them eventually to make ends meet. For a woman who had led an independent life overseas for twenty-five years, that would hardly have been a happy state.

But an accurate impression of her mood is lost along with so many other facts. Bertha was the first member of her immediate family to die, but she was followed within five years by her brother Howard and both of her parents. Lucia and Ernest lived on into the 1960s, and Lorne and Clarence into the late 1970s. Her sister's descendants still cherish memories that once there was an 'Aunt Bertha, the opera singer,' but the details of her life and character faded long ago. Only a handful of souvenirs remain scattered among the family: a poster and brochure from the 1909 tour of western Canada; an enamelled silver Easter egg pendant; an album of Canadian and American newspaper clippings from the 1920s; a blonde-haired porcelain doll wearing a dusty blue coat; and a some Edwardian studio portraits of an optimistic young woman, smiling boldly at the camera.

While Bertha's death was widely reported in the newspapers at the time, attention quickly faded and public memory with it. By the time *The Encyclopedia of Music in Canada* appeared in 1981, Bertha Crawford's life in music had been whittled down to four sentences.

This book has been an attempt to recapture something of the real life and times of a Canadian singer who has been long forgotten. But no matter how many facts are resurrected, there will always remain more questions than answers. Perhaps it was inevitable, given the mythic status of the prima donna, that much of her real story would end up swept under the carpet of time. As it is, there is so much we can never really know, and inevitably readers are left to fill in the gaps with their own imaginations.

ACKNOWLEDGEMENTS

A project of this scope could not possibly be completed without the help of a large team of supporters. So many friends encouraged me in my crazy search for the story of Bertha's life and kept faith that the project would be eventually completed, despite considerable evidence to the contrary. But some people deserve special thanks.

First thanks, of course, go to my editor, Elizabeth Bond, who I think of not so much as an editor (although she certainly is that), but more as a personal trainer for my writing. Without her advice and guidance, the book would have remained a confusing (and perhaps even tortuous) read.

Secondly, I have to thank Bertha's relatives for sharing family memories, copies of documents, pictures, and artifacts from their personal collections. Ernest Pearson, now sadly deceased, was the last person alive who remembered meeting Bertha, and he told me what he recalled over lunch. Paul Mably, also no longer with us, and Sheila Watson, produced scans of invaluable portraits, and photos of Bertha's 1909 tour poster and her 1920s album of clippings. Ellen Mably sent photos of Bertha's jewelry. Beth Sklias sent photos of the doll that Bertha had given to her niece Evelyn (Beth's mother). Judy Marlow, Kathy Bulman, Wayne Marlow, Jayne Crawford Donahue-Regan, and Donald Walton all told me what they knew about their family.

Thirdly, I can hardly begin to thank my family for all the many ways they contributed to the project. For example, Julia joined me in taking out a reader's ticket at the UK National Archives and found the first filing card with Bertha's name on it. Michael put me up when I wanted to visit the New York Public Library and took me to the Metropolitan Opera. Margaret guided me on a cycling 'tour de Bertha' around downtown Toronto. Matt set up my website. Alex doctored scans of photos. Sophia arranged feedback on the second draft from her book club friends, Randi, Cathy, and Danielle. Rita made the Kickstarter video. Auntie Clare commented on an early draft. Sarah left her sick husband's bedside to go to the Archives of Ontario to copy Bertha's will, and she proofread an early version of the manuscript.

Equally important were the many contributions from friends, old and new. Early on, David Gray demonstrated to me the importance of subscribing to a World Deluxe Membership with Ancestry.com by finding Bertha's passenger records from New York. Heather and Irene read and commented on early drafts. Kathy drove with me to Kingston to meet Uncle Ernie. Brian made clever Photoshop repairs to old photos. Connie made the maps. Debbie put me up in Barrie so I could visit the Simcoe County Archives, where I found the photograph of the Elmvale Silver Band. James Neufeld, the only other contemporary biographer of a Canadian opera singer, gave me early advice and encouragement that the story was worth pursuing. Carl Morey, Prof. Emeritus at the University of Toronto, read an early draft for accuracy in musical history. Douglas Gardner gave me a delightful tour of Massey Hall. Greg McKinnon opened up the basement vault at the Metropolitan United Church in Toronto so I could dig into their archives.

Archivists and librarians in collections across Canada provided invaluable professional help in digging out dusty papers from their collections, including: Linda Liima, Toronto Reference Library; Suzanne Meyers Sawa, University of Toronto Faculty of Music Library; Trisha Carleton, Claresholm and District Museum; Ellen Millar and Megan Arnott, Simcoe County Archives; and Gary French, Elmvale Presbyterian Church.

I discovered that traces of Bertha's story can be found all over the world, and people in many countries were happy to help via phone or email. The UK author, Michael Occleshaw, gave me invaluable advice about the Foreign Office card catalogue in the UK National Archives, which led me directly to the key correspondence during my only day in Kew. Simon Demissie at the National Archives followed up by looking for the information I missed that day. In Baltimore, Sandy von Stackelberg delved into the Stackelberg family files to identify who the Baroness Kosińska really was. From Warsaw, Count Karol de Hauke's daughter Maria and granddaughter Anna Szostakieiwcz sent a detailed biography and family photos. From Sweden, Alexander and Henrik de Hauke also contributed memories and more photos. Kristian Stockmann of Helsinki Genealogists found me references from Finnish newspapers, and Reija Lång at the National Library of Finland searched for Bertha in their digital database. Pekka Nutinnen and Matti Heinonen put to the test their best election observation skills, trying to dig up more traces of Bertha in Finland. From as far away as Australia, Jennifer Hill at the Grainger Museum at the University of Melbourne explained the details of the contracts signed with Bertha's New York agent.

Many people I met on my international research trips to Poland and Russia also got caught up in the pursuit of Bertha. Ewelina Hallmann, my enthusiastic translator and guide in Warsaw, brought useful suggestions from her mother every day and, many months later, went twice to the Stare Powaski Cemetery to find and photograph the Baroness's father's grave. Major thanks must go to the leading expert on opera in Poland between the wars, Dr. hab. Małgorzata Komorowska, who, together with her colleague Krystyna Zawadzka of the Music Institute of the Polish Dictionary of Biography, gave me a number of references on Bertha's work in Warsaw. Małgorzata went even further to read and correct the many Polish references in the manuscript. Others in Poland who provided help include: Marta Dziewanowska-Pachowska, Fryderyk Chopin University of Music; Marta Michocka, Poznań Opera Archive; Anna Wypych-Gawrońska and Andrzej Kruczyński, Warsaw Opera Museum; and Joseph A. Herter, the Kosciuszko Foundation.

In St. Petersburg, Elena Ten, my indefatigable translator and guide, found me a friendly home with Lena, Sascha, and Vanya, introduced me at all the libraries and archives, and took me to productions at the venerable Mariinsky and Mikhailovsky theatres. Elena's friends Marina Popova and Yuri Popov took me to visit the Peterhoff Palace and the Peter and Paul Fortress, and Tatiana guided me to the site of the long-lost Pavlovski Vauxhall. Lidia Alder of St. Petersburg Conservatory, named after N. Rimsky-Korsakov, gave me all the technical advice I needed to start my research. Tatiana Vasilevna Vlasova of the St. Petersburg State Museum of Theatre and Music directed me to the

Figner Archive at the National Library of Russia, while Elena Mikhailova of the Manuscript Department arranged special access to Olga Michaelovna Gardner's diary. Marina Mikhailovna Godlevskaya, opera specialist from the Museum of Theatre and Music, provided very pertinent research advice and extracted the dates of some of Bertha's earliest appearances in Petrograd from her database.

All these people, and many more, played a part in bringing this story to light. Credit goes to all who helped, but responsibility for any errors remains my own.

SOURCES

—— Archives and unpublished materials ——

AoO	Archives of Ontario
APW	Archiwum Państwowe w Warszawie [State Archives of Warsaw]
BUW	Biblioteka Uniwersytecka w Warszawie [University of Warsaw Library]
LAC	Library and Archives Canada
MUC	Metropolitan United Church Archives, Toronto
NMB	Sankt-Peterburgskoi gosudarstvennoï konservatorii im. N.A. Rimskogo-Korsakova Nauchnaya muzykalnaya biblioteka (NMB) [Rimsky-Korsakov St. Petersburg State Conservatory Scientific Music Library]
NA	National Archives, United Kingdom
NYPL-PA	New York Public Library for the Performing Arts
PMPC	Paul Mably Private Collection
RGIA	Rossiiskii gosudarstvennyi istoricheskii arkhiv [Russian State Historical Archive]
RNB	Rossiiskoi natsionalnoi biblioteki [Russian National Library], St. Petersburg, manuscripts department
SCA	Simcoe County Archives
SPbG-MTiMI	Sankt-Peterburgskii gosudarstvennyi muzei teatralnogo i muzykalnogo iskusstva [St. Petersburg State Museum of Theater and Musical Arts]

SPbG-TB   Sankt-Peterburgskaia gosudarstvennaia teatralnaia biblioteka. [St Petersburg State Theatre Library]
TPL   Toronto Reference Library, Toronto Public Library
TsGALI   Tsentralnyi gosudarstvennyi arkhiv literatury i iskusstva Sankt-Peterburga [Central State Archive of Literature and Art of St. Petersburg]
TsGIA-SPb Tsentralnyi gosudarstvennyi istoricheskii arkhiv Sankt-Peterburga [Central State Historical Archive]
WPL   Warsaw Public Library, Varsavia Department

Bibliography

"V Serbskoĭ Dobrovol'cheskoĭ Divizii/With the Serbian Volunteer Division 1916", MO "Obedinenaya serbskaya diaspora Evrazii." Accessed March 19, 2013. http://serbska.org/serbia/2009/03/04/v-serbskoj-dobrovolcheskoj-divizii/.

"Adam Dołżycki." *Słownik Biograficzny Teatru Polskiego 1900-1980 t.II* (2010). Accessed August 1, 2012. http://www.e-teatr.pl/en/osoby/49327.html.

"Adelgeim, bratya." *Jewish Encyclopedia in Russian On The Web.* Accessed December 6, 2012. http://www.eleven.co.il/article/10078.

"H. A. Wheeldon." *Musical Canada* 2, no. 6, (1907), Accessed April 20, 2012. Internet Archive

"H. Ruthven Macdonald, Toronto's Favorite Basso-Cantante." (1912). Accessed March 23, 2015. Iowa Digital Library, University of Iowa Libraries.

"Teatr Wielki Im. Stansilawa Moniuszki W Poznaniu, O Teatrze." Accessed August 1, 2012. http://www.opera.poznan.pl/page.php/1/0/show/15/.

Albani, Emma. *Forty Years of Song*. London: Mills & Boon, 1911. Accessed October 2011. Internet Archive.

Allied and Associated Powers. *Treaty with Poland: Treaty of Peace between the United States of America, the British Empire, France, Italy and Japan and Poland*. Washington: Government Printing Office, 1919. Accessed 2012. Internet Archive.

Ambrosius, Lloyd E., ed. *Writing Biography: Historians and Their Craft*. Lincoln & London: University of Nebraska Press, 2004.

Annon. *The Russian Diary of an Englishman: Petrograd 1915-1917*. London: William Heinemann, 1918. Accessed 2012. Internet Archive

Annuaire Des Artistes Et De L'enseignement Dramatique Et Musical, edited by Emile Risacher. Paris, 1909. Accessed November 12, 2011. http://gallica.bnf.fr/.

Arakelyan, Ashot. "Emilia Corsi (Lisbon 1870 – Bologna 1928)". Accessed April 20, 2012. http://forgottenoperasingers.blogspot.ca/2011/10/emilia-corsi-lisbon-1870-bologna-1928.html.

Armstrong, William. *Lillian Nordica's Hints to Singers*. New York: E.P. Dutton and Company, 1923. Accessed November 2011. Internet Archive.

Balińska, Marta Aleksandra. *For the Good of Humanity: Ludwik Rajchman, Medical Statesman*. Budapest: Central European University Press, 1998.

Barker, Alfred. "My Musical Life in Russia." *Music Masterpieces: Gems from the World's Famous Operas and Musical Plays* 28, (1926): 110.

Barnett, Louise. (2000). *Ungentlemanly Acts: The Army's Notorious Incest Trial*. New York: Hill and Wang.

Bell, James Mackintosh. *Side Lights on the Siberian Campaign*. Toronto: The Ryerson Press, 1923. Accessed 2012. Internet Archive.

Bergholt, Ernest. "Albani and Voice Training." *Musical Canada* 5, no. 8 (1911). Accessed 2012. Internet Archive.

Boag, Veronica Strong and Michelle Lynn Rosa, eds. *McClung, Nellie: The Complete Autobiography: Clearing in the West and the Stream Runs Fast*. Peterborough, ON: Broadview Press, 2003.

Bordo, Michael D. and Anna J. Schwartz, ed. *A Retrospective on the Classical Gold Standard, 1821-1931*. Chicago: University of Chicago Press.

Borovsky, Victor. *Chaliapin: A Critical Biography*. New York: Alfred A. Knopf, 1988.

Bourne, Joyce. *Who Married Figaro? A Book of Opera Characters*. Oxford: Oxford University Press, 2008.

Brundage, Dean K. "Sickness among Male Industrial Employees During the First Quarter of 1937." *Public Health Reports (1896-1970)*. 52 no. 35, (Aug. 27, 1937): 1169-1171.

Bryx, Maurycy, "History of Polish Radio." Accessed May 19, 2013. http://www.historiaradia.neostrada.pl/Historia.html.

Buchanan, Meriel. *Petrograd – the City of Trouble 1914-1918*. London: W. Collins Sons & Co. Ltd., 1919.

Canadian Expeditionary Force. *War Diary "E" Anti-Aircraft Battery*. Ottawa: Canadian War Museum, 1917.

Careless, J.M.S. *Toronto to 1918: An Illustrated History*. Toronto: James Lorimer & Company Ltd, 2002.

Charlesworth, H. *I'm Telling You: Being the Further Candid Chronicles*. Toronto: MacMillan Company of Canada Ltd., 1937

Charlesworth, H. *More Candid Chronicles: Further Leaves from the Note Book of a Canadian Journalist*. Toronto: MacMillan Company of Canada Ltd., 1928.

Chosley, Pauline S. *Intimate Letters from Petrograd*. New York: E.P. Button & Company, 1920.

Clemow, Frank. "Notes on Health Resorts and Sanatoria." *Br Med J* 2, no. 1921 (1897): 1189-90.

Cooper, Dorith Rachel. "Opera in Montréal and Toronto: A Study of Performance Traditions and Repertoire 1785-1980." PhD diss., University of Toronto, 1983.

Drynan, Margaret. "Reginald Stewart." *Encyclopaedia of Music in Canada* (2012). Accessed June 4, 2013. The Canadian Encyclopedia Online.

Eaton, Flora McCrea. *Memory's Wall: The Autobiography of Flora McCrea Eaton*. Toronto: Clarke, Irwin & Co. Ltd., 1956.

Esposito, Brigadier General Vincent J., ed. *The West Point Atlas of War: World War 1*. New York: Black Dog & Leventhal Publishers Inc., 1995.

Ezhegodnik Imperatorskikh Teatrov. Vol. 1915, edited by A.E. Molchanov, P.P. Gnedich and S.P. Diailev. Russia: Direktsiia imperatorskikh teatrov, 1915. Accessed 2012. Internet Archive.

Ezhegodnik Petrogradskikh Gosudarstvennykh Teatrov, edited by A.E. Molchanov, P.P. Gnedich and S.P. Diagilev, 1918-1919. Accessed 2012. Internet Archive.

Farmborough, Florence. *Nurse at the Russian Front: A Diary 1914-18*. London: Futura Publications Limited, 1974.

Farrar, Geraldine. *The Story of an American Singer*. New York: Houghton Mifflin Company, 1916. Accessed November 2011. http://gutenberg.org.

Fay, Amy. *Music Study in Germany*. London: Macmillan & Co. Ltd., 1908.

Fedor Chaliapin Memorial Museum. St. Petersburg: Committee of Culture of the Government of St. Petersburg, St. Petersburg State Museum of Theatre and Music, 2004.

Forrester, Maureen and Marci McDonald. *Mureen Forrester: Out of Character*. Toronto: McClelland and Stewart, 1986.

Frame, Murray. "Theatre and Revolution in 1917: The Case of the Petrograd State Theatres." *Revolutionary Russia* 12, no. 1 (1999): 84-102.

Frame, Murray. *The St. Petersburg Imperial Theaters: Stage and State in Revolutionary Russia, 1900-1920*. London: McFarland & Company, Inc., Publishers, 2000.

Fraser, John Foster. *Russia of Today*. London: Cassell and Company, Ltd., 1915. Accessed November 2012. Internet Archive.

Gaisberg, F.W. *The Music Goes Round*. New York: The MacMillan Company, 1942.

Ganz, Hugo. *The Land of Riddles (Russia of Today)*. Translated by Herman Rosenthal. New York: Harper & Brothers Publishers, 1904.

Gardner, Vivien and Susan Rutherford. *The New Woman and Her Sisters: Feminism and Theatre, 1850-1914*: Harvester Wheatsheaf, 1992.

Gidney, R. D. and W. J.P. Millar. "The Salaries of Teachers in English Canada,1900 – 1940: A Reappraisal." *Historical Studies in Education / Revue d'histoire de l'éducation* 22, no. 1 (2010): 1-38.

Glackens, Ira. *Yankee Diva: Lillian Nordica and the Golden Days of Opera*. New York: Coleridge Press, 1963.

Glazebrook, G.P. deT. *The Story of Toronto*. Toronto: University of Toronto Press, 1971.

Godfrey, H.H. *A Souvenir of Musical Toronto, Second Annual Issue 1898-1899*. Toronto: Musical Toronto, 1899. Accessed April 20, 2012. Internet Archive.

Gossett, Philip. Divas and Scholars: Performing Italian Opera. Chicago: University of Chicago Press, 2006.

Graham, Melva, Kenneth Winters and John Derksen. "Anthema, Motets, Psalms." *Encyclopedia of Music in Canada* (2012). Accessed March 9, 2012. The Canadian Encyclopedia Online.

Greenhorn, Beth. "An Art Critic at the Ringside: Mapping the Public and Private Lives of Pearl McCarthy." MA Thesis, Carleton University, 1996.

Guillet, Edwin C. *Toronto from Trading Post to Great City*. Toronto: The Ontario Publishing Co., Ltd., 1934.

Harper, Marjory, "Crossing Borders: Scottish Emigration to Canada", University of London: Institute of Historical Research. Accessed February 8 2012. http://www.history.ac.uk/ihr/Focus/Migration/articles/harper.html.

Hayes, Florence and Helmut Kallmann. "Piano Building." *Encyclopaedia of Music in Canada* (2012). Accessed March 9, 2012. The Canadian Encyclopedia Online.

Hayes, Florence. "Adanac Quartet." *Encyclopaedia of Music in Canada* (2011). Accessed March 24, 2012. The Canadian Encyclopedia Online.

Heard, Christopher. *The Suite Life: The Magic and Mystery of Hotel Living*. Toronto, Ontario: Dundurn, 2011.

Henderson's Alberta Gazetteer and Directory for 1911. Accessed March 24, 2011. Peel's Prairie Provinces.

Henderson's Brandon City Directory, 1907, 1909, 1911. Accessed March 24, 2011. Peel's Prairie Provinces.

Heritage Archives, "Lethbridge Daily Herald." Accessed March 24, 2011. NewspaperARCHIVE.com.

Herlihy, Patricia. *The Alchoholic Empire: Vodka and Politics in Late Imperial Russia*. Oxford: Oxford University Press, 2002.

Hill, Jennifer. "Grainger's Managers." *Hoard House: News from the Grainger Museum* 10, (July 2009): 3.

Howard, Kathleen Baird. *Confessions of an Opera Singer*. New York: Alfred A. Knopf, 1918. Accessed November 2011. Internet Archive.

Jones, Isabel Morse. "Nordic and Latin Contrast." *Los Angeles Times*, Aug 5 1928. Accessed June, 1, 2012. ProQuest Historical Newspapers.

Kallman, Helmut. "Patriotic Songs." *The Encyclopaedia of Music in Canada* (2012). Accessed April 2013. The Canadian Encyclopedia Online.

Kallmann, Helmut, Carl Morey and Patricia Wardrop. "Toronto, Ontario." *Encyclopedia of Music in Canada* (2012). Accessed March 9, 2012. The Canadian Encyclopedia Online.

Kallmann, Helmut. "I. Suckling & Sons." *The Encyclopaedia of Music in Canada* (1981). Accessed October 18, 2013. The Canadian Encyclopedia Online.

Kallmann, Helmut. "Publishing and Printing." *The Encyclopedia of Music in Canada* (2012). Accessed April 2013. The Canadian Encyclopedia Online.

Kellog, Clara Louise. *Memoirs of an American Prima Donna*. New York: G.P. Putnam's Sons, 1913. Accessed November 2011. Internet Archive.

Kilbourn, William. *Intimate Grandeur: One Hundred Years at Massey Hall*. Toronto: Stoddart, 1993.

Know, W.W. "A History of the Scottish People: The Scottish Educational System 1840 – 1940." In *A History of the Scottish People*, 2000. Accessed August 27, 2017. http://searchweb.scran.ac.uk/scotland/pdf/SP2_1Education.pdf.

Komorowska, Malgorzata. *Za Kurtyna Lat: Polskie Teatry Operowe I Operetkowe 1918-1939*. Krakow: Oficyna Wydawnicza "Impuls", 2008.

Kosińska, Malgorzata, "Emil Mlynarski, Polish Music Information Centre." Accessed April 2, 2013. http://www.culture.pl/web/english/resources-music-full-page/-/eo_event_asset_publisher/eAN5/content/emil-mlynarski.

Krzyżanowski, Adam. "Currency Reform in Poland." *Economica*, no. 12 (1924): 316-325.

Kwak, A. "Divorce Law Reform and Public Opinion in Poland: The Case of Legal Separation." *International Journal of Law, Policy and the Family* 13, no. 2 (1999): 213-224.

Kwaskowski, Stanislaw. *Teatr W Toruniu 1920-1939*. Gdansk-Bydgoszcz: Wdyawnictwo Morski, 1975.

Labreche-Labrouche, Michelle. *Emma Albani, International Star*. Translated by Darcy Dunton. Montréal: XYZ Publishing, 1994.

Lamperti, Francesco. *The Art of Singing*. Vol. 1587 Schirmer's Library of Musical Classics. New York: G. Schirmer, Inc., 1890. Accessed November 21, 2011. http://www.free-scores.com/.

Lehmann, Lillian. *My Path through Life*. New York: G.P. Putnam's Sons, 1914. Accessed November 2011. Internet Archive.

Leroux, Gaston. *Phantom of the Opera*. New York: Grosset & Dunlap, 1910. Accessed November 2011. Internet Archive.

Lester, Geoffrey. *Atlas of Alberta Railways*. University of Alberta Press. Accessed March 24, 2011. http://railways.library.ualberta.ca/.

Levik, Sergei Yurevich. *Zapiski Opernogo Pevtsa*. Edited by V. N. Stolnaya. Moskva: «Iskusstvo», 1961.

Library and Archives Canada. "Louise Crummy McKinney." *Celebrating Women's Achievements* 2011, (March 24, 2000). Accessed March 24, 2011. www.collectionscanada.gc.ca/women/030001-1324-e.html.

Library and Archives Canada. "The Berliner Gram-O-Phone Company of Canada." *The Virtual Gramophone – Canadian Historical Sound Recordings* (2010). Accessed January 25, 2012. http://www.collectionscanada.gc.ca/gramophone/028011-3005-e.html.

Lock, William. "Edward Schuch." *Encyclopedia of Music in Canada* (2012). Accessed March 9, 2012. The Canadian Encyclopedia Online.

Lucas, Gail and Gladys Train, eds. *Years of Witness: Elmvale Presbyterian Church*. Elmvale, ON: Elmvale Presbyterian Church, 1985.

Macpherson, Murdo and Deryck W. Holdsworth. "Impact of the Great Depression, 1928-1940." *Historical Atlas of Canada* (1993). Accessed June 2, 2013. http://www.historicalatlas.ca/website/hacolp/defining_episodes/social/UNIT_43/U43_intro.htm.

Maltese, John Anthony. "The Dawn of Recording: The Julius Block Cylinders." Accessed June 25 2012. http://www.marstonrecords.com/block/block_liner.htm.

Marcinkowski, Robert. *Warsaw Then and Now*. Warsaw: Wydawnictwo Mazowsze, 2011.

Massie, Robert K. *Nicholas and Alexandra*. New York: Book-of-the-Month Club, 1967.

McLean, Maud. "Augustus Bridle." *Encyclopaedia of Music in Canada* (1981). Accessed October 15, 2013. The Canadian Encyclopedia Online.

McPherson, James B. "Bertha May Crawford." In *Encyclopaedia of Music in Canada*, edited by Helmut Kallmann, Gilles Potvin, and Kenneth Winters, 241.Toronto: University of Toronto Press, 1981.

McPherson, James B. "Otto Morando." *Encyclopedia of Music in Canada* (2012). Accessed 2012. The Canadian Encyclopedia Online.

McPherson, Jim. "Mr. Meek Goes to Washington: The Story of the Small-Potatoes Canadian Baritone Who Founded America's 'National' Opera." *The Opera Quarterly* 20, no. 2 (2004): 197-267.

Meltz, Noah M. "Section E: Wages and Working Conditions." *Historical Statistics of Canada* (2008). Accessed June 6, 2013. http://www.statcan.gc.ca/pub/11-516-x/sectione/4147438-eng.htm.

Middleton, Jesse Edgar. *Toronto's 100 Years*. Toronto: Toronto Centennial Committee, 1934.

Might Directories Ltd. The Toronto City Directory 1917. Toronto: Might Directories Ltd., 1917.

Mills, Welsey. "Some Reflections on Musical Conditions in Canada and Some Advice to Canadians." *Musical Canada* 4, no. 8 (1909). Accessed April 5, 2012. Internet Archive.

Nowicki, Ron.*Warsaw: The Cabaret Years*. San Francisco: Mercury Houses, 1992.

Nygaard King, Betty. "Songwriters and Songwriting (English Canada) before 1921." *The Encyclopaedia of Music in Canada* (2012). Accessed April 2013. The Canadian Encyclopedia Online.

Occleshaw, Michael. *Dances in Deep Shadows: The Clandestine War in Russia 1917-1929*. New York: Carroll & Graf Publishers, 2006.

Parkhill Baillie, Joan. *Look at the Record: An Album of Toronto's Lyric Theatres 1825-1984*. Oakville: Mosaic Press, 1985.

Plouffe, Hélène. "Canadian Grenadier Guards Band." (2012). Accessed April 13, 2013. The Canadian Encyclopedia Online.

Podolsky, S.H. "The Changing Fate of Pneumonia as a Public Health Concern in 20th-Century America and Beyond." *American Journal of Public Health* 95, no. 12 (2005): 2144.

Potvin, Gilles. "Montréal Opera Company/Compagnie D'opéra De Montréal." *Encyclopaedia of Music in Canada* (2012). Accessed April 16, 2012. The Canadian Encyclopedia Online.

Pskovskii akademicheskii dramaticheskii teatr. imeni A.S. Pushkina. "Vysokii repertuar bratev Adelgeim." Accessed December 6, 2012. http://theater.pskov.org/about/books/book2/art47.

Pycka, Anna, "O Xix Wiecznym Teatrze Warszawskim Słów Kilka..." Accessed May 30, 2012). http://stacjakultura.pl/2,10,329,O_XIX_wiecznym_teatrze_warszawskim_slow_kilka,artykul.html.

Radziwill, Janusz. "Poland since the Great War." *The Slavonic and East European Review* 12, no. 35 (1934): 293-303.

Raszewski, Zbigniew and Wilski Zbigniew eds. *Słownik Biograficzny Teatru Polskiego 1900-1980, Tom II*. Warszawa: Wydawnictwo Naukowe PWN, 1994.

Reade, Arthur. *Finland and the Finns*. London: Menthuen and Co., 1914. Accessed November 26, 2015). Internet Archive.

Roberston, J. Ross. *Robertson's Landmarks of Toronto: A Collection of Historical Sketches of the Old Town of York from 1792 until 1837 and of Toronto from 1834 to 1904*. Toronto: J. Ross Roberston, 1904. Accessed April 20, 2012. Internet Archive.

Rutherford, Susan. *The Prima Donna and Opera, 1815-1930*. Cambridge: Cambridge University Press, 2006.

Sachs, Harvey. "Arturo Toscanini – Biography." Accessed June 3, 2012. http://test.toscaninionline.com/bio.htm.

Sawyer, Antonia. *Songs at Twilight*. New York: Devin-Adair Company, 1939.

Semi-Centennial, Elmvale Presbyterian Church, 1860-1910. Elmvale, ON: Elmvale Presbyterian Church, 1910.

Shorter, G.W. *Ottawa-Hull Fire of 1900*. Ottawa: National Research Council, 1962.

Singher, Martial. *An Interpretive Guide to Operatic Arias: A Handbook for Singers, Coaches, Teachers, and Students*. University Park, PA: Penn State University Press, 2003.

Smith, Lawrence. "The Zloty, 1924-35." *The Journal of Political Economy* 44, no. 2 (1936): 145-183.

St Petersburg Museum of Theatre and Music. *Fedor Chaliapin Memorial Museum*. St Petersburg, RU: Committee of Culture of the Government of St Petersburg, 2004.

St. John, Judith. *Firm Foundations: A Chronicle of Toronto's Metropolitan United Church and Her Methodist Origins 1795-1984*. Toronto: Metropolitan United Church, 1988.

Stackelberg, Baron Constantin. (1955). Genealogy of the Hauke family. Washington, DC.

Stańczyk, Tomasz. "Radziwiłłowie W Dwudziestoleciu." *Uwazam Rze Historia* (2012). Accessed May 14, 2013. http://www.historia.uwazamrze.pl/artykul/857815,873019-Radziwillowie-w-dwudzieseleciu.html.

Stite, Richard. *Passion and Perception: Essays on Russian Culture*. Washington: New Academia Publishing, LLC, 2010.

Struthers, James and Richard Foot. "Great Depression." *The Canadian Encyclopedia* (2012). Accessed June 2, 2013. The Canadian Encyclopedia Online.

Suhm-Binder, Andrea. "Adamo Didur: Polish Bass, 1874 – 1946." Accessed July 12, 2012. http://www.cantabile-subito.de/Basses/Didur__Adamo/didur__adamo.html.

Swaby, John. *Physiology of the Opera*. Philadelphia: W.P. Hazard, 1852. Accessed August 15, 2014. Internet Archive.

Switala, Tadeusz. *Opera Poznanska 1919-1969: Dzieje Teatru Muzycznego*. Poznan: Wydzial Kultury i Sztuki, Prezydium Rady Narodowej Miasta Poznania, 1973.

Taylor, David C. "The Art of Beautiful Song." *Musical Canada* 4, no. 10 (1901). Accessed February 19, 2011. Internet Archive.

The Canadian Academy of Music Limited, Toronto. Toronto: Canadian Academy of Music, 1915. Accessed February 19, 2011. Internet Archive.

The Society Blue Book of Toronto, Hamilton and London – a Social Directory. Toronto, ON: Dau Publishing Co., 1908. Accessed August 3, 2013. Internet Archive.

Tolstoy, Alexei. *Road to Calvary*. Translated by Edith Bone. New York: Alfed A. Knopf, 1946.

Turley-Ewart, John A. and Robert Craig Brown, "Kemp, Sir Albert Edward", University of Toronto/Université Laval. Accessed June 6 2014. http://www.biographi.ca/en/bio/kemp_albert_edward_15E.html.

Uvarova, Elizaveta Dmitrievna, ed. *Éstrada V Rossii. Xx Vek. Éntsiklopediya*. Russia: OLMA Media Group, 2004.

Vickery, Anthony. "Two Patterns of Touring in Canada: 1896 to 1914." *Theatre Research in Canada / Recherches théâtrales au Canada* 31, no. 1 (2010): 1-19.

Villari, Luigi. *Russia of to-Day, Volume III*. Boston: J.B. Millet Company, 1910.

Von Kunits, Luigi. "Otto Morando, Biographical sketch." *The Canadian Journal of Music*, 3, no.5, (Toronto, September, 1916): 304. Accessed November 20, 2011. Retrospective Index to Music Periodicals.

Waghorn. *Waghorn's Guide – Rail-Stage-Ocean-Lake, 1910*. Winnipeg: James Rawlinson Waghorn, 1910.

Wagner, Anton ed. *Establishing Our Boundaries: English-Canadian Theatre Criticism*. Toronto: University of Toronto Press, 1999.

Washburn, Stanley. *Victory in Defeat: The Agony of Warsaw and the Russian Retreat*. New York: Doubleday, Page & Company, 1916. Accessed June 6, 2012. Internet Archive.

WCTU. "Welcome to the WCTU", Women's Christian Temperance Union. Accessed February 27, 2012. http://www.wctu.org/index.html

Westwood, JN. "The Vladikavkaz Railway: A Case of Enterprising Private Enterprise." *Slavic Review* 25, no. 4 (1966): 669-675.

Whitfield, Eileen. *Pickford: The Woman Who Made Hollywood*. Toronto: MacFarlane Walter & Ross, 1997.

Wikipedia contributors, "Riccardo Stracciari." Wikipedia, The Free Encyclopedia. Accessed May 31, 2012. http://en.wikipedia.org/w/index.php?title=Riccardo_Stracciari&oldid=494731279.

Wikipedia contributors. "Kilbirnie." Wikipedia, The Free Encyclopedia. Accessed April 16, 2012. http://en.wikipedia.org/wiki/Kilbirnie.

Wilson, Beatrice. "Student Life in Italy." *Musical Canada* 2, no. 5 (1908). Accessed February 19, 2011. Internet Archive.

Woodward, Chris. *The London Palladium: the Story of the Theatre and Its Stars*. London: Northern Heritage Publications, 2008.

Wynot Jr., Edward D. *Warsaw between the World Wars: Profile of a Capital City in a Developing Land, 1918-1939.* Vol. No. CXXIX East European Monographs. New York: Columbia University Press, 1983.

Závodský, A. ed. *Słownik Biograficzny Teatru Polskiego 1765-1965.* Warszawa: Panstwowe Wydawnictwo Naukowe, 1973

Newspapers

(CA=Canada, US=United States, UK= United Kingdom, PL=Poland, RU=Russia, FI=Finland)

ABC	ABC Pismo Codzienne, Warsaw, PL
BV	Birzhevii Vedomosti, Petrograd, RU
BE	Blairmore Enterprise, AB, CA
Blu	Bluszcz, Warsaw, PL
BIR	Bow Island Review, AB, CA
BDS	Brandon Daily Sun, MB, CA
BC	British Colonist, Victoria, BC, CA
Br Med J	British Medical Journal, UK
CC	Canadian Courier, Toronto, ON, CA
CJM	Canadian Journal of Music, Toronto, CA
CSM	Christian Science Monitor, Boston, MA, US
CR	Claresholm Review, AB, CA
CB	Collingwood Bulletin, ON, CA

CC	Crossfield Chronicle, AB, CA
DBW	Daily British Whig, Kingston, ON, CA
DM	Daily Mirror, London, UK
DP	Dagan Press, Helsinki, FI
EG	Echo Gdanskie, Gdansk, PL
EC	Elmvale Chronicle/Lance, ON, CA
EPT	Ewa: Pismo Tygodniowe, Warsaw, PL
ET	Evening Telegram, Toronto, ON, CA
EP	Express Poranny, Warsaw, PL
FV	Frank Vindicator, AB, CA
GB	Gazeta Bydgoska, Bydgoszcz, PL
BB	Gazeta Gdanska, Gdansk, PL
GW	Gazeta Warszawska, Warsaw, PL
GWP	Gazeta Warszawska Porana, Warsaw, PL
GP	Gazetta Porana, Warsaw, PL
G&M	Globe and Mail, Toronto, CA
G&M	Globe, Toronto, CA
GP	Glos Polski, Lodz, PL
GP(Vlad)	Golos Primoriya, Vladivostok, RU
GN	Goniec Nadwislanski, Warsaw, PL
GW	Goniec Wielkopolski, Poznan, PL
HH	Hamilton Herald, ON, CA
HS	Hamilton Spectator, ON, CA
HStLO	Hastings and St. Leonards Observer, UK
IR	Illustrowana Republika, Lodz, PL

IRC	Illustrowany Kuryer Codzienny, Krakow, PL
KK	Kavkazskii Krai, Piatigorsk, RU
Kzh	Khronika Zhurnala "Muzykanyi Sovremennik", Petrograd, RU
KS	Kingston Standard, ON, CA
KP	Kurier Poznanski, Poznan, PL
Kwil	Kurier Wilenski, Wilna, PL
Kwa	Kurier Warszawski, Warsaw, PL
LPat	La Patrie, Montréal, QC, CA
LPre	La Press, Montréal, QC, CA
LCM	Le Canada Musical, Montreal, QC, CA
LDH	Lethbridge Daily Herald, AB, CA
LM	Lincoln, Rutland and Stamford Mercury, UK
LE	Lodzkie Echo Wieczorne, Lodz, PL
LS	London Standard, UK
LAT	Los Angeles Times, USA
M&E	Mail and Empire, Toronto, ON, CA
MFP	Manitoba Free Press, MB, CA
MV	Moskovskie Vedomosti, Moscow, RU
ML	Moyie Leader, BC, CA
Mucha	Mucha, Warsaw, PL
MC	Musical Canada, Toronto, ON, CA
MCE	Musical Courier and Examiner, Toronto, ON, CA
MT	Musical Times, London, UK
Muz	Muzyka, Warsaw, PL

NE	New Enterprise, Madison, FL, US
NYA	New York American, US
NYT	New York Times, US
NYTr	New York Tribune, USA
NS	Novosti Sezona, Moscow, RU
NP	Nasz Przeglad, Warsaw, PL
NV	Novoye Vremya, Petrograd, RU
NK	Nowy Kurier, Poznan, PL
OT	Obozrenie Teatrov, Petrograd, RU
Ork	Orkiestra, Warsaw, PL
OC	Ottawa Citizen, ON, CA
OJ	Ottawa Journal, ON, CA
PE	Peterborough Examiner, ON, CA
PZ	Polska Zbronja, Warsaw, PL
PTF	Prezeglad Teatralny i Filmowy, Tygodnik Ilustrowany, Bydogoszcz, PL
PK	Priazovskii Krai, Rostov-na-Don, RU
PM	Przegląd Muzyczny, Warsaw, PL
RDN	Red Deer News, AB, CA
RZ	Rzeczpospolita, Warsaw, PL
RL	Regina Leader, SK, CA
RT	Ridgewood Times, New York, US
Roz	Rozwoj, Lodz, PL
Rmg	Russkaya Muzykalnaya Gazeta, Petrograd, RU
SN	Saturday Night, Toronto, CA
SP	Slowo Pomorskie, Torun, PL

SZ	Swiat Zwierzecy, Warsaw, PL
TN	Tammerfors Nyheter, Tampere, FI
Ti	Teatr i Iskusstvo, Petrograd, RU
Tr	Teatr, Moscow, RU
TDS	Toronto Daily Star, ON, CA
TSWeek	Toronto Star Weekly, ON, CA
TSWor	Toronto Sunday World, ON, CA
TW	Toronto World, ON, CA
Vm	Varshchavskaya Mysl, Warsaw, PL
Vd	Varshchavskii Dnevnik, Warsaw, PL
WP	Washington Post, DC, US
WT	Washington Times, DC, US
WinT	Winnipeg Tribune, MB, CA

Notes

Overture—The Inspiration of Albani

3-5 **Albani dressed in court mourning**: "Social events," *G&M*, March 23, 1901, 21.; **program of German, French and English songs**: "Music and Drama," *G&M*, April 27, 1901.

Introduction – The Dream of the Prima Donna

6   **highest paid performers**: Rutherford, *The Prima Donna and Opera*, 15.

7   **Albani's picture featured**: *A Souvenir of Musical Toronto*, 1897.

7   **Emma Albani:** Library and Archives Canada, "Biographies: Emma Albani, Soprano and Voice Teacher (1847-1930)."

8   **singers' autobiographies**: Rutherford, *The Prima Donna and Opera*, 203, describes a "cult in memoirs and autobiographies… towards the end of the nineteenth century."

8   **opera stars of the era published memoirs:** For a sample of contemporary memoirs of opera singers and musicians see: Albani, Emma, *Forty Years of Song.*; Kellog, Clara Louise. *Memoirs of an American prima donna.*; Lehmann, Lillian, *My Path Through Life.*; Farrar, Geraldine, *The Story of an American Singer.*; Howard Baird, Kathleen, *Confessions of an Opera Singer.*; Fay, Amy. *Music Study in Germany.*

8   **absorbed from books**: Rutherford, *The Prima Donna and Opera*, 139.

9   **patrons and protettore:** Rutherford, *The Prima Donna and Opera*, 137.

9   **Albani's terrier**: Labreche-Lasrouche, *Emma Albani, International Star*, 96.

9   **course of study in Europe:** Armstrong, *Lillian Nordica's Hints to Singers.*

10   **popular novels**: DuMaurier, *Trilby*; F. Marion Crawford, *Soprano* (1905), *The Primadonna*, (1908) and *The Diva's Ruby* (1908).

11   **34 bedrooms**: Rutherford, *The Prima Donna and Opera*, 185.

12   **salary…barely adequate:** "The Poor Salaries Paid Opera Singers," TW, June 18, 1911.

13   **compared positively with great stars**: Augustus Bridle, "Miss Crawford Scores Vocal Triumph Here,"*TDS*, November 10, 1921, 13.; "Theatre and Music,", *NV*, February 12, 1915, 5.; "Theatre and Music,", *NV*, April 7(20), 1915, 6.; E.R. Parkhurst, "Music and Drama," *G&M*, November 10, 1921, 9.; "A most successful concert," *TDS*, May 1, 1909, 20.; "Images and pictures - a wonderful invention," *SP*, August 8, 1931, 6.

Entr'acte–A Child Takes the Stage

14   **first concert**: "Entertainment," *EC*, February 14, 1895.

Chapter One – An Inheritance of Ambition, 1858-1895

18   **Bertha's paternal grandparents**: John Crawford (1833-1883) and Mary Crawford (1831-1911).

18   **Kilbirnie:** The description of Kilbirnie owes much to Google Street View and my personal experience of small towns in Scotland and northern England.

18   **Scottish emigration:** Harper, "Crossing Borders: Scottish Emigration to Canada."

18   **Crawford genealogy:** The databases of Ancestry.com were invaluable in reconstructing the family tree of the Crawford family and their relationship to their Walton cousins, and history of their migration internationally, and within Canada. Particularly important were census entries in English, Canadian, and American census, and birth, marriage and death records. Provincial and city directories were also accessed via Ancestry.com, The Internet Archive, and in person at Library and Archives Canada.

21   **Elmvale was a place in flux:** The description of Elmvale is based on information from the *Elmvale Chronicle*.

22   **childhood roots:** Information about the Crawfords children's childhood is based on numerous references in the *Elmvale Chronicle* (1893-1901) and *Elmvale Lance* (1901-1905).

24   **first concert**: "Entertainment," *EC*, February 14, 1895.

25   **estimated the total loss:** "Elmvale's Calamity," *EC*, July 18, 1895, 4-5.

       successful businessman: the information about John Crawford's career in Elmvale is based on numerous references in the *Elmvale Chronicle* (1893-1901) and *Elmvale Lance* (1901-1905).

26   **town fires in Ontario**: Shorter, *Ottawa-Hull Fire of 1900.*; Glazebrook, *The Story of Toronto*, 25.

Entr'acte–Every Phoenix Needs a Fire

28   **1895 fire in Elmvale**: "Elmvale's Calamity," *EC*, July 18, 1895, 4-5.

Chapter Two – Music in the Family, 1895-1903

32   **Elmvale Presbyterian Church:** *Semi-Centennial, Elmvale Presbyterian Church, 1860-1910*. Lucas and Train, *Years of Witness: Elmvale Presbyterian Church*.

33   **piano manufacturing in Ontario:** Hayes and Kallmann, "Piano Building."

34   **brass band:** The rise and fall of the Elmvale Silver Band can be traced through many entries in the *Elmvale Chronicle* and *Elmvale Lance*.

36   **always sang mezzo to my sister's soprano:** "Canadian Girl Sings Opera at Petrograd", *CSM*, September 22, 1915, 4.

38   **public library:** "Public Library and Reading Room," *EC*, August 31, 1899.

39   **Women's Christian Temperance Union:** WCTU, "Welcome to the WCTU."

41   **Pan American Exhibition:** Eck, Susan, "Doing the Pan: Pan-American Exposition at Buffalo in 1901," http://panam1901.org/.

42   **strong, clear, flexible voice:** *EC*, December 3, 1902.

43   **horse racing:** The successes of John Crawford and his horses on the racetrack can be traced through the social columns of the *Elmvale Chronicle*, *Elmvale Lance* and in racing pages of *The Globe*.

Entr'acte–Life is a Gamble

44   **ice race at Barrie:** "'Princevale' Champion of the Province," *EC*, February 22, 1900.

Chapter Three – The First Rungs on the Ladder, 1903-1907

48   **helped build the town:** *EC*, April 15, 1903.

48 **an Elmvale lassie:** *EC*, February 8, 1905.
49 **Merchant's Picnic:** "Merchants Go Merry-Making", *TS*, July 16, 1903, 3.
49 **Toronto's economy:** Glazebrook, *The story of Toronto*, 200-201.
50 **a city dominated by its churches:** Roberston, *Robertson's Landmarks of Toronto*.
50 **Toronto a conservative place:** Kilbourn, *Intimate Grandeur*.; St. John, *Firm Foundations*.
51 **a close relationship between music and religion:** Kallmann, Morey and Wardrop, "Toronto, Ontario." **three prominent music schools:** Godfrey, *A Souvenir of Musical Toronto*.
51 **Edward Schuch:** The details of E.W. Schuch's life and career have been reconstructed from census and vital statistics information accessed via Ancestry.com and from numerous reports in *The Globe* and *The Toronto Daily Star* and *Musical Canada*.
52 **Bel canto:** Taylor, "The Art of Beautiful Song", *MC*, 327-332.
56 **full of promise:** *EC*, February 8, 1905.
56 **deserving special attention:** "Music and Drama," *G&M*, March 28, 1906, 14.; **ease and grace:** "Music and Drama," *G&M*, November 2, 1906, 12.; **Parkhurs**t: Stuart, Ross. "The Critic as Reviewer: E.R. Parkhurst at the Toronto Mail and Globe 1876-1924," in Wagner, A., ed. *Establishing Our Boundaries*, 95-106.
58 **paid soloists at the Metropolitan Church:** MUC The details of Bertha's career at the Metropolitan Methodist Church were illuminated by a visit to the church archives of the Metropolitan United Church.
58 **woman school teachers in Ontario earned**: Gidney and Millar, "The Salaries of Teachers in English Canada, 1900–1940: A Reappraisal," 1-38.
58 **appointed to Sherbourne Street Methodist Church:** "Music and the Drama," *G&M*, April 12, 1906, 14.
60 **Ladell-Fox touring plan:** "Music and the Drama," *G&M*, January 7, 1907, 12.
60 **the economics of the business:** Vickery, "Two Patterns of Touring in Canada: 1896 to 1914," 1-19.

60   The details of the lives and careers of Marietta Ladell, George Fox, Hugh Ruthven MacDonald, Elizabeth MacDonald, and Grace Merry have been reconstructed from census and vital statistics information accessed via Ancestry.com and from reports in *The Globe* and *The Toronto Daily Star* and *Musical Canada*.

61   **splendid rich voice**: "Overflow Locals," *NE*, February 14, 1907, 1.; PMPC, *The H. Ruthven MacDonald Concert Party*, 1909 brochure.

62   **Massey Hall:** Kilbourn, *Intimate Grandeur*.

63   **stage modifications at Massey Hall**: "Music and the Drama," *G&M*, April 13, 1907, 11.

63   **Pirates of Penzance:** "Music and Drama. " *TDS*, April 19, 1907, 8. "Music and Drama," *G&M*, April 19, 1907, 14.

Entr'acte – Competing for the Metropolitan Prize

65   **competition for soloists at the Metropolitan Methodist Church:** PMPC, *The H. Ruthven MacDonald Concert Party*, 1909 brochure described Bertha's soloist position with the Metropolitan Methodist Church as "a position, which she gained in competition with dozens of Canada's foremost sopranos."

Chapter Four – The Pinnacle of Choirs, 1907-1909

69   **Dr. Torrington:** St. John, *Firm Foundations*, 94-95.

70   **Herbert Wheeldon:** Herbert Wheeldon's career in England and Toronto can be traced through census data and numerous reports in *The Globe*, *The Toronto Daily Star*, and *The Musical Times*, and in the archives of the Metropolitan United Church. A particularly useful reference was "H. A. Wheeldon," *Musical Canada*, 2, 1907, accessed April 20, 2012, Internet Archive.

71   **competition:** PMPC, The H. Ruthven MacDonald Concert Party, 1909 brochure.

72   **Metropolitan Methodist Church:** St. John, *Firm Foundations*, 85-106; MUC Correspondence from the Music Committee.

74	**Arthur Blight**: Arthur Blight Fonds, *LAC*, Vol. MUS 31, File 19731, Box 1 and 2.
75	**fourteen 'patronesses'**: "Social Events", *G&M*, March 14, 1908, 13.
75	**a microcosm of the ruling class**: The Society Blue Book of Toronto, Hamilton and London - A Social Directory, (1908), Internet Archive.
75	**good friends with John Craig Eaton**: "Social Events", *G&M*, May 25, 1908, 6.
75	**a fan of opera**: Eaton, *Memory's Wall*, 57.
76	**program**: "Music and the Drama", *G&M*, February 29, 1908, 11; "Music and the Drama", *G&M*, March 30, 1908, 12.
77	**a lack of balance in the ensemble**: *G&M*, March 31, 1908.
77	**fit for the operatic field**: "Social and Personal," *EC*, April 9, 1908.
77	**Peterborough concert**: "Stony Lake", *G&M*, August 8, 1908, 13.; "Zetland's Ladies' Night", *G&M*, January 30, 1909.
77	**Bertha not in Iolanthe cast**: E.R. Parkhurst, "Music and Drama," *G&M*, December 11, 1908, 12.

Entr'acte – A Satisfactory Picture

79	**portrait at the Aylett studio**: PMPC A 1909 advertising brochure for the H. Ruthven MacDonald Concert Party suggests that "it was only after great influence had been brought to bear that [Bertha] was enabled to obtain a leave of absence to make this tour." All the photos of Bertha used in the tour brochure and poster are taken by Charles Aylett (1880-1942), as is the portrait of Wallace Graham printed in *Musical Canada* in 1910. Aylett was a society photographer from about 1900 through to the 1930s, who had a studio on Queen Street West.

Chapter Five – Riding the Rails, 1909-1911

83	**the economics of the business**: Vickery, "Two Patterns of Touring in Canada: 1896 to 1914," 1-19.
83	**Wallace Graham**: The details of the life and career of Wallace Graham have been reconstructed from census and vital statistics information

accessed via Ancestry.com and from reports in *The Globe, The Brandon Daily Sun, the Manitoba Free Press* and *Musical Canada*.

84 **Chautauqua circuits:** Maxwell, Jeffrey S., "The Complete Chautauquan: a Chautaugua Collection". http://www.crackerjackcollectors.com/Jeffrey_Maxwell/alphachautauquan/.

84 **Wallace Graham:** MacGregor, "Chronicle and Comment," *MC*, November 1910, 187.

84 **promotional materials**: PMPC, *The H. Ruthven MacDonald Concert Party*, 1909 brochure.

86 **H. Ruthven MacDonald Concert Party**: The details of the Western Canadian tours undertaken by the H. Ruthven MacDonald Concert Party in 1990-1910 and 1910-1911 have been reconstructed from reports in *Musical Canada, The Manitoba Free Press, The Lethbridge Herald, Brandon Daily Sun, Red Deer News, Crossfield Chronicle, Claresholm Review, Bow Island Review, Blairmore Enterprise, Frank Vindicator, The Calgary Daily Herald, The Regina Morning Leader, The Moyie Leader* and *The Daily Colonist*.

87 **the party favoured songs:** "Theatrical – The H. Ruthven Macdonald Concert Party, " *LDH*, January 28, 1911, 3; "Music and Drama," *MFP*, November 2, 1910.; "H. Ruthven Mac Donald Concert Party," *MFP*, November 2, 1910.

88 **clear as a lark**: E.B.,"H. Ruthven MacDonald Concert Party," *MFP*, November 2, 1909.

89 **the Montreal Opera Company:** Cooper, *Opera in Montreal and Toronto*, 394-471. Potvin.; "Montreal Opera Company/Compagnie d'opéra de Montréal."

90 **God-fearing city like Toronto**: Charlesworth, *More Candid Chronicles*, 378.

Entr'acte – Sailing into Uncharted Waters

93 **travel by ship from Montreal to Liverpool:** Passenger records show a Bertha Crawford travelling in First Class from Montreal to Liverpool on the Allen Steamship Line R.M.S. Virginian, arriving 17 June 1911, UK Incoming Passenger Lists, 1878-1960, Ancestry.com. Detailed

contemporary descriptions of trans-Atlantic travel were accessed April 16, 2012, The Gjenvick-Gjonvik Archives.

Chapter Six – Crossing the Atlantic, 1911-1912

98 **six Canadian girls**: E.R. Parkhurst, "Music and the Drama," *G&M*, May 20, 1912, 8.

99 **safety**: "A Warning to Parents," *MC*, 2 no. 2, May 1907, 33-34.; "Dangers Exist for Young Girl Students," *TSW*, January 1, 1911.

99 **Olga De Nevosky**: *Annuaire des artistes et de l'enseignement dramatique et musical*. (1909). In E. Risacher (Eds.) Available from http://gallica.bnf.fr/; and various other references in contemporary periodicals available through Gallica, and UK census and directories accessed via Ancestry.com.

100 **stepped out of a romance**: "Some reflections in my mirror," *DM*, March 23, 1915, 7.

100 **I sing for her sake**: "Music and the Drama," *G&M*, May 20, 1912, 8.

100 **Otto Morando**: The details of the life and career of Otto Brandeis (Morando) have been reconstructed from census and vital statistics information accessed via Ancestry.com and from reports in *The Globe* and *The Toronto Daily Star*, Von Kunits, Otto Morando [Biographical sketch]," *CMJ*, 304, McPherson, "Otto Morando," *Canadian Academy of Music Limited*, 13-14, and *NYPL-PA*, Otto Morando Papers.

101 **fellow Torontonians**: The details of the lives and careers of Margaret George, Arthur George, Madeline Hunt and Gladys Banks have been reconstructed from census and vital statistics information accessed via Ancestry.com and from reports in *The Globe* and *The Toronto Daily Star* and *Musical Canada*.

102 **Lamperti method**: Lamperti, *The Art of Singing*.; Bergholt, "Albani and Voice Training," *MC*, December 1911, 264-265.; Rutherford, *The Prima Donna and Opera, 1815-1930*, 70-71.

103 **lyric and dramatic roles**: Rutherford, *The Prima Donna and Opera, 1815-1930*, 216-221.

104 **slender girlish figure:** "A Canadian Nightingale," *DBW*, October 27, 1921.

104 **an ideal Gilda in appearance:** "Miss Crawford to Sing in Opera," *WT*, January 23, 1923.

105 **getting notices from London:** Mills, "Some reflections on musical conditions in Canada and some advice to Canadians," *MC*, December 1909, 260-261.

105 **Bromley Choral Society**: "Suburban Concerts", *MT*, February 1, 1912, 116.

105 **National Sunday League**: Woodward, *The London Palladium*, 41-19.

10 **famous Scottish-Canadian soprano:** "Special Arrangements for Christmastide," *HStLO*, December 16, 1911.; "The Winter Orchestra," *HStLO*, December 30, 1911.; "Amongst the Scots," *HStLO*, January 27, 1912, 7.

106 **success in London**: "Society," *TW*, March 30, 1912, 8.

106 **Queen's Hall concerts**: *LS*, January 15, 1912, April 22, 1912, and May 6, 1912

106 **sympathy with victims of the Titanic**: E.R. Parkhurst, "Music and the Drama," *G&M*, May 20, 1912, 8.

107 **first Canadian record company:** LAC, *"The Berliner Gram-o-phone Company of Canada."*

107 **Will Gaisberg:** Gaisberg, *The Music Goes Round*.

108 **neither recording was released as a record:** Personal communication, Sonita Cox, Senior Archives Assistant, EMI Archives, January 10, 2013.

108 **his voice lives on:** A number of recordings by H. Ruthven MacDonald can be heard on the website of Library and Archives Canada.

108 **Widows and Orphans Benevolent Fund**: "Wisbech," *LM*, October 4, 1912, 4.

Entr'acte – The Singing Lesson

109 **Olga De Nevosky:** *Annuaire des artistes et de l'enseignement dramatique et musical*. (1909). In E. Risacher (Eds.) Available from http://gallica.bnf.fr/; and various other references in contemporary periodicals available through Gallica, and UK census and directories accessed via Ancestry.com.; **Lamperti method:** Lamperti, *The Art of Singing*.

Chapter Seven – An Italian Interlude, 1912-1913

116 **Pygmalion project**: while it is enticing to think that Zofia might have been directly inspired by George Bernard Shaw's play, *Pygmalion*, which he wrote in 1912, the play was not produced in London until 1914. However, clearly the idea that the right training in languages and manners could allow a woman to pass as an aristocrat had currency at the time.

118 **Emilia Corsi:** Arakelyan, "Emilia Corsi."

119 *disposizione scenica:* Gossett, Divas and Scholars, 459-61.

119 **advance notices of debut:** "'Tales of Hoffman' Admirably Sung," *G&M*, February 13, 1913, 8.; "Miss Bertha Crawford Makes debut in Milan," *TDS*, February 13, 1913.

119 **controversy about payments**: "A Warning to Parents," *MC*, 2 no. 2, May 1907, 33-34.; "Student Life in Italy," *MC*, 2 no. 5, 210-212.

119 **payments as a necessary investment:** Armstrong, *Lillian Nordica's Hints to Singers, 80-81*.; Michele Fratianni and Franco Spinelli, "Italy in the Gold Standard Period, 1861-1914," in Bordo an dSchwartz, ed., *A Retrospective on the Classical Gold Standard*, 437.; Bank of Canada, *The History of the Canadian Dollar*, 97.

120 **Pagliacci:** Bourne, *Who Married Figaro?*, 222.

120 **debut night**: "Toronto prima donna Makes Italian Debut," *TSWor*, May 3, 1913.

121 **Gilda in Venice and Del Verme, Milan**: Charlesworth, H., "Canadian Prima Donna and Idol in Russia," *SN*, October 1, 1921.

Entr'acte – Backstage at the Opera

125 **drab little dressing room:** The description of the opera star's dressing room in the first decade of the 20th century owes much to contemporary descriptions in France Marion Crawford's *Fair Margret*, 1905, and *The Prima Donna*, 1908.

Chapter Eight – A Year in Warsaw, 1913-1914

130 **event which was to shape her history**: Charlesworth, "Canadian Prima Donna," *SN*, October 1, 1921.

130 **size of Toronto at the time**: Glazebrook, The Story of Toronto, 212.; **size of Warsaw**: Wynot, *Warsaw Between the World Wars*, 38.;

131 **Warsaw was very much a European city**: Marcinkowski, *Warsaw Then and Now*.; Wynot, *Warsaw Between the World Wars*; **water connections**: Wynot, *Warsaw Between the World Wars*, 29.; **gas and electricity**: Marcinkowski, *Warsaw Then and Now*, 7.

131 **lap dogs**: Swaby, *Physiology of the Opera*.

133 **Warsaw Great Theatre main hall**: Pycka,"O XIX wiecznym teatrze warszawskim słów kilka [A few words about theatre in Warsaw in the 19th century]."

135 **Warsaw Theatre Directorate hired all the performers:** Wynot, *Warsaw Between the World Wars*, 22.

136 **Pietro Cimini:** "Nordic and Latin Contrast'" LAT, August 5, 1928, C15.

137 **favourable impression:** "Theatre and Music – Second Guest Appearance of D. A. Smirnov," *Vd*, March 14, 1914, 3.

140 **charity concert:** "Raut.," *KP*, March 1, 1914, 4.

140 **encouragement from Polish audiences**; Charlesworth, "Canadian Prima Donna," *SN*, October 1, 1921.

141 **terrible suspense:** "Miss Crawford Home, War Years in Russia," *TSW*, November 1921.

141 **guns, guns**: "A Canadian Nightingale," DBW, October 27, 1921.

Entr'acte – A Brush with Fame

143 **Shalyapin at the People's House**: A photograph by Karl Bulla showing Shalyapin discussing a performance on the stage of the People's House in 1913 is on display in the F.I. Shalyapin Memorial Apartment in St. Petersburg. Shalyapin performed in *Rusalka* on February 9, 1915 and Crawford appeared in *Rigoletto* in February 10, 1915. Crawford was photographed outside St. Isaac's Cathedral with her two Griffon Belge

dogs, "Canadian Girl Sings in Opera in Petrograd," *CSM*, September 22, 1915, 4. Shalypin was photographed with a Boston Terrier around the same time.

Chapter Nine – A 'Canadian Nightingale' Takes Flight

149 **People's House Opera:** Frame, *The St. Petersburg Imperial Theaters*, 65-73; Villari, *Russia of Today*.

150 **invited a senior Colonel to be God Father:** *TsGIA-SPb* f. 14 Vladimir Afanasievich Cherepanov university file, op. 3, d. 62255, l. 10. The **couple had been maintaining separate addresses:** Petrograd city directories, Russian National Library, retrieved from http://leb.nlr.ru.

150 **steadily worked his way upwards:** *TsGIA-SPb* f. 14 Vladimir Afanasievich Cherepanov university file, op. 3, d. 62255, ll. 23-28.

150 **Guardianship of Public Sobriety:** Herlihy, *The Alcoholic Empire*, 18.

151 **rumours were circulating:** *RNB* f. 1534 N.N. Figner, n. 98-IV+ 80 Diary of Olga Michailovna Gardner, ll. 124-125.

151 **actress with a reputation:** Fraser, *Russia of Today*, 84.

152 **ashamed of their innocence:** Tolstoy, *Road to Calvary*, 3.

153 **Nikolai Figner:** Maltese, "The Dawn of Recording: The Julius Block Cylinders."

153 **wife and friends feared that a *claque* was being organized:** *RNB* f. 1534 N.N. Figner, n. 98-IV+ 80 Diary of Olga Michailovna Gardner, ll. 124-125.

153 **alternating nights with Shalyapin:** Feb 9, Shalyapin in *Rusalka*, Feb 10 Crawford in *Rigoletto*, Feb 11 Shalyapin in *Boris Gudonov*, Feb 13 Shalyain in concert, Feb 14 Crawford in *Romeo and Juliette*, Feb 16 Shalyapin in *Faust*, Feb 17 Crawford in *TheBarber of Seville*, Feb 18 Shalyapin in *Don Quixote*, Feb 19 Crawford in *Rigoletto*, Feb 20 Shalyapin in *Mephistopheles*, reported in daily theatre notices in *Teatr I Iskusstvo*, February 1915.

153 **shared review with Shalyapin:** "People's House," *TI*, February 1915, (8) 128.

153 **Feodor Ivanovich Shalyapin:** Borovsky, *Chaliapin: A Critical Biography*.; F.I. Shalyapin Memorial Apartment.

155   **great crowds had surrounded the British embassy:** Buchanan, *Petrograd - The City of Trouble 1914-1918,* 16.

155   **an Anglo-Saxon coldness:** Nikonov, "Anglo-American-Italian-Russian Alliance (Guest Appearance by Bertha Crawford at the People's House),"*OT*, February 12, 1915, 2672/6.

155   **the Rosina of Northern countries:** "Nikonov, "People's House - 'The Barber of Seville'," *OT*, March 1, 1915, 2694/8-9.

155   **union of our countries:** "Nikonov, "People's House - 'The Barber of Seville'," *OT*, March 1, 1915, 2694/8-9.

155   **an American from Canada**: RNB Gaz. 1-R/2-3, Afishi gosudarstvennȳkh petrogradskikh teatrov: ezhedn. sprav. teatr. organ s pril. obyavl. chast. teatrov i kontsertov [Posters of the Petrograd State Theatres], Petrograd, 1809 – 1917, recital May 8, 1915.

156   **audience was totally unanimous:** "People's House – The farewell performance of Mr. Kamionskiy and Bertha Crawford in 'Traviata'," *OT*, March 14-15, 1915, 2700-2701/4-5.

157   **reduced the government's revenues:** Herlihy, *The Alchoholic Empire*, 145.

157   **scale of their charitable activity:** Frame, *The St. Petersburg Imperial Theaters,* 139-140

158   **large star studded casts:**.; "Theatre and Music," *NV*, April 7(20), 1915, 6.; **guests like the British Ambassador and the French Ambassador:** "Evening at the Palace of His Imperial Highness the Grand Duke Andre Vladimiovich," *NV*, April 15(20), 1915, 6.

159   **Albani meets the Tsar**: Albani, *Forty Years of Song*, 83.

159   **presented with a new decoration**: "Artists at the Winter Palace," *OT*, March 29, 1915 (2709) 11.; **described in a letter home**: "Music," *SN*, June 19, 1915.

160   **worked with Taskin in at least four charity concerts:** RNB Gaz. 1-R/2-3, Afishi gosudarstvennȳkh petrogradskikh teatrov: ezhedn. sprav. teatr. organ s pril. ob"yavl. chast. teatrov i kontsertov [Posters of the Petrograd State Theatres], Petrograd, 1809 – 1917, concerts April 4, 24, May 8, 24, 1915.

160   **sings in Russian amazingly:** Nikonov, B. "People's House - 'The Barber of Seville'," *OT*, March 1, 1915, 2694/8-9.

160 **noted for his ability**: Uvarova, *Éstrada V Rossii. Xx Vek. Éntsiklopediya* [Encyclopedia of the Russian Stage in the 20th Century], 650-651.

161 **May 8th program**: TsGALI-SPb f. 162 A.V. Taskin, op. 1, d. 69, ll. 8- 9.

162 **winning honours**: Parkhurst, "Toronto Singer in Russia," *G&M*, May 1, 1915, 15; **Charlesworth**: Salter, Denis. "H. Willoughby Charlesworth and the Nationalization of Cultural Authority," in Wagner ed., *Establishing Our Boundaries*, 137-176.; "Music and Drama," *SN*, June 19, 1915, 6.; **French translation**: Parkhurst, "Bertha Crawford's Success," *MC*, 19(3) July 1915, 64.

163 **normal musical season in Warsaw**: D.C., "Warsaw (Correspondents)," *Rmg*, May 1915, 358-9.

163 **Aleksander Rajchman**: Balińska, *For the Good of Humanity*:; "Music and Drama," *G&M*, October 20, 1906, 17.; Maltese, "The Dawn of Recording: The Julius Block Cylinders."

164 **La Traviata**: Bourne, *Who Married Figaro?*, 298.

164 **a voice of crystal purity**: "Benefit for the Chorus," *KW*, June 21, 1915.

164 **Germans launch another major attack**: Esposito, *The West Point Atlas of War: World War 1*, 54.

Entr'acte – A Narrow Escape

166 **escape from Warsaw**: Dr. Julian Kosinski's memorial in the Stare Powązki Cemetery, Warsaw, was kindly located and photographed in by Ewelina Hallman. The correspondent for the *London Times*, Stanley Washburn described in detail his final days in Warsaw prior to the German occupation in Washburn, *Victory in Defeat*, 101-113.

Chapter Ten – Adrift in a Storm of Change, 1915-1918

171 **difficult to make a living**: Charlesworth, *More Candid Chronicles*, 198.

171 **Pavlovski Vauxhall:** Stite, *Passion and Perception: Essays on Russian Culture*, 517-521.; **speech is almost without reproach:** "Theatre and Music," *NV*, September 10, 1915, 6.

171 **debuted new Russian material:** "Chronicle," *OT*, October 1915, 2897/12.

172   **secured a three night test run with Zimin:** "Chronicle," *OT*, October 1915, 2927/12.

173   **1915-1916 Moscow opera season:** F-tov', N.N., "Opera Results in Moscow 1915-1916," *Rmg*, 1916, 24-25/503-504.

173   **damning with faint praise:** "B. Crawford Performs at Zimin's," *NS*, November 17, 1915, 3154/4.; **not a virtuoso:** "Touring Artist Bertha Crawford," *Tr*, November 19, 1915, 1771/7.

174   **Sibelius, nature and music**: Reade, *Finland and the Finns*, 175.

176   **Nordica**: Glackens, *Yankee Diva*, 295.

176   **Tampere review**: "Bertha Crawford's Concert," *TN*, March 6, 1916.

177   **shell shock:** What we would now call post-traumatic stress disorder, or operational stress injury.

177   **charity concert at A.S. Suvorin's private theatre:** "Theatre and Music," *NV*, April 5 (18), 1916, 6.

177   **Adelheim tour of 25 towns**: Barker, A., "My Musical Life in Russia," *Music Masterpieces: Gems from the World's Famous Operas and Musical Plays* 28, 1926, 110.

177   **Robert Adelheim**: Jewish Encyclopedia In Russian On The Web, "Adelheim Brothers"; Pskov Academic Drama Theatre, named after A.S. Pushkin, "High Repertoire of the Adelheim Brothers."

178   **spontaneous invitation:** Barker, "My Musical Life in Russia," 110.

179   **every town has an opera house:** "A Canadian Nightingale: Miss Bertha Crawford Who Appears in Grant Hall Thursday Evening," *DBW*, October 27, 1921.; **musical enthusiasm:** Charlesworth, "Canadian Prima Donna, " *SN*, October 1, 1921.; **intense appreciation**: "Bertha Crawford has a most charming manner," *PE*, March 1922.

179   **this meandering railway:** Westwood, "The Vladikavkaz Railway: A Case of Enterprising Private Enterprise," 669-675.

179   **an area of state managed hot springs:** Clemow, "Notes on Health Resorts and Sanatoria," Br Med J, 1921, 2/1189-1190.

179   **a suitably multinational program**: "Tragic Concert – Robert Adelhiem," *KK*, May 12, 1916, 1.

181   **Nickola Pashitch presents regimental banners:** MO "Ob"edinenaya serbskaya diaspora Evrazii", "With the Serbian Volunteer Division 1916.; **Serbia overrun in 1915:** Esposito, *The West Point Atlas of War:*

World War 1, 80; Parkhurst, E.R., "Toronto Singer in Russia," *MC*, August 4, 1916, 59.

182 **delighted the audience**: "First Symphony Concert," *DP*, September, 22, 1916.

182 **family in the dark**: Charlesworth, "Canadian Prima Donna," *SN*, October 1, 1921.; **the problem of getting food**: Charlesworth, "Canadian Prima Donna," *SN*, October 1, 1921.; **met Rasputin**: "A Canadian Nightingale," *DBW*, October 27, 1921.

183 **Bertha was in Helsinki**: Charlesworth, "Canadian Prima Donna, "*SN*, October 1, 1921.

184 **the party had hoped to continue their tour all the way to Japan**: "Miss Crawford Home, War Years in Russia, " *TSW*, 1921.; **another Russian concert party**: "Our Concert Tour to Siberia and Japan," *Rmg*, 1916, 590-593.

184 **on the Trans Siberian railway**: This description of the trip to Vladivostok relies heavily on the contemporary account of: Bell, *Side Lights on the Siberian Campaign*, 18-33.

187 **A.E. Kemp**: Turley-Ewart "Kemp, Sir Albert Edward"; **Enquiries of the Foreign Office**: NA, FO 371/3739, Foreign Office, Political Departments, General Correspondence from 1906-1966. Finland, pages 35631, 37660, Letter from A.E.Kemp, telegram from Bell.

187 **slashed tapestries**: "A Canadian Nightingale," *DBW*, October 27, 1921.

187 **let artists alone**: Charlesworth, "Canadian Prima Donna," *SN*, October 1, 1921.

188 **decorations null and void**: Farmborough, *Nurse at the Russian Front*, 385.

188 **leaving Petrograd**: *OT*, June 14, 1918, 3763/6.

188 **lost everything in Russia**: Prav. V., "Miss Crawford's Russian Success," *KS*, October 27, 1921.

189 **doesn't like to talk of the war**: "A Canadian Nightingale," *DBW*, October 27, 1921.

Entr'acte – The Great Train Robbery

190 **invitation to the Winter Palace:** "Artists at the Winter Palace," *OT*, April 8, 1915, 2721/9.; **the train robbery:** "Miss Crawford lost everything in Russia, her money, baggage and private belongings. She could not even draw her money from the bank, as the law was then that only 500 roubles a month could be drawn out of the bank." *KS*, October 27, 1921.; description of the train robbery is loosely based on incidents in: Tolstoy, *Road to Calvary*, 391-395.; Farmborough, *Nurse at the Russian Front*, 360-369.; **keeping war time awards out of sight after the revolution:** Farmborough, *Nurse at the Russian Front*, 385.

Chapter Eleven – A Return to Stability, 1918-1921

195 **advertising singing lessons:** *KW*, August 11, 1918, 220/13.

195 **constant companions:** "She made many friends in Warsaw and among the dearest are her tiny dogs, four Griffon Belge...Two have been the singer's constant companions." "A Canadian Nightingale," *DBW*, October 27, 1921.

197 **massive damage:** Radziwill, "Poland Since the Great War," 293-303.

197 **enquiries of the Foreign Office:** NA, FO 371/3739, Foreign Office, Political Departments, General Correspondence from 1906-1966. Finland, pages 35631, 37660, Letter from A.E. Kemp, telegram from Bell.

198 **culture consolidated and events celebrated with opera:** Komorowska, *Za Kurtnyna Lat*, 321.

198 **Emil Mlynarksi:** Kosinska, "Emil Mlynarski,"; "Emil Mlynarski," *MT*, May 1, 1915, 265-268.

200 **favourite meeting places of music lovers:** Nowicki, *Warsaw: The Cabaret Years*, 19-20.

201 **Aflred Strauch:** "Suicide of Director A. Straucha," *IR*, June 6, 1934, 1.

202 **Spontaneity:** Felix Halpern, "At the concert hall," *GP*, February 13, 1919 (43), 5.

203 **her coloratura vocal technique:** "At the Philhamomic, Concerts in the Period 28/II 1919 to 28/III," *PM*, April 1, 1919, 11.

203 **her vocal training**: P.K., "At the Philhamomic," *GW,* October 1, 1920, 2.
205 **fears that Warsaw would fall to the Soviet army:** "Miss Crawford Home, War Years in Russia," *TSW,* 1921; Charlesworth, "Canadian Prima Donna," *SN,* October 1, 1921.; **Krakow concert**: "In the concert hall," *IKC,* October 18, 1920, 6.
208 **Poznan *Teatr Weilki* :** (2012) *Poznan Great Theatre, Named After Stansilawa Moniuszki, About the Theatre,* accessed August 1, 2012 from http://www.opera.poznan.pl/page.php/1/0/show/15/
208 **Adam Dolzycki**: "Adam Dołżycki," *Biographical Dictionary of the Polish Theater 1900-1980 Volume II,* accessed from http://www.e-teatr.pl/en/osoby/49327.html.
209 **outstanding performer**: "At the Theatre," *GW,* January 21, 1921 44 (3), 2.
209 **guest soloist with the Poznan Opera**: Switala, *Opera Poznanask 1919-1969,* 435-436.
209 **Gounod's Faust:** Singher, *An Interpretive Guide to Operatic Arias.*; Bourne, *Who Married Figaro?,* 91.

Entr'acte – The Myth in the Making

211 **Kingston newspaper interview**: "A Canadian Nightingale," *DBW,* October 27, 1921.

Chapter Twelve – Transatlantic Times, 1921-1923

216 **French accent**: "Bertha Crawford Has a Most Charming Manner," *PE,* March 1922.
217 **had enough of Eastern Europe**: Charlesworth, "Canadian Prima Donna," *SN,* October 1, 1921, 12.
218 **Toronto Operatic Chorus**: Cooper, *Opera in Montreal and Toronto,* 712.
219 **Suckling**: Kallmann. "I. Suckling & Sons."
220 **renewed concert management**: "Issac E.Suckling Quits Steamships," *G&M,* March 1, 1919, 9.

220 **inferiority complex about Canadian artists**: Charlesworth, *I'm Telling You*, 102.

221 **most distinguished coloratura soprano**: Charlesworth, "Canadian Prima Donna," *SN*, October 1, 1921, 12.

223 **Bridle**: McLean, "Augustus Bridle."

223 **frock of silver cloth**: "Very Smart Audience Greets Toronto Singer," *G&M*, November 10, 1921, 10.

224 **bouquets piled up**: "Toronto Singer Scores: Triumph for Miss Crawford," *ET*, November 9, 1921.

225 **Women's Musical Club**: "Social Events," *G&M*, December 2, 1921, 14.

225 **Montreal debut**: "Les Grenadiers," *LCM*, February 4, 1922, 13.; "Un Pieux Hommage a Saint-Saens," *LPat*, January 30, 1922.; **Grenadier Guards Band**: Plouffe, "Canadian Grenadier Guards Band."

226 **appearing with Damrosch in New York**: "Music: Holiday Opera and Concerts," *NYT*, December 18, 1921.

228 **Canadian song publishing**: Kallmann, "Publishing and Printing."; Nygaard King, "Songwriters and Songwriting (English Canada) Before 1921."; Kallmann, "Patrioic Songs."; **Alberta "Bertie" Aikin-Green**: The details of the life and career of Bertie Aikin-Green have been reconstructed from census and vital statistics information accessed via Ancestry.com, and from sheet music in the collection of *LAC*.

230 **the rational school**: "Great Theatre: Rigoletto – The Barber of Seville – Carmen," *KP* (118), May 23, 1922.

231 **freshly returned**: *SN*, October 28, 1922.

231 **Albion and the Washington Opera**: McPherson, "Mr. Meek Goes to Washington", 197.267.

234 **had a cold**: "'Rigoletto' Has Thrills for Audience," *WP*, January 1923.

234 **recently returned**: "Concert with Bertha Crawford," *KW* (142), May 24, 1923, 4-5.

234 **masterly vocal techniques**: P.R. *GW*, May 27, 1923.

234 **chords of deeper feeling**: Szopiki, F., "At the Phiharmonic," *KWar*, May 26, 1923.

THE CANADIAN NIGHTINGALE

234 **popular press credited Didur:** Jack, "At the Theatre: Adam Didur, On the Occasion of his Performance at the Warsaw Opera", *Blu*, July 1923, 27/229.

235 **hyper-inflation took over the economy:** Smith, "The Zloty, 1924-35," 145-183.; Krzyżanowski, "Currency Reform in Poland," 316-325.

235 **newsstand price of *Bluszcz*:** Issues of Bluszcz magazine for 1923 were consulted in the Varsavia Department of the Warsaw Public Library.

236 **Sawyer is known to have charged:** Hill, "Grainger's Managers."; **managers providing a personal touch:** Sawyer, *Songs at Twilight*.

236 **cerise chiffon velvet:** "Musical Club Opens Season," *WinT*, November 6, 1923, 9.

238 **significant nest egg:** "Estranged friends – case for $10,000 between p. Bertha Crawford and p. Kosinska," *ABC*, 1 December 1933, 2.

Entr'acte – Wrapping up the Album

239 **album of newspaper clippings:** The album referred to in this vignette is in the private collection of Paul Mably.

Chapter Thirteen – Choosing Poland, 1924-1926

243 **successes in Poland:** "Former Elmvale Girl May Wed Polish Count," *CB*, September 11, 1924.

243 **Warsaw following:** Ibid.

244 **Warsaw circus:** contemporary pictures of the Waraaw circus can be found in the online collection of the National Photographic Archive.

245 **1924 performance with Didur:** "Chronicle of the Opera," *PTF*, June 1924, 19-21.

246 **Karol de Hauke:** The details of the life and career of Karol de Hauke have been reconstructed from information accessed at Archiwum Państwowe w Warszawie [State Archives of Warsaw], http://szukajwarchiwach.pl/ and Archiwum Korporacyjne [Archive of Polish Academic Fraternities], http://www.archiwumkorporacyjne.pl/en/, and personal communications and family photographs from descendants, Alexander and Henrik de Hauke in Sweden; **looked after the**

dog: Anna Szostakwska, Karol Hauke's granddaughter, personal communication, May 2016; **remembered by his daughter**: Maria Hauke, unpublished memoir.

248 **Orange Lodge influence:** "For nearly a century the Orange Lodge has been so strong in Toronto that the greater part of almost every City Council have been those appearing on the Orange 'slate'...the policies of Conservative and Protestant Orangeism have usually been considered... to be the public opinion of the city as a whole", Guillet, *Toronto*, 389.; **unheard of to marry a Catholic**: personal communication from Paul Mably who had compiled an extended family tree of the Crawford and Pearson families.

249 **personal letter to Suckling**: "Former Elmvale Girl May Wed Polish Count," *CB*, September 11, 1924.

250 **Jerzy Bojanowski:** Draft entry for Polish Dictionary of Biography, Volume III, Bojanowski, Jerzy, consulted at the Instytut Sztui Polskiej Akademic Nauk, Warsaw.

250 **Opera Pomorska:** Komorowska, *Za Kurtyna Lat*, 137-140.; Kwaskowski, *Teatr w Toruniu 1920-1939*, 78-79.

Entr'acte – A Stage in the Air

252 **radio program in honour of American Independence Day:** "Warsaw Radio Concert Program," *NP*, July 4, 1926, 8

Chapter Fourteen – Public Lives and Private Dramas, 1926-1934

256 **earliest years critics argued:** various essays published in Muzyka in 1926-27.

257 **supremely successful:** "Musical Broadcasts 'Polish Radio," *Muz* June 6, 1927 (4), 292.

257 **offering voice lessons:** "News of the Day," *NP*, September 30, 1926, 8.

258 **loans money to Zofia**: "Estranged friends – case for $10,000 between p. Bertha Crawford and p. Kosinska," *ABC*, 1 December 1933, 2.

259 **finally her own apartment:** "Warsaw Grand Opera Singer Visits Parents in Toronto," *TDS*, July 26, 1934, 28.

260 **founders of the Polish League of the Friends of Animals:** "Polish League of the Friends of Animals in 1927," *SZ*, November 1929, 12.

260 **great and wonderful vocal technique:** "In the Concert Halls: Warsaw Symphony Orchestra at the Philharmonic," *GWP*, October 4, 1927, 4.

261 **vote for the top Polish musicians:** "Echo of the Myzyka Plebicite," *Muz*, May 20, 1928, 215.; "Results of Music Poll," *Muz*, June 28, 1928, 265.

262 **Strauch hangs himself:** "Suicide of Director A. Straucha," *IR*, June 6, 1934, 1.

262 **ironic commentary:** "Is the word 'inquisition' an insult?," *RZ*, January 22, 1931, 9; "P. Trajdosiewicz versus Judge Lauter," *PZ*, May 10, 1931, 6.

262 **launch of Radio Poland:** Bryx, "History of Polish Radio."

263 **vignette published after an August radio concert:** "Images and pictures - a wonderful invention," *SP*, August 8, 1931, 6.

263 **although she is a 'Berta':** apparently a reference to 'Big Bertha', slang for the biggest guns produced by the Germans during the First World War.

264 **stars of the first magnitude**: "Radio," *EPT*, October 9, 1932, 5.

264 **Janus Radziwill:** Stanczyk, "Radziwill in the Past Twenty Years."

264 **castle and estate at Nieswiez:** Neiswiez Castle is now in Belarus.

265 **performing for the other guests:** "Warsaw Grand Opera Singer Visits Parents in Toronto," *TDS*, July 26, 1934, 28.

265 delicate **innuendo**: "Estranged friends – case for $10,000 between p. Bertha Crawford and p. Kosinska," *ABC*, 1 December 1933, 2.

Entr'acte – The Final Return

267 **Mary Pickford parade:** Mary Pickford visited Toronto as part of the Centennial Celebrations in May 1934, and was treated to a full day of activities including a parade, as well as a civic reception and luncheon, etc., just two weeks before Bertha returned to Canada. See for

instance, "Rousing Welcome is Given to Favorite Daughter," *G&M*, May 11, 1934, 1.

Chapter Fifteen – An Uneasy Return, 1934-1937

271 **sacrificed a family life**: "Polish Women's Status Bettered," *WP*, June 7, 1934, 14.
271 **social column**: "Over the tea cups," *TDS*, June 6, 1934, 24.
271 **interview at her parents' home**: "Warsaw Grand Opera Singer Visits Parents in Toronto," *TDS*, July 26, 1934, 28.
272 **attractive hesitancy**: "Warsaw Grand Opera Singer Visits Parents in Toronto," *TDS*, July 26, 1934, 28.
273 **Lucia recorded in her date book**: *PMPC*, Lucia Pearson Date Book, 1930s.
273 **one visit Lucia's home**: Ernest Pearson, personal communication, December 2011.
273 **Pearson family**: Paul Mably, Ellen Mably, Beth Sklias, Wayne Marlow, Judy Marlow, personal communications, 2011, 2012.
274 **unemployment and relief**: Struthers and Foot, "Great Depression."; Macpherson and Holdsworth, "Impact of the Great Depression, 1928-1940."; Glazebrook, *The Story of Toronto*.
274 **putting on an optimistic show**: Middleton, *Toronto's 100 Years*.
275 **letters to Morando from ex-students**: *NYPL-PA*, Otto Morando Papers.
276 **Reginald Stewart**: Drynan, "Reginald Stewart."
277 **he set high standards**: Mason, L., "Prom. Orchestra Concerts," *G&M*, May 25, 1935, 10.
278 **McCarthy**: Greenhorn, "An Art Critic at the Ringside."
278 **homecoming**: "Prom is delighted by Bertha Crawford," *TDS*, August 23, 1935, 1.; **everyone began to sit up**: Pearl McCarthy, "Crawford holds Prom Spotlight," *M&E*, August 23, 1935.; **spontaneous welcome**: "Prom Concert is Invigorating," *ET*, August 23, 1935.
279 **a home which pulsed with life and activity**: Heard, *The Suite Life*.
280 **pneumonia**: Podolsky, "The Changing Fate of Pneumonia," 2144

280 **death rate from pneumonia:** Brundage, "Sickness among Male Industrial Employees during the First Quarter of 1937," 1170.
280 **ate sparingly:** "Warsaw Grand Opera Singer Visits Parents in Toronto," *TDS*, July 26, 1934, 28.
281 **unnoticed by thousands:** "Once great singer passes in Toronto," *G&M*, May 28, 1937.
281 **representatives of Toronto musical circles**: "Canadian Diva Buried," *TDS*, May 29, 1937, 28.
281 **Inventory of personal estate**: a microfilm copy of Crawford's was located in the Archives of Ontario; **equivalent to ten months average earnings:** Meltz, "Section E: Wages and Working Conditions."

Picture credits

7   **Emma Albani**, retrieved from Wikimedia Commons, July 24, 2017.
17 **Crawford family**, c. 1889, personal collection of Paul Mably.
24 **Elmvale Presbyterian Church**, image published on Flicker by Mike Wessesman, March 2013.
33 **Elmvale Silver Band**, c. 1895, Simcoe County Archives.
36 **Lucia Crawford**, c. 1902, personal collection of Paul Mably.
47 **Bertha Crawford**, c. 1907, personal collection of Paul Mably.
55 **Massey Hall**, c. 1902, Library and Archives Canada, in Kilbourn, *Intimate Grandeur*, 45.
59 **Marietta Ladell**, retrieved from Iowa Digital Library, University of Iowa Libraries, March 23, 2015.
68 **Bertha Crawford**, c. 1907, (photographer Charles Aylett, Toronto) personal collection of Paul Mably.
70 **Herbert Wheeldon**, *Musical Canada* 2, no. 6, (1907): 265. Internet Archive.

72	**Metropolitan Methodist Church,** c. 1873, Toronto Public Library, E 9-233 small, retrieved July 30, 2017.
73	**Massey Hall Stage,** c. 1900, Library and Archives Canada, in Kilbourn, *Intimate Grandeur*, 36.
82	**Bertha Crawford,** c. 1909, (photographer Charles Aylett, Toronto) personal collection of Paul Mably.
85	**Bertha Crawford tour poster,** c. 1909, personal collection of Paul Mably.
86	**H.R. MacDonald,** c. 1909, from the tour brochure, personal collection of Paul Mably.
97	**Bertha Crawford,** c. 1909, (photographer Charles Aylett, Toronto) personal collection of Paul Mably.
101	**Otto Morando,** New York Public Library for the Performing Arts.
102	**Lamperti book title page,** Internet Archive,
112	**Bertha Crawford,** c. 1912, (photographer F.A. Swaine, London) personal collection of Paul Mably.
114	**HH Zofia (Zolka) z Kosinskich Slubicka,** personal collection of Anna Szostakieiwcz, Warsaw.
118	**Emilia Corsi,** personal collection of Ashot Arakelyan.
129	**John, Maud and Lucia Crawford,** c. 1914, personal collection of Paul Mably.
133	**Warsaw Great Theatre,** c. 1900, University of Warsaw Library digital collection.
135	**Stracciari-Rigoletto,** c. 1915, Library of Congress, LC-B2- 4812-10
146	**Bertha Crawford,** c. 1915, from the program for a concert May 8, 1915, in the file of Alexei Taskin, TsGALI SPb, f. 162, op. 1, d. 69, l. 9
148	**General-Lieutenant Baron Constantine Karlovitch von Shtakelberg,** retrieved from Wikimedia Commons, August 8, 2017.
154	**Feodor Chaliapin,** c. 1917, in Borokovsky, *Chaliapin*, 171.
158	**Ioakim Tartakov,** in costume as Figaro in the Barber of Seville.
169	**Bertha Crawford,** c. 1915, personal collection of Paul Mably.
170	**Russian army leaving Warsaw,** July, 1915, postcard from the author's personal collection.
172	**Alexei Taskin,** retrieved from russian-records.com, August 8, 2017.
180	**Robert Adelheim,** unknown Internet site.

194	**Bertha Crawford**, personal collection of Paul Mably.
199	**Emil Mlynarski,** Zbiory Narodowe Achiwum Cyrowe.
200	**Warsaw Philharmonic,** c. 1907, postcard from the author's personal collection.
205	**Dr. Violette Berger**, c. 1919, personal collection of Paul Austin Orleman.
208	**Adam Dolzicki,** c. 1925, Zbiory Narodowe Achiwum Cyrowe, SM0_1-K-6459.
214	Bertha Crawford, c. 1921, personal collection of Paul Mably.
216	**Bertha Crawford,** c. 1921, in costume as Gilda (photographer Herman Miskin, New York), personal collection of Paul Mably.
222	**Harry Adaskin,** c. 1933, retrieved from Women's Musical Club of Toronto website, August 8, 2017.
230	**Poznan Theatre,** postcard from the author's personal collection.
231	**1922 concert program,** collection of the Toronto Reference Library.
242	**Karol de Hauke,** c. 1925, personal collection of Henrik de Hauke, Sweden.
245	**Adam Didur,** c. 1915, Library of Congress, LC-B2- 2905-16.
255	**Prof. Ludwik Urstein,** c. 1930, Zbiory Narodowe Achiwum Cyrowe, SMO_1-K-6992.
260	**Parade for the Day of Kindness to Animals, Warsaw,** c. 1929, from the newsletter of the Polish League of Friends of Animals, National Library of Poland.
270	**Bertha Crawford,** c. 1935, collection of the Toronto Reference Library.
276	**Promenade Concert program,** c. 1935, collection of the Toronto Reference Library.